Thomas Ritchie

THOMAS RITCHIE

A Study in VIRGINIA POLITICS

By

CHARLES HENRY AMBLER, Ph. D.

Author of

"Sectionalism in Virginia, 1776 to 1861", etc.

Richmond, Va.
BELL BOOK & STATIONERY CO.
1913

TO

My Mother

PREFACE

The political history of the United States for the period of its inception, infancy, and youth can be found in the numerous biographies of illustrious Virginians. Notwithstanding the fact that many Virginians preferred to serve their country in the capacity of local legislators and administrators, others gave up their lives and fortunes to the general government. It was their own darling child. Historians have written the names of those who took the latter course, Washington, Madison, Jefferson, Marshall, Monroe, Randolph, and others in large letters in the annals of the republic and have ascribed all the prestige and renown to the state of their nativity. In weaving these lives into that of the nation they have forgotten, however, those other illustrious sons who remained at home to preserve those conditions which made possible the state's greater prominence and her national influence. They have forgotten also that Virginia continued to have a history separate and distinct from that of the nation. The fact that there is no written history of the state for the period since the federal government began is significant, but it does not mean that there were no events worth recording or that she gave all her talents and genius to the common country.

It is not the purpose of this brief biography to rescue her second sons from oblivion or to give a comprehensive political history of the state, as its sub-title might suggest. These commendable undertakings would necessitate the writing of volumes similar to Hammond's and Alexander's Histories of Political Parties in New York and to the numerous lives of our national heroes. A humble effort will be made to render tardy recognition to one of her lesser lights who devoted practically the whole of a long, tempestuous, and eventful life to maintaining the ascendancy of Virginia among the states and to making possible the national career

PREFACE

The political history of the United States for the period of its inception, infancy, and youth can be found in the numerous biographies of illustrious Virginians. Notwithstanding the fact that many Virginians preferred to serve their country in the capacity of local legislators and administrators, others gave up their lives and fortunes to the central government. It was their own darling child. Historians have written the names of those who took the latter course, Washington, Madison, Jefferson, Marshall, Monroe, Randolph, and others in large letters in the annals of the republic and have accorded a due prestige and renown to the state of their nativity. In weaving these lives into that of the nation they have forgotten, however, those other illustrious sons who remained at home to preserve those conditions which made possible the state's greater luminaries and her national influence. They have forgotten also that Virginia continued to have a history separate and distinct from that of the nation. The fact that there is no written history of the state for the period since the federal government began is significant, but it does not mean that there were no events worth recording or that she gave all her talents and genius to the common country.

It is not the purpose of this brief biography to rescue her second sons from oblivion or to give a comprehensive political history of the state, as its sub-title might suggest. These commendable undertakings would necessitate the writing of volumes similar to Hammond's and Alexander's Histories of Political Parties in New York and to the numerous lives of our national heroes. A humble effort will be made to render tardy recognition to one of her lesser lights who devoted practically the whole of a long, tempestuous, and eventful life to maintaining the ascendency of Virginia among the states and to making possible the national careers of her more illustrious sons. As he taught his people "to think his own thoughts, to speak his own words, to weep when he wept, to wreathe their faces with his smiles, and above all to vote as he voted," this biography will of necessity deal largely with local political conditions and happenings. But the life of that man who did more than any other to keep both Clay and Calhoun from the presidency cannot be told separate and apart from the history of the federal government. Chief emphasis will, however, be placed upon local conditions and events, and it is hoped that the brevity in reference to national events and conditions, necessitated by a lack of space, will not add greatly to the other difficulties which may be encountered in reading these pages.

In the preparation of this biography I have been greatly aided by the authorities of the Virginia State Library and the Library of Congress. I have also received assistance from Dr. W. C. Rives of Washington, D. C., Miss Mary Campbell of Dunnsville, Va., Mrs. George E. Harrison of Brandon, Va., Miss Margaret Ritchie Harrison of Washington, D. C., Mrs. M. W. Simmons of Younge's Island, S. C., Professor W. E. Dodd of Chicago University, and numerous other persons, to each of whom I gladly make a hearty acknowledgement. Through the kindness of the libraries I have been able to secure access to the files of the *Richmond Enquirer* for the forty-one years during which Thomas Ritchie was its editor and to the *Washington Union* for the seven years he edited it and the use of other valuable sources, such as the Jackson, Van Buren, Stevenson, and Polk manuscripts in the Library of Congress and the public archives in the State Library of Virginia. Individuals have aided me by their helpful suggestions and by placing at my command manuscripts and other source material now inaccessible to the public.

CHAS. H. AMBLER.

Ashland, Virginia, May, 1913.

CONTENTS

		PAGE
I.	The Beginnings	9
II.	The Peace Regime	25
III.	Nationalism and Particularism	53
IV.	President Making	85
V.	Reform and Nullification	118
VI.	Jackson and the Whigs	155
VII.	Van Buren and the Independent Treasury	187
VIII.	Tyler and Texas	219
IX.	The National Spokesman	246
X.	The Great Compromise	273
XI.	The Editor and the Man	290
	Appendix . . . Genealogy	301

ILLUSTRATIONS

Thomas Ritchie . . . . Frontispiece

Thomas Ritchie's Birthplace 12

Spencer Roane 82

Lower Brandon 276

THOMAS RITCHIE

CHAPTER I.

THE BEGINNINGS.

Thomas Ritchie was born on November 5, 1778, in the only brick residence then in Tappahannock, Virginia. To-day this house may be seen on the main thoroughfare of that town and is used as a residence and a butcher-shop. Though located near other fine residences, notably the Parker house, the Anderton house, and the Brockenbrough house, the superior quality of the Ritchie residence marked its owner, Archibald Ritchie, as the chief business man of his community.

Archibald Ritchie, the first of his family in America, was a Scotchman who emigrated to this country to engage in the mercantile business. The year of his arrival is not known, but he seems to have been a man of affairs from the beginning and to have found a place in the best social circles of Virginia. Under date of August 21, 1753, Francis Jerdone wrote, "Last week Mr. Arch[d] Ritchie was married to a daughter of Capt. Roane, with whom he gets £500 down, and as much at her father's death."[1] Already he was a large exporting and importing merchant, exchanging articles of foreign manufacture for the corn, wheat, and tobacco produced in a large part of the Rappahannock valley and thus scattering industry and prosperity throughout Essex and the surrounding counties. He also owned negro slaves and did not hesitate to sell a "likely negro" to replenish the family exchequer. The records show that he left a considerable fortune to his wife and children.

Years after Archibald Ritchie's death and after one of his sons had lost his life in the defence of his country and another had seen gallant service in the same cause, John

[1] *William and Mary College Quarterly*, XI., 240.

Floyd and John Hampden Pleasants, for political purposes, accused Thomas Ritchie of being the "son of a Scotch Tory." Their accusation seems to have been founded upon the fact that Archibald Ritchie violated the Association of 1774, entered into to prohibit the importation of British goods into Virginia, and incurred the enmity of Richard Henry Lee who had raised a mob in 1766 to destroy his business, after he himself had mysteriously seen the light of a new day.[2] That Archibald Ritchie was among the last to break away from the mother country is probably true. He was a Scotchman and moved with all the conservatism of his kinsmen. Besides few of those interested in commerce were anxious for war. In many instances it involved the loss of their own and their neighbors' fortunes. But there is no evidence that he opposed the cause of the patriots after war had been declared. In fact, the evidence points to the opposite conclusion. In 1776 he was appointed by the General Assembly a member of the Committee of Public Safety of Essex county, and at a later date he supplied Colonel Landon Carter with gunpowder with which to fight the British.[3] Tradition has it that his wife commanded him to stand behind her while she got at a party of British pillagers with the butcher knife, but it is not certain that he obeyed even this authority.

Like many another man of distinction, Thomas Ritchie owed much, if not most, of his success to his mother. To that conservatism and interest in worldly affairs, which he inherited from his father, she added a taste for letters and for society, all of which later contributed to make her son an influential and efficient public servant. These sterling natural qualties were not, however, the least of the maternal gifts. She supplied an environment for the development of the tastes which she gave. Among her relatives and connections were some of the ripest scholars, the profoundest thinkers, and the most upright and honest men and women

[2] *William and Mary College Quarterly*, II., 238.

[3] *Ibid.*, V., 254; *Ibid.*, XVI., 266.

to be found in Virginia. She herself was a Roane, whose family had either intermarried with or was on most intimate terms with the Brockenbroughs, the Ruffins, the Brookes, the Parkers, and the Latanés, representatives of a younger generation which in due time formed an "Essex Junto" that virtually governed Virginia through its power to control her courts, legislatures, and financial policies. Unlike the planters who surrounded them on all sides, they were progressives. Among them were patriots of the revolution and ambitious youths. From the lips of the former young Ritchie caught that spirit which had revolutionized America and Europe, and from his younger associates he caught a vision of the future greatness of the nation and the part his native state was to play in it.

Besides, from another standpoint, it meant something in Ritchie's day to be born in old Tappahannock. It was located fifty miles from the Chesapeake upon a bluff overlooking a broad expanse of the Rappahannock river, and was then, as it now is, one of those modest and retiring towns which hides itself from the world under the dense foliage of its large and beautiful trees. A century ago it was a port of entry for all the surrounding country. Hence there went to the remotest parts of the world trading ships which supplied material wants and brought daily suggestions of the dependence of man upon man and of nation upon nation. In this small village, as in few others of colonial Virginia, there intermingled the best in the plantation life with the energy, initiative, and sagacity of the Scotch tradesmen. The product of this single local environment in time reshaped the character of the Old Dominion.

Thomas Ritchie's father died when he was only six years old, and the responsibility for his education and rearing fell consequently to his mother and her family. She planned first to put him to the law under the guidance of his distinguished cousin, Spencer Roane, who later became head of the Court of Appeals of Virginia and Jefferson's first choice for Chief Justice of the Supreme Court of the United States and for his own successor in the presidency. A short apprenticeship sufficed to convince young Ritchie that he had neither talents nor tastes for distinction in the field of his distinguished kinsman. Consequently he turned to the study of medicine, but a short course of lectures at Philadelphia convinced him that this profession was even more distasteful than the law. Reversing the practice of the present day, which makes teaching a stepping stone to the other professions, he then became a pedagogue. At the age of twenty-one he took charge of an academy at Fredericksburg and improved the opportunities which this position afforded to make deeper and broader his knowledge of the classics and the best modern authors.

Ritchie regarded the teaching profession as one of the most honorable and respectable. He was imbued with the idea that the superstructure of wisdom and virtue in a republic is the architecture of its schoolmasters. Moreover, he opposed confining the benefits of education to men and, from the very beginning of his career, made an honest plea for greater opportunities for women. In defence of this plea he pointed to the constellation of feminine genius which had arisen in Europe: the Edgeworths, the Macaulays, the de Genlis and the de Staëls. Henceforth he lost no opportunity to promote the cause of public free instruction in Virginia. Such an enthusiast naturally endeared himself to his students and to their parents. Had he been permitted to follow the path of his inclination, as did his great contemporary, Horace Mann, the history of popular education in the South might to-day be written differently. As will be shown later, his ideas on educational problems were modern and none doubted that he had the courage of his convictions. But ill health would not permit his remaining in the teaching profession, and he sought more agreeable employment in Richmond as the owner and proprietor of a small book-store.

When Ritchie came to Richmond in 1803 he cast his lot with a people through whom he was in time to influence the whole commonwealth and indirectly the whole nation. As if by fate his tastes and training had fitted him for a large and important place in this metropolis. Consequently a passing notice of Richmond, as it was one hundred years ago, might

BIRTHPLACE OF THOMAS RITCHIE, Tappahannock, Va.

contribute much to a proper understanding of his subsequent life and services.

Of industrial Richmond the Duke de La Rochefoucauld-Liancourt wrote in 1796 as follows: "At present there are few wooden houses at Richmond. The trade of this town consists in the purchase of the country products, and in selling at second hand the articles of domestic consumption, which are generally produced in England. The number of merchants who carry on a direct commerce with Europe is inconsiderable. They keep their ships at Norfolk, and send down the produce of the country in small vessels. The commission trade may be considered as the real business of the place. It is from the merchants of Richmond and Petersburg that those of Norfolk most commonly purchase the grain, flour and tobacco which is later exported. The country produce is paid for by the merchants in ready money or on short credit: they even frequently obtain it on cheaper terms by furnishing the planters with an advance of money on their crops. The Richmond merchants supply all the stores through an extensive tract of back country. As they have a very long credit from England, they can allow a similar indulgence of six, nine or twelve months to the shop keepers whom they supply. All the merchants deal in bills of exchange on Europe.

"The falls of the James which obstructed its navigation from the distance of seven miles above Richmond, hitherto imposed the necessity of employing land carriage for that space. At present a canal, running parallel with the course of the river for those seven miles, connects the communication by water, and opens a navigation which extends without interruption 200 miles above Richmond. I have seen one of the two mills at Richmond. It stands below the falls of the river, receives a great power of water, and turns six pair of stones. It is a fine mill, and unites the advantages of all the new inventions; the cogs of the wheels are clumsily executed. It costs a yearly rent of near $6,000 to Monsieur Chevalier, a Frenchman from Rockefort, hitherto director of the French paquets to America, and now settled in

Virginia. Flour mills are more numerous at Petersburg than at Richmond, and the mills there are also upon a good construction. The exportations of Petersburg are more considerable than those of Richmond, although generally speaking, the produce it receives is inferior in quality. Tobacco, for instance, which sells at Richmond for $6 or $7 per hundred weight, does not fetch quite $5 at Petersburg. City Point or Bermuda Hundred, is the spot where the custom house is established for these two places."

Thus it will be seen that industrially and commercially Richmond was then the clearing house of the surrounding country which was then tilled by thousands of negro slaves, the "happy wards" of the most indulgent masters that ever lived. The James was the main thoroughfare "to town," but all roads, however insignificant led to Richmond. The brick row on lower Main Street was not then opulent enough to call forth the scorn of the country folk who could find hospitable treatment and comfortable lodging at the Bird in the Hand, the City Tavern, or the Union Hotel. Meanwhile they could enjoy a concert of the Musical Society at Tanbark Hall, witness a play at the theater, invest their savings in lottery tickets, or read the columns of the *Enquirer* and the *Gazette*.

Richmond was more than a mere industrial and commercial center. It was also the social and intellectual clearing house of a plantation aristocracy with ample leisure to drink deeply at the fountains of learning and culture. In April, 1791, when on his fourth visit to this country, Dr. Thomas Coke preached "in the Capitol where the Assembly sits, to the most dressy congregation" he had ever seen in America, and it gave "great attention." There was then no other place of considerable area in the United States where copies of the standard authors, both classic and modern, could be found in large numbers in the private libraries of its rural population. Many Virginia planters could then read and speak Latin and French and rivaled the English squires in their knowledge of history and jurisprudence. Since 1779, when Richmond became the capital, the annual sessions of the General Assembly, which usually extended from the first of December to the first of March, marked the height of the social season. Thither came the great planters and the political solons with their wives and daughters to aid Cupid in those amorous delights which have made one great family of all Virginians. If three months did not suffice to complete the match-making and the case seemed urgent, the interested parties usually repaired to the springs for the summer season.

Although it is to-day one of the many cities of seven hills, Richmond of a century ago was confined mainly to three, namely: Gamble's Hill, Shockoe Hill, and Church Hill. Each had its own social circle which knew no bounds on great occasions and when Cupid came to town. The first named hill overlooks the islets in the falls of the James. The social life there centered in the "Grey House," built by Colonel John Harvie and purchased after his death by Major Robert Gamble. Elizabeth and Agnes Bell, his daughters, became the wives of William Wirt, later Attorney-General of the United States and candidate for the presidency, and William H. Cabell, later governor of Virginia. During the period of Ritchie's early days in Richmond the two families, each with several children, occupied the Grey House jointly. Here William Wirt wrote his "Letters of the British Spy," and hence went forth the wives of many influential men and the progenitors of such distinguished sons as James Branch Cabell, the novelist.

Shockoe Hill was adorned by the Capitol building and was the chief residential district. The social life of this area centered in the palatial residence of Dr. John Brockenbrough, which was erected in 1818, later used as the White House of the Confederacy, and the Confederate Museum. In the heyday of Jacksonian Democracy it was the rendezvous of the Richmond Junto. Here the Randolphs and the Harrisons were entertained when in the city, Dr. Brockenbrough having married Gabriella Harvie Randolph and being on most intimate terms with the Harrisons. A reception at the Brockenbrough mansion was one of the highest distinctions that could be extended a stranger when visiting

Richmond. The neighborhood was unsurpassed. In full view were the homes of Chief Justice Marshall and his father-in-law, Jacqueline Ambler; Colonel John Harvie of Revolutionary fame lived near; on Clay street, near Eleventh, lived Colonel Edward Carrington, also a distinguished soldier; and nearly opposite his residence were the homes of Lewis Burwell and Major John Ambler. This same section included among its residents Judge Philip N. Nicholas, Dr. James B. McClurg, Benjamin Watkins Leigh, Alexander McRea, Conway Robinson, Thomas Ritchie, and Bishop Moore. Many a young girl was given in marriage in the Brockenbrough mansion with Bishop Moore, of the Diocese of Virginia, officiating. On such occasions Chief Justice Marshall, Dr. Brockenbrough, Benj. W. Leigh, Thomas Ritchie, and other distinguished men of the vicinity were usually recorded as among the guests.

Just opposite Shockoe Hill and connected with it by a heavily built wooden bridge was Church Hill. Since the middle of the eighteenth century it had been owned by Colonel Richard Adams who seems to have been a prosperous man of affairs. He always claimed that his purchase contract with William Byrd was made with the understanding that the Capitol building was to be erected on his lands. The failure of Thomas Jefferson to respect this private arrangement caused a complete estrangement between himself and the Adamses, which later became a source of political annoyance to the former. The social life of Church Hill centered in the Adams mansion, which was erected in 1799 by Dr. John Adams when he married Geddes Winston of Hanover county. In its lofty ceilings, spacious drawing rooms, library, and bed chambers, and its colonial architecture it rivaled the Brockenbrough house, which stood upon the opposite hill. In other lines that rivalry continued even into the period of war. When the latter became the White House of the Confederacy, the former was the home of an influential abolitionist and northern spy, Elizabeth Van Lew. In Ritchie's early days Governor George William Smith, who lost his life in the fire which destroyed the Richmond Theater in 1811, was a member of the Adams household.

Politics rarely marred the social circles of Richmond. They were not half so disturbing an element as the "loo mania," which raged in 1806 and caused the ladies of the first families to lose their pin money and their tempers. Although they had met meanwhile on scores of occasions and were members of the same social clubs, Chief Justice Marshall and Thomas Ritchie never engaged in a political discussion before 1820. The leaders did not hesitate to attack each other through the columns of the press and upon the hustings, but all was forgotten when they approached a common punch-bowl. True, there was much greater unanimity of political opinion in Richmond than might be suspected. It was, in fact, a Federalist stronghold. A review of the names already given will disclose the fact that her leading citizens were either soldiers or officers of the Revolutionary Army. These were, for the most part, loyal to Washington and Hamilton in their efforts to establish a strong central government. Thus silence may have been the better part of discretion on the part of the young Republican interlopers, who, like Brockenbrough and Ritchie, had come to Richmond to seek their fortunes.

Despite their boasted democratic principles and equal rights, the aristocrats of Richmond in 1800, as in 1900, were ever ready to pay obeisance and court to royalty and to rank. They received such recognition from those beneath them in their social and political castes. Why not pay them to others? Reluctant to concede these traits of the body politic Republicans attributed them to a desire on the part of the Federalists for monarchy. On the contrary, the Federalists saw in them only an expression of Virginia's far-famed hospitality. But Wirt observed in his "British Spy" that "notwithstanding all this, it was easy to discern in the look, the voice and the whole manner, with which gentlemen as well as ladies of both parties saluted and accosted young ——— (the son of an English lord) a secret spirit of respectful diffidence, a species of silent, reverential abasement, which, as it could not have been excited by his personal qualities, must have been homage to his rank."[4]

[4] Wirt, *The Letters of a British Spy*, 14.

As in the present day, inequalities in property had produced their corresponding social and political inequalities which penetrated every phase of life and entered into the political contests between the geographic sections, notably that between the cis-montane and the trans-montane counties. On this subject the "British Spy" also observed that, "however, they may vaunt of equal liberty in church and state, they have but little to boast on the subject of equal property. Indeed there is no country," said he, "where property is more unequally distributed than in Virginia. This inequality struck me with peculiar force in riding through the lower counties on the Potomac. Here and there a stately aristocratic palace, with all its appurtenances, strikes the view: while all around, for many miles, no other buildings are to be seen but the little smoky huts and log cabins of poor, laborious, ignorant tenants. And what is very ridiculous, these tenants, while they approach *the great house,* cap in hand, with all the fearful trembling submission of the lowest feudal vassals, boast in their court-yards, with obstreperous exultation, that they live in a land of freemen, a land of equal liberty and equal rights." Need one go farther for an answer to the question now frequently asked, "Why did the poor non-slaveholders follow their leaders into secession?"

Engrafted as it had been upon these sterile beds of Federalism and surrounded here and there by the thorns and rocks of self-interest and tradition, the democratic revolution of 1800 was in grave danger of meeting a premature death in Virginia. For lack of support the mouthpiece of the reform party, the *Examiner,* under the editorship of Skelton Jones of dueling fame, had gone down to a natural death, and the office where it had been published had been consumed in flames. Henry, who had himself become a Federalist was dead, and Jefferson, Madison, Giles, and Randolph were devoting their energies and talents to the federal councils. Under these conditions Jefferson, who had every reason for keeping Virginia true to the teachings of republicanism, appealed to the young book-seller, Thomas

Ritchie, as a proper person to watch the vestal fires in her state capital. As yet Ritchie had made no entangling alliances with the aristocrats; he was fitted by nature, training, and previous association for such a calling; and he had a number of promising friends and connections among the younger generation. Accordingly, the *Richmond Enquirer* arose Phoenix-like from the ashes of the *Examiner,* and in its resurrection Ritchie found a life work. The first office of the *Enquirer* was to echo and to re-echo the utterances of the *National Intelligencer* and the thoughts of the federal administration until they became the utterances and the thoughts of the common people. Meanwhile the power and influence of the *Gazette,* the Federalist organ, was to be crippled.

The first copy of the *Enquirer* appeared on May 9, 1804. It was announced to appear bi-weekly, but supplementary half-sheets were promised for the weeks covering the sessions of Congress and the General Assembly. The price of subscription was four dollars per annum, in advance, which was soon raised to five dollars. Advertising space was sold to non-subscribers at seventy-five cents per "square in length" for the first insertion, fifty cents for each of three subsequent insertions, and thirty-three cents for each additional insertion, "long ones in the same proportion." Rates to subscribers were fifty for the first insertion and thirty-three for each subsequent one. Little attention, however, was paid to advertising. The *Enquirer* was to be maintained by official patronage and by subscriptions, which were raised during the first eighteen months from five hundred to fifteen hundred.

From the very beginning the *Enquirer* fell under the influence of party patronage. The initial number contained certified copies of federal laws and extracts from speeches made on the anniversary of Jefferson's election to the presidency. Without official patronage it could not have lived in so strong a Federalist atmosphere as Richmond and in competition with a well established and popular press. From the first Ritchie did not disguise his purpose to speak for the administration and his expectation of compensation for such service. On the other hand, he did not propose to become a political vassal. "Principle not men" was to be his motto, and he boldly announced his purpose to sail the turbid political stream alone with the constitution for his compass and the Union for his chart.

The disavowals of any temporary allurements and transitory convictions, which appeared in the first number of the *Enquirer,* made it clear that young Ritchie had found a life work. Without advancing any pretensions to unbounded and varied resources he characteristically refused to disclaim them. For his lack of knowledge in practical things and in the "ways of the world" he hoped to make a temporary compensation by drawing upon the results of his "theoretical research." Of only one thing was he confident, and that was the unfailing quality of his zeal, a confidence which he never betrayed. Like his great prototype, Jefferson, he knew that the frailty of human wisdom would often lead him wrong and cause others to think him wrong when he was right. For each contingency he asked only the indulgence of a grateful people and expressed the patriotic desire to be able, when his course had ended, to lay his hand upon his heart and indulge the reflection that he had not injured his country, dishonored his profession, or sullied his personal honor.[5]

Though in full accord with its social regime, Ritchie's great service to Virginia and incidentally to the Union came from the leaven which he, as an editor, injected into aristocracy and conservatism. Like the raindrops against the mountain boulder his pleas for republicanism and greater equality beat in vain upon that old Federalist stronghold, Richmond, but they cast sprays beyond, which brought political life and virility to all the surrounding country. Unlike most Virginians of his day, he was a disciple of Adam Smith, being well versed in the principles of his "Wealth of Nations" and in the writings of the other great thinkers of

[5] *Richmond Enquirer,* May 9, 1804.

the liberal school of political economy, Ricardo, Malhus, and Say. He was equally well informed in the writings of Voltaire, Rousseau, and Paine who, with the economists above mentioned, had already revolutionized society. With them he believed that governments had long had too much power and individuals too little. This he thought the chief difference between despotic and republican governments, between those of Europe and that of the United States. In the former, agriculture was shackled by entails, primogeniture, and tithes; manufacturing was restrained by corporation and apprenticeship laws; and commerce was stifled by the abuses of privilege. He was determined that Virginia should throw off whatever relics of feudalism lingered in her society and conform her thought and legislation to the genius of republicanism.[6] To this end he considered popular education, local reforms in the existing laws and customs, and the development of the state's natural resources as indispensable prerequisites. He was thus ready to take up these subjects where Jefferson and Madison had been forced to abandon them a quarter of a century before. In him the theorists of 1776 had at last found a champion who did not tremble or quail before the realities of democracy.

Our unexampled freedom and opportunity, Ritchie maintained, could be endangered by one or all of four evils: war, luxury, the fitful violence of party spirit, and the dismemberment of the Union. War offered an opportunity for a designing president or an ambitious party leader to usurp the government; luxurious indulgence would unnerve the zeal that watched over the public welfare; when carried to the point of persecution and riot, party spirit might lead to a despotism like that in France; and dismemberment was certain to be followed by border warfare between the states and a return to dependence upon Europe. To avoid war he advised adherence to Jefferson's counsels for peace and to the well known injunctions of Washington's Farewell Address; he found an antidote for the rising tide of luxury in enlight-

[6] *Richmond Enquirer*, April 14, 1807.

ened minds and in the maintenance of equal industrial and political opportunities for all; and he would have avoided unnecessary and dangerous manifestations of party spirit by a strict adherence to the compromises of the constitution and to the conciliatory spirit in which it had been drawn. In this early stand for conciliation and compromise he struck the key-note of his subsequent career.

With these diagnoses and specifics thus carefully made and set forth Ritchie took his place as a sentinel upon the watch-tower of the rights of the individual states. Circumstances and conditions had more to do with placing and keeping him there than inclination or personal preference. In ordaining and establishing the federal government the fathers had attempted to avoid each of the two well recognized evils in all government, the tendency to centralization on the one hand and to decentralization on the other. Observation and study had taught them that one led to despotism, the other to anarchy. They had thus resorted to a division of powers between the central and the state governments, evolving the idea of a dual sovereignty in a single state. In contemplating the result of their efforts, Gladstone later pronounced it "the most wonderful work ever struck off at a given time by the brain and purpose of man." Had Ritchie been able to ignore facts and conditions, he would have been a neutral, guarding alike the rights of both the central and the state governments. But the exigencies of our growing and expanding country had caused statesmen of all parties to depart from the letter of the constitution, by which alone the government of the fathers could be maintained. Under the general welfare license they were rapidly sweeping the country toward the dreaded maelstrom of centralization. Even Jefferson had passed dangerously near that pit on more than one occasion. If the government of the fathers was to be preserved, Ritchie had thus no choice, except to defend its vulnerable points. It is as a strict-constructionist of the conservative type that he will live in history. With that same spirit of conciliation and compromise which had characterized the federal convention of 1787, he continued to be a patriot of the ancient type and to see in our original plan of government what Gladstone and Madison saw. Had we adhered to that plan, his precepts would today be watch-words on the tower of civic liberty and his name a commonplace in every household. Who can now look into the lesson of the past and contemplate the problems of the future and deny him positively and unreservedly the right to such a distinction?

In his defence of the powers and the rights of the states, which in its broadest sense was a plea for the preservation of the Union, Ritchie drew his chief information and inspiration from Madison's Report of 1799 to the Virginia Assembly and from Edmund Pendleton's celebrated essay written shortly after Jefferson's first election to the presidency and entitled "The Danger Not Over." These documents were the Old and the New Testaments of his political faith. The former is accessible to all readers, but the latter is an unexploited source of the "Virginia doctrines." Though brief, it is a matchless presentation of the evils of centralization and decentralization. It was frequently referred to by Ritchie in his editorials and was republished in the *Enquirer* after Jackson's election to the presidency in 1828 to serve as a warning to him, as it had served as a warning to Jefferson.

Among all the companions of Ritchie's early years there were few if any who did more to instruct him in the tenets of sound republicanism than Henry Clay. The "mill boy of the slashes" and the studious son of the Scotch merchant-man were kindred spirits. They had each sat at the feet of a Gamaliel. The former was a disciple of George Wythe, the latter of Spencer Roane. When young Ritchie had found it convenient to visit Richmond, they discussed together grave political and economic questions in a manner which made it plain that they had each caught the progressive spirit of the age. They were each imbued with the idea and the feeling of a new era, in which government would be improved and the civil happiness of man enlarged. They were each tired of that narrow and dastardly coasting which had kept legislatures close to usage and to precedent. They yearned to hazard a voyage in search of the treasure of public felicity. Though they later ceased to be friends, they followed the same roads, each tempering his actions by a spirit of conciliation and compromise.[7]

[7] See *Richmond Enquirer*, December 6, 1828; *Ibid.*, September 10, 1852.

CHAPTER II.

THE PEACE REGIME.

The intervention of the French revolutionists in San Domingo and the bloody scenes which followed the overthrow of French authority there fixed the eyes of the slaveholders of the United States upon that unhappy island. The conditions there, together with an occasional rumor regarding local uprisings at home, caused the slaveholders of Virginia to tremble for their own security and dictated silence on this all important subject to the columns of the *Enquirer*. At first Ritchie had promised full accounts of the massacres and complete texts of the proclamations being made by the black chieftain, Dessalines. His conception of the freedom of the press left no other alternative. A brief experience revealed, however, that such a promise was not in harmony with the feelings and sentiments of Virginia, which had already decided upon a policy of studied silence upon the subject of negroes and negro slavery. Accordingly his promises were never kept, and he expressed the wish that no one "would demand the reason."

Thus early Ritchie fell into that great reaction against the anti-slavery movement which had attended and followed the American Revolution and given liberty to thousands of those in bondage. The current with which he had cast his lot, in time, eradicated those sentiments and theories which caused Washington, Jefferson, Randolph, and others to emancipate their slaves and made the South a pro-slavery section. Ritchie now began the first contribution to these ends by advocating the enactment of laws making it more difficult for slaves to gain their freedom and restricting the liberty of the free negroes.[1]

[1] *Richmond Enquirer*, January 9, 1804; *Ibid.*, January 15, 1805.

Even at this early date it is evident that Ritchie recognized in the slavery problem a negro problem as well. Thus he raised a voice of protest when South Carolina and Georgia, in response to the increased demand for negroes caused by the purchase of Louisiana and the invention of the cotton gin, opened their ports to the foreign slave-trade. Virginia had too large a surplus of that "melancholy race of men, whose fate we may deplore but can not redress," to permit her to sit quietly by and see Africa supply a demand which she could supply equally well, though not so cheap. Plainly this was not a time for silence from the *Enquirer* which now advocated an amendment to the Federal Constitution to forbid the foreign slave-trade after 1808.[2] It also condemned that spirit of avarice which was driving the slave-dealers from the western to the eastern coast of Africa in their search for human prey. Within two weeks, from May 1st to May 15th, 1806, one newspaper in South Carolina had advertised for sale seven hundred and forty negroes newly imported from Zanzibar and other points on the east coast of Africa. His interested denunciations of these "horrible crimes" to humanity were potent factors in procuring the enactment of a federal law to prohibit the foreign slave-trade after January 1, 1808.

Meanwhile the chronic fear of the Virginians toward banks and banking had subsided enough to permit the Assembly to charter a state bank which was established in Richmond in 1804 and was called the Bank of Virginia. Hitherto the fabulous profits of the West India trade and the demands for credit had not induced them to embark upon such enterprises. With a characteristic conservatism they had adhered to their rural simplicity and feared banks, because it was believed that they fostered monopoly, increased the cost of living, and paved the way to luxury and extravagance. As a consequence the routes of commerce did not terminate in their ports, and they themselves had become as

[2] *Richmond Enquirer*, June 28, 1805; *Ibid.*, June 3, 1806.

dependent upon the bankers of London as they are today dependent upon those of New York.

Ritchie shared many of the local prejudices of his countrymen against the banks, but his experiences and observations as the son of one of the largest exporting and importing merchants of colonial Virginia had taught the value, nay the necessity, of institutions of credit. Besides his cousin, Dr. John Brockenbrough, who was also born and bred in the old commercial center, Tappahannock, and who later became president of the proposed bank, was now interested as one of its directors in putting it into operation. The opportunity for fixing the hold of an Essex Junto upon Virginia was at hand and was too tempting to let pass. His uncle, Spencer Roane, also from Essex county, was president of the Court of Appeals; several friends were influential in both the Assembly and in Congress; and with Brockenbrough at the head of the financial interest and Ritchie at the head of the press, there was no reason why the influence of these stalwart sons of the younger generation could not be made permanent in Virginia. True, their methods were clannish, but which one of the large family of Virginians could object to that? Accordingly Ritchie endorsed the proposed departure, ostensibly that the country might have sufficient capital to develop its natural resources. To prevent the dreaded monopoly in the banking business he recommended the freest competition and the public sale of bank stock.

It was not long, however, after the Bank of Virginia had been established and put into successful operation before Ritchie experienced a complete change of mind regarding the banking business. This change was doubtless shared, if it was not induced, by his relatives and friends. He now became a conservative, in modern terms, one identified with the interests, and in the face of his democratic theories set himself squarely against that free competition which he had formerly recommended and to which the state of New York later resorted in an effort to remove her banking business from politics. He now defended Richmond's monopoly, insisted that bank directors should be Republicans, and denied banking privileges to towns under the control or even the influence of the Federalists.[3] In defence of Richmond's monopoly he referred to the worthless "out of town bank bills" which had demoralized the finances of Massachusetts, despite the wholesome influences of Boston.[4]

Strange as it may seem in view of the prominent part he later played, Ritchie buckled on the armor of national politics reluctantly. It was generally conceded that the *Enquirer* had been established with the sanction and by the aid of Jefferson. Consequently its early silence on national questions became a matter of concern and comment. "Index" demanded information about the threatened schism within the Republican party and the censures which were being daily directed toward Mr. Jefferson.[5] A series of essays defending Virginia against the attacks of New England was the only answer. Ritchie's silence came not from a lack of information in practical politics or from ignorance on the subject of statecraft. He was well versed in the latter and in a position to know all that was to be known about the former. It is more than likely that his silence was due to a deference to Jefferson's wishes. The questions relating to the Yazoo frauds, the occupation of Florida, the purchase of Louisiana, and the renewal of war in Europe had clouded the political horizon, and it is doubtful if he saw his way clearly out of any one of the perplexing situations. Silence was therefore the better part of discretion on the part of a party organ.

There came a time, however, when silence ceased to be a virtue. Luckily for Ritchie the Louisiana purchase was a closed incident when he entered public life. He could therefore pass over the question of its constitutionality without comment. But not so with the petitions requesting a repub-

[3] *Richmond Enquirer*, January 7, 9, 11, 1806.

[4] *Ibid.*, April 15, 1807.

[5] *Ibid.*, September 22, 1804.

lican form of government for its inhabitants. Like the modern politician he would have accorded them a respectful hearing without thought of granting their requests. With Jefferson he considered them unfit for self-government, and saw in the anxiety of those who advocated their requests for it attempts to embarrass the administration. Unlike the English colonists in America, the scions of a free country and the heirs to democratic institutions, they knew not the ways of republics. No colleges or private schools adorned their land; the press had not diffused the lessons of reason among them; and not more than half of their number could even read and write. In the light of the great barriers which lie between all extremes he saw no inconsistency with his own theories or any injustice or lack of wisdom on the part of the administration in the policy to extend representative government to Louisiana by degrees, to be determined in each case by the fitness of its inhabitants to receive it.[6]

Regarding the wisdom, yea the necessity, of the Louisiana purchase Ritchie entertained not a doubt. Consequently he sought to gain the greatest possible advantages from it. Thus Spain's efforts to restrict us to the western bank of the Mississippi met in him a patriotic resistance. By reference to the treaties of 1719 and 1763 he tried to prove that West Florida had always been a part of Louisiana. He preferred compromise, however, to war as a means of settling that question. Unlike Jefferson he was not temperamentally opposed to war. In this case he considered it a poor method to promote the federal interests. True, Spain was not formidable and could not defend even East Florida against an attack by American frontiersmen. But our republican institutions were yet in an experimental stage and might not weather the vicissitudes of a great international war and the consequent indebtedness which it would involve. Accordingly he suggested that Spain be given a clear title to the land between the Mobile and the Perdido rivers in

[6] *Richmond Enquirer*, October 3, 1804.

exchange for the remaining part of West Florida. In case of a refusal to accept this offer he would have given her lands west of the Sabine river, the present territory of Texas, in exchange for both East Florida and West Florida. The latter proposition was especially attractive, because acceptance would have given us an unbroken coast line east of the Mississippi and extended our possessions into the very heart of the West Indies.[7]

His equivocal attitude on the Yazoo affair caused Duane, editor of the *Aurora* and leader of the insurgents in Pennsylvania, to pronounce Ritchie "a wolf in sheep's clothing" and "a temporizer" with schemes of plunder and iniquity.[8] Though the *Enquirer* condemned the alleged attempt of the Yazoo claimants to defraud the federal government and praised Randolph's genius in opposing them and in keeping pure the principles of the republic, it did not publish his speeches made in December, 1804, in opposition to their claims. They were the first signals of schism, and as such were passed over in the hope that they would be the last. Later, when Randolph made his chief effort in this case, Ritchie's attitude toward him remained unchanged, but he continued to defend Madison's integrity and good intentions in favoring the Yazoo claimants. This unusal stand of the *Enquirer* was doubtless due to a desire on the part of its editor and those for whom he spoke, to maintain harmony and accord within the administration party. Randolph had a large following in Virginia, who concurred in his opposition to the centralizing tendencies of the federal government and were willing to follow him into any insurgent movement. Besides he had been more irritable than usual in attacking the "Yazoo thieves," and he yet had a great service to perform to the Republican party in sustaining the impeachment of Judge Chase. Success in this effort would doubtless elate him and redeem him with Jefferson.

[7] *Richmond Enquirer*, September 15, 1804; *Ibid.*, October 13 17, 1804.

[8] *Ibid.*, April 13, 1805.

Thus there was a prospect of avoiding schism, and the *Enquirer* lost no oportunity to improve it.[9]

All of Ritchie's precautions were useless. Randolph did not succeed in sustaining the impeachment charges and retired from the troublesome eighth Congress distrusted by and disgusted with Jefferson and Madison and the rank and file of his party. The sudden announcement of Jefferson's intention to retire with a second term, placed Madison in line for the succession and aroused all the bitterness and jealousy in Randolph's nature. From his home at Bizarre in the summer of 1805 he poured out his discontent and dissatisfaction to his friends, Nicholson, Macon, and Gallatin, and indulged in talk about "more union and decision among the real friends of freedom." This was the atmosphere in which was born the "Quid" party which now turned to Monroe as the only person capable of defeating Madison for the presidency. It effected no formal organization and was held together only by a common feeling of dissatisfaction on the part of its leaders.

Notwithstanding the formidable characters, who were arraying themselves against the administration, and Randolph's fulminations, Ritchie continued his efforts at conciliation. To this end he refused to concede the possibility of Randolph's complete defection and shrewdly placed all opposition Republicans into a class with the Federalists. Considering the ultimate outcome of this third party movement his comments upon the political conditions following the adjournment of the eighth Congress show true political insight. In the proposed "union of honest men" he saw only "the chorus of a Federalist ditty." Because of her uniform population and freedom from the infection of popular elections he feared no third party in Virginia. Unlike their kinsmen in Pennsylvania and New York the German and Irish elements in Virginia's population could not be organ-

[9] *Richmond Enquirer,* December 15, 1804; *Ibid.,* April 13, 1805.

ized into "clans and tribes for political purposes."[10] He expected differences of opinion as well as a "censurable spirit of moderation" among those "who lived in the towns," but he was certain that the yeomen of Virginia would not desert the ranks of the Republican party. In general these observations were correct, but the forces making for accord and union within the party were too slow moving to prevent the Federalists and the Quids from uniting in the Assembly of 1805-'06 to elect W. H. Cabell to the governorship and to defeat Ritchie for election to the office of public printer.

Meanwhile international relations had taken a turn which would eventually increase Randolph's hostility to the administration and render schism within the Republican party inevitable. Our claims to West Florida and the act of Congress making Mobile a collection district for duties and customs had called forth a terrible castigation from the Marquis of Casa Yrujo, minister from Spain to the United States, and had produced a warlike attitude toward us on the part of both Spain and France. While Randolph was pouring out his dissatisfaction to his friends and receiving consolation in kind, the leaders at Washington were talking about war with Spain and contemplating the possibility of defeating Macon's re-election to the speakership of the House. The approach of the war cloud had, however, allayed the intense feelings on all sides, and Macon and Randolph returned to the ninth Congress, the former able to effect his re-election to the speakership and the latter willing to co-operate, as chairman of the Ways and Means Committee, in preparations for war with Spain. Accordingly the regular annual message, sounding the war cry, was popularly received.

Ritchie had seized upon the bellicose spirit of the country as another means of avoiding faction within the administration party. Though counseling the prudence of Polycrates of Samos, he praised the annual message.[11] He had

[10] *Richmond Enquirer*, November 8, 1805.

[11] *Richmond Enquirer*, December 17, 1805.

now abandoned all idea of compromise with Spain, and following the popular demand, possibly with an idea of directing it, had advised the conquest of West Florida and so much of East Florida as would insure the payment of a war indemnity. He now insisted upon an increase in the standing army and the construction of an efficient navy.

To the utter surprise of Randolph and his small tribe, and without consulting a single one of them, Jefferson sent a secret message to Congress three days after the regular message, in which he invited it to make preparations for the purchase of Florida and said not a word about war. The proposed purchase was to be made either through France or as a bribe to her, and had a secret origin in the cabinet. When Randolph grasped the situation he saw that the Spanish dispute had been converted into a French job. At once he began a series of amusing tactics to defeat the object of the special message and to bring reproach upon Madison. After a hurried interview with the President and Madison, in which he made it plain that he would not bribe one nation to rob another, he delayed a week and then made a visit to Baltimore before calling a meeting of his committee to which the matter had been referred. When the committee did meet, which was not until late in December, he secured the adoption of a report adhering to the original plans for war with Spain. After a prolonged session behind closed doors the President's request was finally granted.

During the enactment of this comic drama, in which Randolph had behaved like a spoiled boy and Jefferson himself had not escaped the political mire, the *Enquirer,* in common with the press of the whole country, maintained a profound silence. The mysterious secret session, preceded as it had been by what seemed to be a popular and official demand for war, left no doubt about some hitch in the workings of federal machinery. Considering the possibilities for war it was no time for idle conjecture. Shortly before Pitt had revolutionized the rules hitherto recognized as regulating neutral commerce, and Sir William Scott had handed down a decision which render American ships fit subjects for British prizes. Accordingly Ritchie sought to ease the public mind by leaving doubt as to whether the mysterious actions of Congress related to Great Britain or to Spain.[12]

At length the cloud of secrecy passed, and Ritchie was forced to look upon a discordant party. After hitting some desperate blows and hurling Jefferson and dozens of Congressmen headlong into the mire, Randolph had placed himself beyond the pale of the Republican party, and his likeness to the porcupine rendered a continuation of the efforts to caress and fondle him extremely dangerous. Thus Ritchie assumed a studied indifference toward him and made haste to proclaim the "glorious news" of a peaceful settlement of our difficulties with Spain and to divert the hostile tendencies of the country toward Great Britain which, he said, should be taught that "the sovereignty of the seas is an absurd and dangerous dogma."[13] At the same time he praised the wisdom and the statesmanship of the President. Later he published, without comment, Randolph's celebrated speech upon Gregg's resolution for prohibiting the importation of British goods, which marked his final breach with the Republican party.

As the election for members of the General Assembly drew near Ritchie began to look with alarm upon the prospects of the administration party in Virginia. He saw clearly that inability to control the Assembly might endanger Madison's chances for reaching the presidency. Accordingly he made a conservative and conciliatory review of the proceedings of the late Congress with a view to influencing the local election. At the head of the factional opposition he saw a Virginian "whose conduct had been not unworthy of Bayard himself, *sans peur, sans reproche,*" and he was confident that we could not and should not rely upon France to interpose her good offices between us and Spain. He also ridiculed the idea entertained by some blind partisans that

[12] *Richmond Enquirer,* January 14, 1806.

[13] *Ibid.,* January 14, 16, 1806.

Jefferson could do no wrong. His method of dealing with Spain had certainly been a "melancholy example" of his human frailties. Nevertheless he recognized in Jefferson "a man of most unblemished integrity, a man whose administration had manifested no less vigilance than virtue," and he predicted that it would be months and years before we would have a president who would be more worthy or in whom we could repose more confidence.[14]

Randolph had taken leave of his party never to return so long as Jefferson and Madison directed its councils. Henceforth he voted almost uniformly with the Federalists and did not scruple at a resort to the most "diabolical and ingenious arts" to defeat the measures of the administration. Both in the national House and on the local hustings he became a flowing gargoyle of vituperation which attracted attention because of its sparkling illustration. Not content with his verbal denunciations of Jefferson and his administration, he went into print over the signature "Decius." In the series of essays which followed he laid bare the contents of the President's secret message regarding Spain, praised the minority which had dared to oppose it, and poured out vials of sarcasm upon the "idol" who ruled in the White House.[15] In fact these essays were the first, if not the only, formal statement of the principles of the Quids.

A due consideration for the freedom of the press admitted Decius to the columns of the *Enquirer,* but the answers to his essays show clearly that Ritchie had given up all hope of healing the schism within the Republican party, and that he had returned to his original ideas of our proper policies in dealing with Spain. Henceforth he spoke of Randolph as lacking the tempering influences of experience requisite in a statesman and defended Jefferson unqualifiedly. Even the lately lamented secret message now became wise and patriotic and a statesman-like method of dealing

[14] *Richmond Enquirer,* May 13, 1806.

[15] *Ibid.,* August 15, September 2, November 18, and December 9, 1806.

with the conditions as they existed in December, 1805. Questions of diplomacy were not for the common herd, much less John Randolph. Again Ritchie entertained the hope that Spain might sell the Floridas to keep them from falling into the possession of the mistress of the seas. He also revived the idea of exchanging a part of Louisiana for them.[16] In terms which suggest the Monroe Doctrine he warned his countrymen against allowing them to become the property of Great Britain in any event.

The regular Republicans had triumphed in the local elections of 1806, and when the Assembly met in December of that year efforts were made to censure the insurgent Republicans. To this end resolutions were introduced, one to commend the President, another to condemn his critics.[17] While disavowing any intention to protect or defend Randolph, Ritchie again came forward in his role of the conciliator. He heartily approved the resolution commending the President, but as earnestly opposed the other. He did not believe all the members of the factional minority equally culpable and therefore feared that a general resolution of censure might be unjust to some. Then, too, the fact that Mr. Randolph "held no terms whatsoever with Madison" did not necessarily make him and his followers uncompromising enemies of Jefferson. Had not Decius himself spoken of the "illustrious" President? Ritchie's councils prevailed, and only the resolution commending Jefferson received a majority of the Assembly.[18]

In the meantime the efforts of General Miranda in behalf of the revolting Spanish patriots in America were attracting general attention. Sympathy for him and his cause ran high in the southern states, whence both men and means were sent to his aid. Even the inland city of Richmond sent aid under the guise of a trading expedition, and Vir-

[16] *Richmond Enquirer*, November 28, 1806.

[17] *Ibid.*, December 9, 1806.

[18] *Ibid.*, December 20, 25, 1806.

ginians expected Jefferson to become the god-father of his filibustering expeditions.[19]

Though in sympathy with the revolting Spaniards, Ritchie believed Miranda an arch intriguer and warned Jefferson to have nothing to do with his expeditions. Even at this early date he believed that the Spanish possessions in America would eventually become free, though not under his leadership. He therefore tried to dampen the ardor of his countrymen in their zeal to help him, and insisted that their proposed expedition would be a palpable violation of international law and result in another South Sea Bubble.[20]

At this juncture attention was suddenly diverted from Randolph and South America to our own West. After his fatal encounter with Hamilton, Burr had retired from the vice-presidency to seek new fortunes and new friends on the frontier. There he met General Wilkinson, the arch-traitor of American traitors. What transpired between them will never be known, but it is certain that Burr returned from this trip filled with new ambitions and a determination to return to the West with a band of adventurers. All this happened just after Randolph's tirade against the "Yazoo thieves" and his failure to sustain the charges of impeachment against Judge Chase, and while he was yet sulking in his tent. Consequently, he, Macon, and Nicholson looked on with an anxiety intermingled with delight while Burr, Dayton, and their friends in the West hatched their treasonable plots and worked upon the "easy credulity" of Jefferson in an effort to destroy him. In the operations of these adventurers Randolph saw a "conjunction of malign planets" which "bodes no good."

Ritchie shared Jefferson's credulity in dealing with Burr. Contrary to the opinion of his closest friends he now refused to believe that Burr had shown bad faith in the election of 1801, and that he now sought to erect an empire

[19] *Richmond Enquirer*, March 7, 1806.
[20] *Ibid.*, March 4, 1806.

in Mexico and to dismember the United States by adding a large portion of the Mississippi valley to his proposed dominions.[21] He saw in Burr no Napoleon, and thought it impossible for him, with his limited resources and with no other following than a band of adventurers, to conquer an extensive and populous empire and dismember a great republic.[22] He insisted therefore that Burr's expedition was simply the last resort of a forlorn and friendless man to find a new new home and new friends.

The Federalists, especially the Marshalls of Kentucky, who were doubtless prompted and aided by their distinguished kinsman, the Chief Justice, shared the suspicions of Randolph and his friends regarding Burr, and seized upon the occasion as a suitable one for exposing Jefferson and freeing their country of the odious presence of Wilkinson, whose treasonable transactions with Spain were known to or suspected by them. To this end a Mr. Wood of Richmond, Virginia, was invited to Kentucky and made editor of *The Western World,* a newspaper devoted to the interests of Federalism in the "Dark and Bloody Land." Associated with him as a fighting partner, such a coadjutor being more necessary to an editor in that day and climate than a printer's devil, was a Mr. J. M. Street, also of Richmond. The very first issue of the *World* gave a history of the Spanish Association and of Wilkinson's treasonable connection therewith, and made it evident that the West had been honeycombed with treason and conspiracy for a quarter of a century.[23] It required no stretch of imagination to apply its revelations and deductions to the questionable acts of the ambitious vice-president who was then returning to the western land.

Though admitting that Burr's military talents, intriguing disposition, and inordinate ambition rendered him a dangerous resident on the frontier, especially in times of

[21] *Richmond Enquirer,* April 2, 1805.

[22] *Ibid.,* November 14, 28, 1806.

[23] *Ibid.,* September 5, 1806.

war, and deploring Wilkinson's frivolous pomp, his obsequious court to parties and to administrations, and his hauteur toward inferiors, Ritchie still insisted that the former entertained no treasonable designs and excused the latter for his connection with the Spanish Association. In that venture he now saw only a natural revolt against the Jay-Gardoqui negotiations of 1785 and the untold neglect and iniquities which had been heaped upon the West. Jefferson had recently made Wilkinson governor of the Upper Louisiana Territory and permitted him to retain his command in the regular army. But it is not plain that Ritchie sought to shield his chieftain by defending Wilkinson, because he now condemned the practice of combining the civil and military functions of government in the same hands, and criticised most severely Wilkinson's abilities and private character.[24]

The account of Burr's warlike preparations on Blennerhassett's Island, sustained as it was by reliable witnesses and accompanied by the belated anxiety of the President, revolutionized Ritchie's ideas regarding the purposes of Burr's expedition. After a strange somersault the Federalists and the Quids could now see no cause for alarm and quietly prepared themselves for Jefferson's humiliation. They now used the mild term, "Burr's Project," while Ritchie spoke of "Burr's Conspiracy" and pronounced its author the "American Cataline," whose true history could be written only by a Sallust.[25] When Wilkinson's keen scent for the course of events finally led him to turn state's evidence and testify against Burr, the Federalists raised the question, "How can one traitor convict another?" Such taunts did not disconcert the President or his spokesman in Richmond. Whatever they may have thought about Wilkinson's acceptance of a commission in the Spanish army and a pension from the Spanish government, while he yet held a commission in the American army, they now extended to him a safe conduct and placed in him their chief reliance

[24] *Richmond Enquirer*, September 5, 1806.
[25] *Ibid.*, February 13, 1807.

for convicting Burr, who was already in Richmond awaiting trial in John Marshall's court on the charge of high treason.[26]

For the Quids and the Federalists the period of Burr's imprisonment and detention in Richmond was a gala time. The *Virginia Gazette* pictured him as a patriot foiled in an honest attempt to fight our battles with Spain by an attack upon Mexico. We had extended local aid to Miranda in his filibustering expeditions, and the Federalists saw no reason why Burr should be arraigned as a traitor for a similar undertaking. They stood ready to furnish bail for him in any sum. He was "wined and dined" in the homes of the "first families" and received other attentions fit for a conquering hero. Although he was to preside at the proposed trial, Marshall thought it no desecration of his high office to dine with Burr at the home of his chief counsel, John Wickham.[27]

Burr's hospitable treatment in Richmond worried Ritchie quite as much as it did Jefferson. He shared the President's distrust in Marshall, and could not therefore see in him that "noble candor" and those "god-like talents" which were being ascribed to him by others. Although he occupied a place at the head of the social life of Richmond and was lavish in his distribution of hospitality, Ritchie considered Marshall's act in dining with Burr a reprehensible and willful prostration of his own dignity and a wanton insult to his country. When partisan feeling was willing to pay court to a traitor, he thought it a time to be concerned for the liberties of the country.[28]

During the four months which the politicians required to find out that Burr was not guilty of treason, the *Enquirer* confined itself to a publication of the court proceedings and scrupulously refrained from comment upon them. It did not even side with the President in his controversy with the court. It would be difficult to say that its refusal to do so

[26] *Richmond Enquirer,* March 3, 1807.

[27] *Ibid.,* April 10, 15, 1807.

[28] *Ibid.,* April 10, 28, 1807; *Ibid.,* May 8, 1807.

was a silent disapproval of the President's refusal to testify before John Marshall. The verdict came, however, as a surprise to Ritchie. Indeed, he refused to accept it, and insisted that Burr was guilty at heart if not by an "overt act." In a series of essays entitled "Cursory Reflections" he attempted to show that Burr had planned the separation of the West from the East, and that his proposed settlement in Louisiana was only a temporary device to conceal his ulterior purposes. He condemned Marshall's conduct during the trial and his instructions to the trial jury as reprehensible. The court had held that a traitor under the constitution was a principal in levying war against his country or in adhering to its enemies. To be a principal the court had also held, in this case, that the accused had to be present at the time and place where the warlike preparations had been made. As Burr had not been at Blennerhassett's Island when the alleged treasonable transactions took place, there was nothing left to the jury but a verdict of acquittal. But Ritchie insisted that the English law, upon which our own was based, knew no accessories or seconds in crimes of treason. Under such a ruling as that of Marshall he pointed out the impossibility of the English King's levying war upon his subjects in America, since he had never been here in person, and concluded therefore that the Declaration of Independence was a lie and the American Revolution a misnomer. In the light of these apparent contradictions he demanded Marshall's impeachment.[29]

Meanwhile our relations with Great Britain and France in our efforts to become the neutral carriers of the commerce of warring Europe had become alarming. Notwithstanding the fact that Napoleon threatened the peace of the world, and that the French vessels vied with the English in committing depredations upon our commerce, Ritchie shared the common prejudice toward England and placed the chief blame upon her. Randolph's fulminations against the non-

[29] *Richmond Enquirer*, October 30, 1807; *Ibid.*, November, 3, 6, 10, 17, 1807.

intercourse act and the intensity of the opposition to it, doubtless heightened his hatred for the mistress of the seas. Like Jefferson he did not, however, regard war as the proper means of redress in dealing with either nation. The battle of Trafalgar had ended the power of France upon the seas, and he now thought it possible to starve England into better treatment for American seamen. Accordingly he heartily endorsed the non-importation act with Great Britain. Dependent as she had been in the past, he felt that she could not now operate her mills without raw materials from America. The weavers of Springfield had been thrown into distress by a change of fashion from silk to muslin, and a million workmen had been thrown out of employment in Sheffield and Birmingham by a change from buckles and metal buttons to strings and covered buttons for shoes. He saw no reason, therefore, why the withdrawal of 25,000,000 pounds of raw cotton would not effect the textile industries and bring her government to terms.[30] Relying upon the policy of non-intercourse, he endorsed the President's summary disposal of Monroe's treaty with Great Britain, because it had not safeguarded the rights of American seamen.[31]

The attack of the *Leopard* upon the *Chesapeake* aroused young Ritchie's maternal fighting blood and demonstrated the futility of the peace policy as a restraining force upon the leaders of the younger generation in a time of crisis. As in the twinkle of an eye he became an insurgent, demanded war, and even found a commander for the federal army in the person of the gallant Moreau, then sojourning in America. An "extra" announced the news of the attack and summoned the people of Richmond to the Capitol Square. Though confronted by a vigorous opposition under the leadership of Charles Fenton Mercer, who did not hold the British government culpable for the attack upon the

[30] *Richmond Enquirer*, October 18, 1805; *Ibid.*, February 25, 1806; *Ibid.*, December 11, 1806.

[31] *Ibid.*, March 10, 13, 1807.

Chesapeake, Ritchie, Roane, and Brockenborough secured the adoption of resolutions which pledged the lives and sacred honor of those present to the patriotic duty of securing justice. A later report brought the news that the commander of the *Leopard* was blockading Norfolk. Without waiting for a confirmation of this report, which proved to be false, Ritchie deserted his young bride of a few weeks, turned the management of the *Enquirer* over to a friend, and shouldered his musket to fight with the "Republican Blues" in the defence of his country.[32] He requested that Congress be called immediately in extra session to deliberate upon the means of enforcing our rights and of extorting reparation.

The President was not moved by the bellicose demonstations in Virginia or elsewhere and held tenaciously to the peace policy. He accepted the disavowal of the British minister, waited patiently to hear from England, and set the date of the proposed extra session three months hence. When Congress did assemble the war sentiment had subsided, but the news of fresh aggressions from England and France, and of the enforcement of the Berlin Decrees and the British Orders in Council again fanned it into red heat. Even then the President did not yield, but quietly sent to Congress a confidential message asking for an embargo.

Though he himself preferred war, Ritchie defended the peace policy in its new garb with all the zeal of a partisan. The embargo was his only alternative to war. He might and doubtless would have said the same of a non-intercourse act, had it been deemed adequate to meet the exigencies. On the contrary the Federalists and Randolph, after another queer flip-flop, now opposed the embargo, arguing that it was partial to France, that it would bring distress and bankruptcy to business, ruin our commerce and agriculture, and bring war with the greatest and freest nation on the globe and withal our best friend, Great Britain. Ritchie defended the embargo by practically the same arguments used

[32] *Richmond Enquirer,* July 1, 27, 1807.

in defence of the non-importation act, but now insisted upon the necessity for a patriotic self-denial even at the expense of agriculture and commerce. He likened those who went to Great Britain for lessons of liberty and freedom to those benighted souls accustomed to consult the Lama of Thibet about religion, denounced Randolph as " the veriest slave alive to his passions and antipathies," and predicted that the petitions then being prepared in London, Manchester, and Liverpool against the operation of the Orders in Council marked the beginning of the end of British tyranny.[33] When the expected redress did not come, he issued a declaration of independence based upon that of 1776 setting forth our national grievances and pledging the lives, fortunes, and sacred honor of Virginia to maintain the embargo.[34]

Strange as it may seem, in view of his subsequent course, Ritchie now advocated protection for American manufactures. The suspension of free intercourse with England had necessitated the erection of cotton mills in the North and a resort to domestic manufacturing in the South. Under the existing conditions it became evident that the United States could be made a self-sufficing and consequently a truly independent nation. But every one knew that a resumption of free intercourse, which was expected to follow the repeal of the embargo, would be destructive of the new born industries in America. Consequently he would have preserved the beneficent results of the embargo by resort to a permanent protective tariff. In our abundant resources, mechanical genius, ample supply of slave labor, rapidly accumulating capital, growing tendencies to form corporations, and the rise of the wool-growing industry, he saw all the domestic requirements for a great manufacturing nation.[35] Accordingly he made proud mention in the columns of the *Enquirer* of those patriots who wore homespun and denominated the generally accepted belief that manufactures

[33] *Richmond Enquirer*, May 10, 1807.

[34] *Ibid.*, June 3, 1808.

[35] *Ibid.*, December 27, 1808.

could be made to flourish only in a densely populated country, a delusion propagated by Great Britain to aid her own selfish interests. His views on the subject of manufacturing were ably set forth in "An Address to the People of Virginia" signed by himself, W. H. Cabell, William Wirt, William Foushee, and Peyton Randolph. His enthusiasm for protection led to the call of a mass meeting in Richmond which petitioned Congress to intervene in behalf of the American manufacturer.

Ritchie's interest in the manufacturers was, however, due mainly to a desire to maintain the embargo which was now being attacked in all parts of the Union. As has been seen it was his only alternative to war or submission. Now he had an additional motive. Repeal meant condemnation of Jefferson's pet policy. Nevertheless a hostile Congress was openly defiant. To Ritchie it mattered not that a storm was rising in the East where the shipping interests were suffering. The arm of the federal government was not to be palsied by "the lowering aspect of political discontent," and John Randolph and his band of blind partisans were to be given no opportunity to prostrate the nation at the feet of Great Britain. Finally a partial repeal, which would have permitted trade with Spain and Portugal only, was proposed as a compromise. He opposed even that. In such a step he saw the virtual repeal of the embargo itself, because it would then be possible for Great Britain to ship her goods to Spain and Portugal and thence by reshipments to America.[36] In a vain effort to counteract the tide which was about to overwhelm the administration he led the citizens of Richmond in a formal protest against the proposed repeal, but Congress had already acted. To Ritchie's great gratification it had spared the President the deepest humiliation by making the repeal operative after his retirement from office.[37] Even then repeal was a bitter pill. Henceforth Ritchie became an insurgent against the peace policy and an advocate of war.

[36] *Richmond Enquirer*, November 18, 1808.

[37] *Ibid.*, March 3, 1809.

The operation of the embargo caused the New Englanders to "calculate the value" of the Union. A spokesman, John Park, editor of the *Boston Repertory,* had gone so far as to recommend that the states of that section take "just, honorable, and fair ground" in setting forth their grievances and the conditions on which alone the Union could be maintained. The Force Act, which provided for the enforcement of the embargo, caused a storm of protests and brought concerted action against the federal government. The residents of Bath called for civil war; the fishermen of Gloucester prepared to arm themselves in defence of their rights; Hadley expressed the belief that a perseverance in the hostility to commerce, which arose from jealousy of New England, would dismember the Union. In brief, New England had assumed an attitude not unlike that of Virginia in 1798.

Ritchie's response to the anti-Union sentiment resembled the response of New England at a later period. He denominated her Essex Junto, a hot-bed of treason, and warned its adherents that the South would not stand idly by and see them dismember the Union. It was not sufficient that they quoted the example of Virginia in 1798 and incorporated the very words of her celebrated resolutions in their own. He did not deny the right of a state to interpose to arrest a breach of the constitution. But he was certain that the embargo was not a "palpable and dangerous" exercise of power not granted, and that the conditions of 1809 were in no way similar to those in 1798. Besides Virginia had protested as a sovereign state, whereas New England proposed to speak as a geographical section.[38]

Meanwhile, the efforts to select Jefferson's successor in the presidency gave Ritchie an opportunity to develop his political instincts and to give evidence of those abilities which were later to become a power in Virginia politics. In the earliest stages of the campaign he had opposed the pretensions of the heir apparent. His attitude toward the Yazoo claim-

[38] *Richmond Enquirer,* January 24, 1809; *Ibid.,* April 4, 1809.

ants caused Ritchie to agree with the *Aurora* "that no virtuous republican can support any man who has a concern directly or indirectly in the stupendous scheme of plunder, or who is a supporter thereof, or who may give a tacit countenance to that fraud."[39] Then, too, the presidency had been filled sixteen out of twenty years by Virginians, and expediency demanded that it should go to another state. Accordingly he and Giles had favored the pretensions of George Clinton of New York.[40] But the defection of the Quids, the uncertainties connected with Burr's conspiracy, the growing strength of the Federalists, and the tactics of its chief trumpeter, W. C. Nicholas, drove them into the Madisonian bandwagon. At no time did Ritchie look kindly upon Monroe's candidacy. On the contrary, he lost no opportunity to keep him from the snares of the Quids. Upon his return from England in December, 1807, he had warned him against the danger of building for the future upon "the trembling ruins of John Randolph's reputation." On January 21, 1808, a largely attended caucus of the Virginia Assembly nominated Madison for the presidency, while a smaller caucus placed Monroe in nomination for the same office. Two days later a congressional caucus, attended by eighty-three senators and representatives, confirmed the action of Virginia in nominating Madison, which was the work of Nicholas, Ritchie, and Giles. The next issue of the *Enquirer* announced the Republican electoral ticket, and expressed surprise at the thought of opposition to it.[41]

As in many a subsequent case, Ritchie's expression of surprise at the presence of and necessity for an opposition meant that it was unusually abundant. Both the motives and the tactics of the legislative caucus which had nominated Madison were soon the objects of a severe attack, Over the signature "Opecancanaugh," Benjamin W. Leigh charged that W. C. Nicholas had gone to Congress for the express

[39] *Richmond Enquirer*, October 7, 1806.
[40] *Ibid.*, April 21, 1826.
[41] *Ibid.*, January 26, 1808.

purpose of making Madison President, and that the letters from Washington which had appeared with such regularity in the *Enquirer* had been written by him with a view to shaping the political sentiment of Virginia. At the same time "A Constant Reader," either George Hay, who was Monroe's son-in-law, or John Randolph, assailed the political and editorial character of the *Enquirer,* and openly accused its editor of apostacy to the Yazoo thieves and of subserviency to the administration.[42]

Ritchie was never more at home than when resenting attacks upon his political record and methods, and was consequently now ready with a reply. He denied the use of unfair tactics in the state legislative caucus which had nominated Madison, but said not a word about Nicholas' purpose in going to Congress or about his alleged connection with the *Enquirer.* As at all times he could not be induced to defend the Yazoo claims, but he could not see in them an Aaron's rod to swallow up the just claims of an able and upright man to the presidency. He now took a turn which is one of the most unique in his whole political record. Formerly he had diverted the censure of the anti-Yazoo men from Jefferson to Madison. Now he sought to place it wholly upon Gallatin, in whom the discontented saw no guile. Frequent mention was made of the fact that Gallatin had, as one of a commission of three with Madison and Levi Lincoln, prepared the report upon which the Yazoo claims were based. It was true that Madison had made a grave political blunder in signing the report, but the point was now made that he had simply deferred to Gallatin's judgment.[43]

After the nominations for the presidency had all been made, Ritchie entertained little fear of the Federalists and the Quids. Except a few "sly bodies" which crept into the columns of the *Norfolk Ledger* or a "blushing rose" which occasionally adorned the *Charleston* (S. C.) *Courier,* he noted with delight that Federalism had practically disap-

[42] *Richmond Enquirer,* February 11, 1808; *Ibid.,* March 1, 1808.
[43] *Ibid.,* February 11, 1808.

peared in the Southland. The Quids confined their activities to North Carolina and to eastern Virginia, and were at no time formidable. Each of the opposition parties cared more for party success than for party principles. Ritchie's only cause of alarm came from the interest and the alleged activity of the British in the campaign. In their co-operation with the Essex Junto to defeat Madison, he saw a menace not to the Republican party but to the whole country. Success in that event would be followed by an attempt to dismember the Union. He found, therefore, more than the joy of a partisan in Madison's election, and it afforded him an exquisite pleasure to stand by the side of his old friend, Henry Clay, to see their common choice take the oath which made him President.[44]

After the contest had ended, an incident of the campaign was revived and occasioned an interesting exchange of personalities which threw light upon the political conditions in Virginia and revived some of her history. In an effort to force Colonel John Taylor of Caroline into line for the regular nominee of the Republican party, the non-suspecting young editor of the *Enquirer* had commented upon the fact that, unlike most of the prominent men who had formerly supported Monroe, Taylor was not then, September, 1808, supporting Madison. The true cause of this defection, the nationalistic tendencies of the times, was overlooked, and it was intimated that Colonel Taylor had sustained "private griefs" at the hands of the administration. In a private letter Taylor protested against the unauthorized use of his name in a public print, and denied that he had ever asked or expected any favors of Jefferson. The matter would probably have rested there, had not friends prevailed upon Colonel Taylor's son to permit the publication of his father's letter in *The Spirit of '76*, which was then edited by one of Ritchie's personal enemies. It now became necessary for the public to hear the whole story.

[44] *Richmond Enquirer*, September 10, 1852.

In a paternal and philosophical manner peculiar to himself and characteristic of the attitude of the older toward the younger school of Virginia politicians, Taylor warned Ritchie against the danger and folly of appropriating to himself undue credit for Madison's success and of posing as an arbiter of public merit. He was certain that the public would never permit an insignificant editor to squirt his filth like a Hottentot conjurer, nor would it kiss the rod of a pedagogue. He saw in Ritchie only a demagogue intoxicated by flattery and goaded into error by partisan zeal. He saw no future for him as an editor, and predicted that his glowing editorials, "like glass beads, painted in gaudy colors to dazzle and cheat ignorance," would in due time be accepted at their true worth.

But the Sage of Carolina had met his match in the use of invective and sarcasm. To this generally recognized "quibbler" and "sophist" Ritchie was willing to accord the privilege of railing, the prerogative of monks and women, but he would not permit any one to assail the high calling and permanent usefulness of the teacher and the editor. They were each essential to the life and purity of a republic. Ritchie was not content, however, to deal in mere personalities. With the ardor of youth he attacked the record of his venerable assailant. He openly accused him of being the original Quid, of leading John Randolph into schism, of directing the attacks upon Madison from garbled extracts from the *Federalist,* and of willfully absenting himself from the polls in November, 1808. He was the one of whom "the world was telling sad stories." Despite the fact that Ritchie had recommended him for the premiership in the new administration, in case it was not offered to Giles, he now admitted that Taylor had not sought office, but he insisted, nevertheless, that he was green with envy and jealousy. To heighten the ravages of these mental diseases, Ritchie tauntingly added that Taylor's Resolutions of '98 had not been half so favorably received as had been Madison's Report of '99.

Colonel Taylor's reply revealed the fact that there were things which the older politicians had not revealed even to their chosen spokesman. To his great surprise, Ritchie now learned that Madison had written the Resolutions of '98 as well as the Report which followed, and that a man's politics were not necessarily good or bad according to whether or not he read the *Enquirer*. Taylor had read the *Federalist* upon the suggestion of Ritchie, and had never used them or anything else in alienating Randolph's affections from Madison. Ritchie was also surprised to learn that it was Jefferson himself who had first informed Colonel Taylor about the threatened schism within the administration party. Doubt about the propriety of voting for himself as an elector upon the Monroe ticket, and the conviction that opposition was futile as well as needless, had kept him from the polls in November, 1808.[45] His later replies took the form of philosophical essays.[46] They protested against the centralizing tendencies of the federal government and against either war or non-intercourse with England. He insisted that the latter was ruining American commerce, and ridiculed the audacity of those who would win the liberty of the seas by "an expedition to the North Pole (Canada)."

No quantity of metaphysical writing could convince Ritchie that Taylor was not a conceited sophist whose absurdities were worthy only of ridicule, and that he had not been the original Quid. For a time all friendly intercourse between them was suspended as a result of the personalities exchanged on this occasion.

Ritchie sympathized, nevertheless, with Taylor's attacks upon the new nationalism, which was now demonstrating itself in many ways, and particularly in a movement for the recharter of the Bank of the United States. As the first bank had approached a natural death Gallatin, the Secretary of the Treasury, had recommended a recharter. Now that Jefferson had made his official exit and that the Bank of Vir-

[45] *Richmond Enquirer*, March 14, 1809.

[46] These essays were published in pamphlet form.

ginia was in successful operation, Ritchie was free to protest against the proposed recharter on constitutional grounds. Gallatin's former intimacy with Randolph had not been forgiven, and Ritchie now objected to acknowledging him as "the pope of the constitution." Besides the political activity of the federal bank and its predilection for things European had rendered it dangerous. Then, too, a recharter might pave the way to other things national: roads, canals, and schools. A federal bank was also unnecessary so long as there were specie paying state banks which could be used for depositories for federal moneys and as mediums for regulating the currency. That the Bank of Virginia might serve these ends, Ritchie and Dr. Brockenbrough united their energies in a successful effort to increase its capital stock and to establish tributary banks in the leading towns of the state.

CHAPTER III.

NATIONALISM AND PARTICULARISM.

Like his predecessor in the presidency, Madison loved peace and was willing to secure it by any slow process of law or negotiation. What seemed to be a triumph for his ideas and policies came, when, after repeated conferences with Erskine, the British minister to the United States, he was able to issue a proclamation repealing the embargo and non-intercourse acts against Great Britain and her colonies after June 10, 1809. On that date more than a thousand ships, already loaded and anxiously waiting the signal for flight, spread their wings and, like a flock of long-imprisoned birds, flew to the sea. Congress had met in extra session on May 22d to prepare for war, but the President was then able to assure it that there would be no war, that foreign intercourse would speedily be restored, that domestic tranquillity would again smile upon the land, that the gun-boats would be laid up, and that the militia had been discharged. During this brief period of enthusiasm he was the most popular man in the country. True, it was a Federalist triumph, but the demands for peace were so urgent that it brought joy to Republicans also, who now joined with the Federalists in proclaiming Madison the superior to Jefferson in statesmanship and diplomacy.

Since the attack of the *Leopard* upon the *Chesapeake,* when he had shouldered his musket and marched to Norfolk, Ritchie had been an insurgent and in favor of war as the only means of redress for the wrongs and indignities heaped upon us by Great Britain. Nor was he now carried away by the temporary prospect for peace. In the promised success of the Spanish uprising against the power of Napoleon he saw a menace to our peace with England. With no ally except the "corrupt and selfish" English cabinet, with the foot of the lion of Europe upon her neck, and with no

Kosciusko to lead her patriots he had at first feared that the fate of Poland would be that of Spain. But, when success finally came as the result of British aid, he saw that the markets of Spain and of her colonies would at once be opened to British trade and that the mistress of the seas would be no longer dependent upon the United States for her raw materials and foods stuffs, if indeed she ever had been. As early as January, 1809, he had noticed that the riots in Manchester were ceasing and that British seamen, conscious of their independence, were constantly assuming a more defiant attitude toward American commerce.[1]

The course of events fully justified Ritchie's contentions. By a new order in council, that of April 26, 1809, the previous order of November 11, 1807, was revoked, but the ports of Holland, France and Italy were declared to be blockaded. Shortly afterward, Canning repudiated Erskine's arrangement with Madison, whereby the latter had been induced to revoke the embargo and non-intercourse acts, and Erskine was himself recalled. Then there came as his successor the haughty and despotic Jackson with his servants, horses, and carriages and a set of instructions which would have justified the United States in a declaration of war. His subsequent conduct, together with a renewal of the depredations upon our commerce came near precipitating war with both England and France, and when Congress met again in extra session on November 27, 1809, the whole country was in a turmoil.

Ritchie urged Congress to use decisive measures. He defended Madison's summary refusal to continue intercourse with Jackson and demanded the recall of Wm. Pinkney, our minister to England, on the ground that he was guilty of coquetting with British royalty. As the reports of depredations upon our commerce multiplied, he asked for letters of *marque* and *reprisal,* as the only means of defence for our merchant marine. The time seemed opportune to strike.

[1] *Richmond Enquirer,* August 12, 26, 1808; *Ibid.,* October 7, 1808; *Ibid.,* January 12, 1809.

The British fleet then stood foiled in the Scheldt; her troops were being driven from Portugal; France ignored her paper blockade; and her greatest ally, Austria, lay prostrated.[2]

As early as May, 1810, Ritchie saw a solution of the perplexing problems growing out of our foreign relations only in the election of a progressive and patriotic Congress which would not hesitate to defend the national honor and interests by a declaration of war. The "imbecility" of the tenth and the eleventh Congresses disgusted him.[3] The former had repealed the embargo, and the latter had "piddled" with the "Macon Bills" and revived the cowardly policy of non-intercourse with England. It was plainly one of those congestions which have frequently appeared in our history and lingered until relieved by a free and independent use of the suffrage. It has always necessitated a complete change in the personnel of those in authority. The following directions to the voters, accompanied by denunciation of John Randolph and the peace loving Federalists, appeared in the columns of the *Enquirer* on the eve of the election of that memorable twelfth Congress. They leave no doubt about Ritchie's remedies for the situation.

"Take 40 grains of virtue, principally of that sort called disinterestedness, and 30 grains of firmness, which is distinguished by a man's thinking for himself and doing what he thinks right—blend these with a portion of talents and a sufficiency of eloquence, and you have a composition something like an American representative."[4]

Ritchie's sentiments were those which actuated the voters in the newer parts of the Union. Filled with a consuming hatred for England, "the young men," the generation born after the Revolution, came forward to assert and, if necessary, to fight for a more complete independence. The result was a political revolution. Of the one hundred and forty-two men who sat in the eleventh Congress, sixty-one were not

[2] *Richmond Enquirer*, December 19, 1809; *Ibid*, June 12, 1810; *Ibid.*, July 17, 1809.

[3] *Ibid.*, May 15, 1810; *Ibid.*, July 4, 1810.

[4] *Ibid.*, September 7, 1810.

returned to the twelfth. On the roll of the new House were some of the most illustrious men who have appeared in our history, men who for years to come were to control national legislation and administration, lead parties, and rival each other for the honor of a residence in the White House. Among the young "war hawks" were Henry Clay, John Caldwell Calhoun, Richard M. Johnson, Felix Grundy, Langdon Cheves, George M. Troup, and Peter B. Porter.

Practically all the states held their congressional elections before Virginia, hers coming in April of the odd years. Accordingly Ritchie and his friends felt it incumbent upon them to place her in line with the states of the West and the South, which had responded so nobly to the new born spirit of independence by sending insurgents to Washington. To them it meant more than a mere effort to keep abreast with the times. Virginia's power and prestige among the states was at stake. Thus a vain effort was made to defeat the Quids—Randolph and Gray, and the Federalists—Breckenridge, Sheffey, Lewis, Baker, and Wilson, for a re-election. Notwithstanding his failure and what it meant to Virginia in a loss of influence, Ritchie readily acquiesced in the results and magnanimously welcomed into public life Calhoun and Clay, the youthful leaders upon whom the scepter of power had fallen. Though he later came to fear and distrust Calhoun and was a power in keeping him from the coveted presidency, Ritchie now saw in him "one of those master spirits, who stamp their name upon the age in which they live."[5] His only regret was that this "promising South Carolinian" was not a Virginian.

After giving effective aid in the election of a Congress which could be trusted to guard the welfare of the nation Ritchie began a crusade upon the executive department of the federal government in an effort to relieve it of its dead wood. Nothing was to be expected of a "President de jure" under the influence of a cabal composed of such "weaklings" as William Duane, Michael Leib, and Robert and Samuel

[5] *Richmond Enquirer*, December 24, 1811.

Smith. As a protest against the feebleness of the chief executive Gallatin, the only man of talent among Madison's advisers, was on the point of resigning his place in the Cabinet. It was an intolerable condition and the ties of friendship or locality did not shield the venerable President from condemnation in the columns of the *Enquirer*. When Madison was finally made to see the light, Ritchie approved few of his proposed remedies. He agreed that Smith's incompetence rendered his services as secretary of state valueless, but he desired neither Gallatin nor Monroe, Madison's first and second choices, to succeed him. They each had talents, but their former affiliations with Randolph rendered them objectionable to a "died in the wool" Republican.[6] Ritchie would have preferred Calhoun or Clay for this high honor.

Like many of the best movements in the ante-bellum history of Virginia the war sentiment of 1812 took form in her western counties and gradually extended itself to the Lowlands, where it found a ready exponent in the *Enquirer*. As if in protest against the attitude of the New England Federalists the eighth regiment of militia, in mass-meeting assembled at Lexington, had early expressed a desire to buckle on the "armor of the nation" and to fight upon the shores of the Atlantic or in the wilds of Canada.[7] Others gave expression to their militant feelings in petitions to the Assembly, which was finally induced to adopt a resolution calling for war.[8] Shortly thereafter the citizens of Richmond, under the direction of Ritchie and Spencer Roane, assembled in mass meeting to consider our foreign relations and to strengthen the courage of the President, then on the point of abandoning his traditional peace policy.[9] Prominent among the leaders of the war movement were also: William Wirt, Geo. Hay, Samuel Pleasants, P. N. Nicholas, William Foushee, Peyton Randolph, P. V. Daniel, and Dr. Brockenbrough.

[6] *Richmond Enquirer*, May 10, 1811; *Ibid.*, April 16, 26, 1812.

[7] *Ibid.*, January 4, 1812.

[8] *Ibid.*, February 6, 1812.

[9] *Richmond Enquirer*, May 3, 1812.

Both Giles and Randolph had seen the handwriting on the wall. Without seeking a re-election the former had retired to the "woods and vales" of Amelia, while the latter, in a long letter addressed to his constituents, tried to defend his course in Congress and to allay the rapidly increasing war sentiment. Though Giles' presence in the Senate was of no particular advantage to the country and of none to Virginia, since he had put himself out of harmony with the administration and drawn about himself "a cloud of suspicion which all his eloquence and ingenuity could not dispel," Ritchie sarcastically reminded him in his "Letters from the Simple to the Great" that "those who are not for us are against us."[10] He now found a suitable position for Randolph as the "chief horuspex" in a proposed college of Augurs to be modeled after that of ancient Rome and to be an oracle for "grannies" and the feeble hearted. As a last resort Randolph tried to show that there was as much reason for a declaration of war upon France as upon England and that Napoleon was using the United States to further his own selfish ambitions. Ritchie denied positively that we were being offered up as an idolatrous sacrifice on the altar of French rapacity, perfidy, and ambition and insisted that those who favored war—Macon, Crawford, Troup, Bibb, Lowndes, Cheves, Grundy, Calhoun, and Clay, were not, as was claimed, the minions of France but the honest and patriotic representatives of enraged constituency.[11]

Though the Virginians were no longer the leaders in Congress, the formal declaration of war upon Great Britain was a signal triumph for Ritchie. Henry Clay was among the first to congratulate him upon the event and to thank him for his part in bringing it about.[12] Ritchie himself hailed war as the beginning of a new era and implored God to let fall the lightning of the nation upon the editors of the *Baltimore Republican,* the *Boston Repertory,* and all others

[10] *Richmond Enquirer,* May 22, 1812.

[11] *Ibid.,* February 6, 1812; *Ibid.,* June 12, 1812.

[12] *Ibid.,* September 10, 1852.

who deserted their country in its time of need. In his support of an agressive war he spoke simply for that spirit of nationalism and independence, then abroad in the land, which he believed would carry us as conquerors into Canada and bring about the annexation of that country to our own.[13] His brothers, John and Archibald, now atoned for whatever of Toryism may have lingered about the home of the Ritchies in 1776 by accepting commissions in the regular army.[14] The former lost his life while gallantly fighting on the plains of Bridgewater, and the latter rendered distinguished services in the campaign about Norfolk. The records show that Thomas Ritchie himself received pay for services in this war, and in 1827 the state of Virginia in recognition of the distinguished services of Captain John Ritchie presented a sword to his heirs. As editor of the *Enquirer,* Thomas Ritchie's energies were untiring in efforts to arouse the valor of his countrymen, to encourage the soldiers under difficulties and dangers, to nerve and stimulate them to noble achievements and to laud and chronicle their deeds. He had always looked upon the federal government mainly as an instrument for combining the resources of the whole country in efforts to withstand foreign enemies. Therefore the refusal of the New Englanders to permit their state militia to pass under the command of the President was, to say the least, a violation of the spirit of the federal compact. He urged a united and patriotic defence on the part of the whole country and advised the New Englanders to impeach the President, if they thought him incompetent to command the army, rather than desert their common country.[15]

The times are few during the period of actual hostilities when Ritchie was satisfied with the manner in which the war was conducted, but they are fewer still when he despaired of ultimate success. Man to man and gun to gun he was certain that the tried red coats were no match for the American

[13] *Richmond Enquirer,* June 23, 1812; *Ibid.,* July 21, 1812.
[14] *Ibid.,* May 29, 1827.
[15] *Richmond Enquirer,* July 10, 1812.

volunteers. He was equally certain that the generous principles which animated the breast of free men contending for their country, her rights and her independence, would prove "too powerful for the mercenary principles of the hired slaves," who composed a large part of the British army. In the incompetency of Dr. Eustice, the Secretary of War, Ritchie saw a greater cause of Hull's defeat before Detroit than the incompetency of that general, and he manfully placed the blame where it belonged—to an unwise use of the appointive power. In adhering to the tendency, as old as the government itself, to parcel out the loaves and fishes of office without regard to the ability and peculiar fitness of the appointees, he saw the most fatal blunder of Madison's whole administration. To his mind there was just as much reason for choosing the Secretary of War, or any other official, by the color of his eyes or the length of his nose as by the place of his domicile.[16]

It was with keen disappointment that Ritchie announced the surrender of Napoleon and his banishment to Elba.[17] That the greatest warrior of the age should become an humble sovereign and the recipient of the bounties of his enemies was revolting to him. Besides, he now saw that the war dogs of England would be turned upon America. Although negotiations to end the war were in progress, he warned his countrymen against the siren voice of peace, contending that the British would concede nothing until the fate of their expedition to our southern states had been determined. In the hostile tone of the British press, in the presence of armed vessels in our waters, and in the arrival of Wellington's tried veterans upon our shores he saw no harbingers of peace. In a sort of ultimatum to Congress he demanded an aggressive continuation of the war, and, yet hopeful of winning Canada, he made bold to suggest that

[16] *Ritchie Manuscripts.* Thomas Ritchie to Archibald Ritchie, September 1, 1812, and August 31, 1813.

[17] *Richmond Enquirer,* June 11, 1814.

the scenes of operations be carried from the gates of Rome to the gates of Carthage.[18]

The rumors of peace which found their way from Ghent, where negotiations to that end were in progress, made little impression upon Ritchie, so firmly did he believe that the British meant to continue the war. In the white flag sighted off Cape May he saw only "a hoax, an invitation to traitors to furnish the enemy with provisions." At length the disappointing treaty arrived, and denial of the facts was no longer possible.[19]

Ritchie accepted peace with a gratitude intermingled with shame and humiliation, but found solace for his wounded feelings in urging a continuation of preparations for war. He firmly believed that "as long as America preserves a name amongst the nations of the earth, she would be opposed by a foe, haughty and cruel, and more faithless than Carthage." Already there were rumors of British designs upon Florida and the Northwest Territory. Our only security lay, therefore, in a strong navy. To this end Ritchie favored the construction of two "seventy-fours" and four "Guerriers" annually. In our second war for independence experience had proved the value of a navy, and Ritchie now insisted that further delay in building men-of-war was as suicidal as it was unnecessary. The South abounded in naval stores and live oak; the West furnished cordage and canvass; and the North had sailors "who would not give up the ship."

From Jefferson and Madison, Ritchie had come a long way in arriving at the conclusion that a time of peace is a time to prepare for war,[20] but a vast gulf lay between the generation for which he now spoke and that for which he had formerly spoken. Born in the midst of the Revolution and reared in an atmosphere of hatred to England he now spoke for himself. It was plainly a time to venerate the name and the deeds of "the fathers" but not to follow them.

[18] *Richmond Enquirer*, September 7, 14, 18, 21, 1814.

[19] *Ibid.*, February 22, 1815; *Ibid.*, March 25, 1815.

[20] *Ibid.*, May 20, 1815; *Ibid.*, October 11, 1815.

The attitude of the New Englanders toward the war and the utterances of some of their leading prints and statesmen regarding it, caused the *Enquirer* to assume a tone not unlike that of the northern prints in 1860. The "Holy Union" was now as dear to Ritchie as "the ruddy drops that warm our hearts." It was our "pillar of Peace, our Safety, our Prosperity." Without it he saw a country divided, belligerent, with its borders stained by the blood of its own citizens as had been the borders of the Grecian states, England and Scotland, France and Holland, Austria and Prussia. Under such conditions a contest for self-preservation would inevitably follow; standing armies would appear; demagogues and usurpers would be unscrupulous; and vassalage upon a foreign monarch the inevitable result.[21] A time of national danger was evidently inopportune for a discussion of the rights of the sovereign states, and Ritchie accordingly deplored the course of the New Englanders.

Peace had hardly been restored in America and the danger of disunion averted before the prints heralded the triumphant return of Napoleon from Elba. In the hope that adversity had made him a better man, Ritchie welcomed the return of the defender of self-government and the despoiler of the rights of legitimate princes. He saw no reason why Napoleon could not succeed in re-establishing his rule over France. Murat would welcome him; Belgium, now trembling for her independence, stood ready to enlist under his banners; France would rise again in the strength of her might; and the Corn Laws and the Income Taxes had exhausted England's resources. The result of the "hundred days" was therefore disappointing, because experience had taught that France could expect more from Bonaparte than from a Bourbon.[22]

With peace assured at home and abroad Ritchie faced about with his countrymen to enjoy a new-born nationality. From Europe, the prey of the legitimate princes, he gladly

[21] *Richmond Enquirer*, August 27, 1813; *Ibid.*, March 2, 1814.
[22] *Richmond Enquirer*, May 24, 1815.

pointed his fellow countrymen and the oppressed of other lands to "happy America," with its boundless West and matchless resources. His answers, made in the form of questions to the self-imposed query, "What will you do for news now that Napoleon is vanquished?" tell the story of the great change which had taken place. "Have the Americans no water-courses to clear?" asked he. "No canals to construct? no roads to form? no bridges to erect? Where are the public schools which we have erected? Where are the collegs which Virginians have endowed? Where are our public libraries? Where are the shrines which we have erected to the honor of Science.[23]

Any attempt to answer these questions made Ritchie blush with shame. Already Virginia had taken a back seat in politics and statesmanship, and was rapidly sinking into a star of second and third magnitude. All these things grieved Ritchie who had already undertaken, as a life work, the task of maintaining the ascendency of the state of his nativity. To this end he now urged a greater interest in education and internal improvements and established a new journal, the *Richmond Compiler,* which he continued to edit to 1833, to be devoted exclusively to the local and industrial interests of Virginia.[24] Had she followed his advice more closely and paid less attention to the loquacious statesmen who attempted to direct her councils, she would doubtless have fared better in the race for material gain.

Under these altered conditions the question of the presidential succession demanded immediate attention. Monroe's enviable record as Secretary of State had not yet wrought an absolution for his former political sins, and Ritchie remained consequently indifferent to his candidacy. Whether he shaped the indifference of Virginia or Virginia his attitude would be difficult to determine. Possibly they were mutual. Be that as it may, the Assembly of 1816, which

[23] *Richmond Enquirer*, September 20, 1815.

[24] *Ibid.*, September 20, 1815; *Ibid.*, July 25, 1854. The *Compiler* was established in 1816.

had just made Ritchie public printer and given him other contracts for printing, out of which he made large sums, now named presidential electors in legislative caucus, but refrained from expressing a choice for the presidency. This course can not be attributed wholly to a desire to placate those who complained about "the scepter of Virginia." Many of the younger school of politicians discredited Monroe and preferred Crawford. It was not until after the congressional caucus had decided in favor of the former that Ritchie said much in his praise. Even then he did not deny that the nomination had been brought about by an alliance between the politicians of New York, Pennsylvania, and Virginia, and made bold to suggest a more democratic method of nominating and electing the President than that afforded by the congressional caucus and the electoral college. Thus Monroe's election appeared to him to be more of a tribute to Virginia and to Jefferson and Madison than a triumph for republicanism.[25]

With a statesmanlike foresight, Ritchie now turned to a solution of the great problems connected with the internal development of the country. A casual survey revealed the beginnings of a contest between rival states for commercial advantages. Love of the Union and sympathy for the prevailing nationalism carried him beyond state boundaries and caused him to see in closer ties between the East and the West greater security and prosperity for the whole country. Yet Ritchie thought that Virginia could not afford to stand idly by and see the other states tap the granary of the nation, the Mississippi valley. Pennsylvania was already reaching in that direction with her turnpikes, New York with her canal, and Maryland with the Cumberland Road.[26] The zeal with which he spoke, nay pled for a line of communication to connect the East and the West by way of the James and the Kanawha rivers achieved little for Virginia, but it did much to win for Ritchie the affection of those living

[25] *Richmond Enquirer*, March 20, 1816; *Ibid.*, November 6, 1816.
[26] *Ibid.*, August 8, 1817.

in the western counties, whose sentiments he had voiced in 1812 and who were rapidly becoming his political henchmen.

Interest in the growing West naturally directed attention to the public lands which Ritchie feared had already become the prey of speculators. To one who had resided practically all his life in the land of "fair prices," $120 an acre for unimproved land, the price then paid in Alabama for certain choice tracts, seemed anything but normal. Accordingly he recommended the enactment of laws to safeguard the public domain, leaving it at the same time open to a free and liberal use of home seekers. He thought it should be made the basis of credit in times of war and of security for contemplated internal improvements in times of peace,[27] and he therefore oposed any gratuitous distributions. Like Jefferson, he had always regarded the West as the refinery for our republicanism and our national virility and could not tolerate corruption, either in disposing of or administering it. Nay, it was more than that. It was the refinery in which the immigrants were to be wrought into American citizens. Behind the stream of humanity, which was now flowing into the United States at the rate of two hundred daily, the editor of the *New York Evening Post* saw an overpopulated Europe casting off a superfluous and undesirable growth, but Ritchie denied that Europe was overpopulated and could see behind this living stream only the attractions of our great West with its cheap lands, low taxes, and abundant opportunities.[28]

Nevertheless the effect of the westward migration upon Virginia alarmed Ritchie. As the bands of immigrants from the armies of Napoleon and Wellington had passed over the Alleghanies, thousands of his fellow countrymen had joined them in search for new homes. With their negro slaves some had gone to the far South, while others had been content to stop in the Ohio and the Missouri valleys. As a result, realty values had declined in eastern Virginia; per-

[27] *Richmond Enquirer*, October 6, 1818.

[28] *Ibid.*, August 21, 1818.

sonal property was disappearing; and "likely" negroes were not worth half as much as in the lower South. In the migration of the slave owners, Ritchie saw an opportunity to rid the state of the "fearful curse" of negro slavery, but he feared that the process would rob her of her sons and cause her further decline in the councils of the nation. To avert these calamities he now pled for more scientific farming and set in motion that interest and enthusiasm which resulted in the formation of numerous agricultural societies.[29]

On the other hand, western Virginia was sharing the development and growth of the greater West of which it was really a part. The conditions there produced demands for credit and for banking legislation which the East could not understand, coming as it did at a time of financial and industrial depression in that quarter. During and immediately following the second war with Great Britain specie and bank-notes had become as scarce in the western counties as martins in the month of December. The iron makers, the salt and wool manufacturers, cattle raisers and small farmers now demanded some kind of money to carry on their legitimate operations and to aid in the completion of their contemplated works of internal improvement. The danger of dependence upon their northern neighbors was not considered sufficiently menacing to warrant granting their demands for relief. Consequently, they resorted to a sort of "moonshine" enterprise to obtain it. They now supplied the demands for a currency by the use of illegal banks which sprang into existence in every small town and flooded the whole western country with worthless currency. Later these banks sought to sustain themselves by an appeal to the Assembly which was asked to accept the *status quo* and to legalize their issues. The refusal of these requests called forth other acts of defiance. The banking monopoly of Richmond was severely attacked; the immediate resumption of specie payment was demanded; grand juries presented the Assembly as an unjust and tyrannical body; and associa-

[29] *Richmond Enquirer*, August 25, 1818; *Ibid.*, October 6, 1818.

tions, not unlike those which went into the West at an earlier date and set up pioneer governments, were formed to protect the illegal banks.[30] Persistance in their efforts brought about the enactment of a law to compel the banks of Virginia (there were only two each located at Richmond) to resume specie payment on or before November 15, 1816.

The demands of the westerners, accompanied as they were by a movement in the country at large for the recharter of a national bank, greatly embarrassed Ritchie. The national bank he considered unconstitutional, and to grant the request of the westerners would endanger the banking monopoly of Richmond, which had been built up by the genius of his cousin, Dr. Brockenbrough. In his opposition to the proposed increase in the number of the state banks he was actuated, however, by more than local and family interests. His arguments were unanswerable. First, he pointed to Kentucky then in the midst of financial and political chaos because of her unwise banking operations. So long as the old ones were unable to pay specie, he considered it the heigth of folly to incorporate new banks, but he desired the repeal of the law requiring the banks of Virginia to pay specie on a fixed day. If the other states did not resume at the same time, he saw plainly that Virginia would be drained of her specie in a short time by conforming to a suicidal act of the Assembly. It was at this juncture that he called upon Thomas Jefferson to publish his writings upon the subject of banking and classed the illegal bankers of western Virginia with the Tory traitors of New England.

Ritchie's bold stand on this occasion, which was doubtless maintained through the aid of Dr. Brockenbrough, was most salutary in its effect upon Virginia. The Assembly was called immediately to repeal the law requiring the resumption of specie payment. But it completed its work by incorporating two new banks in western Virginia, one at Winchester, the other at Wheeling, and the illegal state

30 *Richmond Enquirer*, April 13, 27, 1816; *Ibid.*, June 8, 1816; *Ibid.*, July 13, 1816.

banks were required to go out of business. Thus Virginia was spared the unenviable experiences of Kentucky and those other states which had been liberal in granting bank charters.[31]

The unsuccessful movement for state banks was immediately responsible for a demand on the part of the westerners for a reform in the state constitution. They were convinced that a more democratic distribution of representation in the Assembly would enable them to obtain redress. Accordingly a convention, composed mainly of representatives of the illegal banks, assembled at Winchester and issued a call for a larger and more representative convention to be held at Staunton, August 19, 1816. The slogan of the reformers was equal representation for equal numbers of free whites. Jefferson was appealed to and responded with his famous letters to Samuel Kercheval, in which he again espoused the cause of reform. Dismemberment was now threatened. But Ritchie again appeared as a compromiser and a peace maker. For an increase in their representation in the state Senate he urged the westerners to consent to a more equitable reapportionment of the land taxes. Feeling between the sections was thus temporarily allayed, and Ritchie was henceforth the friend and advocate of a constitutional convention, which he had at first opposed because he thought it a Federalist enterprise in behalf of the illegal state banks and the bank of the United States.[32]

The new-born spirit of nationalism did not exhaust itself in demands for banks and for reforms in the organic law. It carried settlers into the remotest parts of the far West, led to the acquisition of Florida, and eventually constituted the United States the guardian of the new-born sovereignties which were now making their appearance in America. Though in sympathy with every movement which made for a larger national greatness, Ritchie could not

[31] *Richmond Enquirer*, June 21, 1815; *Ibid.*, February 8, 1816; *Ibid.*, March 30, 1816; November 16, 1816; *Ibid.*, February 6, 1817.

[32] *Ibid.*, July 20, 1816; *Ibid.*, August 7, 1816; *Ibid.*, February 8, 1817.

endorse General Jackson's invasion of Florida and the popular demands which followed for the conquest of that country. His high sense of international honor, his traditional distrust of the military power, and what was possibly more effective, his confidence in the efficacy of peaceful negotiations as a means for acquiring Florida revolted against the blood and thunder methods of the Old Hero. In a strong editorial entitled, "Arbuthnot and Ambrister," which was later published as an appendix to the letters of Algernon Sydney, he laid bare Jackson's unenviable record as military governor of Louisiana and demanded that his conduct in Florida be reviewed by a court of inquiry. At no time did he question the General's patriotism and good intentions. Nor did he deny that the Spaniards, in the violation of their treaty obligations, had given just cause for an attack. He simply insisted that the dignity of our newborn republic, yet in its experimental stage, and a proper regard for our international obligations could not be subjected to the passions or the whims of a zealot and that Yankee tactics should not be employed even to extend the common territory.[33]

It should be noted, by the way, that this attack upon Jackson, mild as it was, was one of Ritchie's greatest political blunders. Though not a culpable act, it later cut him off from all chances of promotion at a time when his services were most needed and would have been most effective. Others, notably Calhoun, who had looked with disfavor upon Jackson's conduct in Florida, were able for a time at least, to conceal their designs and to avoid his displeasure. But the publicity and freedom demanded of the press placed Ritchie in disfavor from the beginning with the man who rarely forgave and never forgot a criticism, even of his public acts, and who was destined to be the commanding figure of his times. Thus, Francis P. Blair was later preferred as the national spokeman of the Republican party,

[33] *Richmond Enquirer*, May 11, 1830; *Ibid.*, December 15, 1818.

and Ritchie, who was called in his day the "Napoleon of the Press," was passed over.

The press of the lower South naturally sympathized with Jackson in the Florida matter. Accordingly they made haste to pronounce Ritchie's talk about the national honor and the superior duties of our new-born republic "a deceitful stratagem," designed to aid a futile plan for securing Florida by peaceful negotiation. They also asserted that he was actuated by a desire to enhance Monroe's popularity, that he was influenced by the Federalists, that the siren voice of Algernon Sydney, his cousin, Spencer Roane, had lulled him into a false security, and that the policy of the *Enquirer* was determined by one of Jackson's personal enemies in Washington. The press was unable to reconcile Ritchie's preference for negotiation, as a means of securing Florida, with the fact that Pensacola was being fortified. None of the many attacks disturbed Ritchie, except that which charged him with subserviency. This he denied vehemently. To prove his complete independence he referred his critics to editorials which had appeared in the *Enquirer* as early as June 30, 1818, before the opinions of any other editor or public man regarding Florida were known in Richmond.[34] He traced the demands for "Florida or war" to the activity of certain business houses in New Orleans and defiantly predicted that, whatever the outcome of the negotiations then in progress might be, Jackson would be withdrawn and Florida would be restored to its rightful owners. He attributed the fortification of Pensacola to Jackson's ignorance of international law and of the policies of the President. The *Enquirer* doubtless spoke for the administration, and its influence upon the South in allaying the prevailing spirit of hostility toward Spain was a potent factor in the purchase of Florida.

During the long period of waiting for the Cortes to ratify the treaty for the sale of Florida there were frequent demands in the South for its conquest by arms. Rumor had it that British intrigue prevented favorable and speedy

[34] *Richmond Enquirer*, October 9, 1818; *Ibid.*, February 2, 1819.

action on the part of Spain and that Florida would never be surrendered to us until Great Britain had acquired Cuba. Rumor also gave credence to the belief that Spain was anxiously waiting for us to seize Florida to relieve her of the embarrassment of selling it and of the consequent demands which would be made upon her for other slices of her rapidly disintegrating empire. Ritchie continued, however, to adhere to the peace policy. He did not anticipate a resort to arms on the part of Great Britain in her efforts to possess herself of Cuba, and no other foes were formidable. Had any nation attempted to seize Florida, he would have consented to war to protect our claims to it. Under other conditions he feared that war with Spain would compel her to sell Cuba to Great Britain and to permit Russia to gain a foot-hold on the Pacific. He was thus willing to "bide our time" in the hope that by so doing not only Florida but Cuba also would become a part of the United States. Indeed, he now regarded Cuba as a more desirable possession than Florida, commanding, as did the former, the free access to the Mississippi and to the shortest land routes between the Atlantic and the Pacific.[35]

The complications regarding Florida had a very noticeable effect upon Ritchie's attitude toward the efforts of the Spanish colonies in America to secure their independence. Before the war with the Seminoles and the beginning of negotiations for the purchase of Florida he had spoken enthusiastically of their efforts and successes. In the midst of the stirring scenes of 1813, he had called attention to the revolution in Mexico and commended the Virginians who were leading it.[36] As early as 1817 he saw that England preferred her own commercial advantages in Spanish America to Spanish rule. Recognition of the independence of the Spanish American states had therefore become necessary to preserve the influence of the United States.[37] But, when

[35] *Richmond Enquirer*, October 26, 29, 1819; *Ibid.*, December 16, 1819; *Ibid.*, May 9, 1820.

[36] *Richmond Enquirer*, August 31, 1818.

[37] *Ibid.*, October 17, 24, 1817; *Ibid.*, April 3, 1818.

negotiation to secure Florida began, following the outbreak with the Seminoles, this attitude suddenly changed. Clay's efforts, formerly commendable, in behalf of the revolting patriots were now traced to a desire for self-aggrandizement, and the independent sovereignties were apparently forgotten. Instead attention was directed to our trade with China and to the proposed Panama canal.[38]

Under the spell of an awakened independence and self-reliance, which had temporarily eclipsed the power and the importance of the individual states, carried settlement into the far West, and increased the area of the national domain, Congress had rechartered the Bank of the United States, enacted a protective tariff law, and increased its appropriations to works of internal improvement. Deserted by both Jefferson and Madison and confronted by the peculiar exigencies of the times, Ritchie had raised only a feeble protest against these violations of the constitution, which this wave of nationalism had made possible.[39] His original conception of the nature of the federal government had not changed, but the tastes of his readers had. Party distinctions were rapidly disappearing, and under the direction of Clay, Calhoun, and Crawford, we were moving harmoniously and unitedly to a national greatness, the very thought of which inspired every patriot. What could Ritchie say against the new-born nationalism, when his friends and associates, Andrew Stevenson, W. C. Nicholas, P. N. Nicholas, and Thomas Rutherford had so far departed from their former prejudices as to become directors of a branch bank of the Bank of the United States to be located at Richmond, and when no voice was raised against the tariff.[40]

Underneath the calm of this "Era of Good Feeling" and little politics there was, however, a conscious dissatisfaction and distrust. In addition to the acts of Congress already noted and to the spirit of the times, this feeling was height-

[38] *Ibid.*, May 12, 1820.
[39] *Ibid.*, March 9, 1816; *Ibid.*, July 31, 1816.
[40] *Richmond Enquirer*, February 1, 1817.

ened in Virginia by the decisions of the federal Supreme Court and by the local discontent which had manifested itself in a demand for an increase in the number of the state banks, for reforms in the fundamental law, and for the industrial awakening of the East. Notwithstanding the fact that Monroe was the Chief Executive of the federal government, Virginians were no longer formidable in national councils. As in 1798 they, therefore, turned again to the good old days before the federal government had become powerful. The leader in this new movement was Spencer Roane, head of the Virginia Court of Appeals. By his numerous letters attacking Marshall's decisions and the centralizing course of events he revived the Democratic-Republican party and those dogmas of state rights so familiar to the fathers. This reaction carried most of the politicians of the old school out of Congress and replaced them by young men imbued with the particularistic theories of government. Most prominent of the new lights who now found a place in public life, as representatives of Virginia in Congress, were P. P. Barbour, John Floyd, and John Tyler. The occasion also called forth, from his involuntary retirement, John Randolph, who henceforth became Virginia's recognized apostle of republicanism. There now began to be talk throughout the whole country of a "Virginia party" and of a revival of the Virginia doctrines. In the beginning neither Jefferson nor Madison were popular with the leaders of this new movement. Monroe was not even considered. But the course of events, accompanied as they were by a change in his attitude toward the tariff and other nationalistic measures, brought Jefferson into good standing with the particularists. After the death of Roane, which occurred in 1822, he became, despite his age, one of the recognized leaders in the new movement.

The particularistic reaction called out the best that was in Ritchie, who now entered upon his real life work, the preservation of the ascendency of Virginia. Temperament, education, and association fitted him for this peculiar service. Only reluctantly had he consented to the nationalistic tendencies of Jefferson's and Madison's administrations.

After enjoying such unusual opportunities it pricked him to the heart to see Virginia dropping behind. Thus he became the natural spokesman of his companion and relative, Roane, of the young men who now entered Congress, and of Dr. Brockenbrough and others who, through their influence upon courts and legislatures directed the political, financial, and industrial efforts of Virginia in her lonely crusade against nationalism. Under the conditions he had no difficulty in renewing his friendship with John Taylor of Caroline, who was one of Roane's ablest lieutenants. The tone of the *Enquirer* changed completely, becoming positive and aggressive. The able essays from the pens of Taylor, Stevenson, Roane, and Brockenbrough, which now illumined its columns were reflected in every editorial. A crusade was commenced to crush out the remnants of Federalism which continued to linger in the borders of Virginia and to eradicate that "hankering" after the stars, garters, and titles of nobility which was daily creeping into the White House.[41] Thus a wholesome discontent had added its leaven to the crucible of national interests, and as its spokesman, Ritchie began to be recognized in national politics.[42]

The strict constructionists made their first united assault upon the Bank of the United States. After two years of trial it had failed dismally to establish a uniform circulating medium and to equalize exchange; many state banks had suspended specie payment or failed; a panic was abroad in the land; and some of the western and southern states were trying to drive the federal bank out of existence by imposing confiscatory taxes upon its branches. The fact that Ritchie's friends had resigned from the directorship of the branch bank in Richmond is indicative of the change of attitude which had come over Virginia. This was followed by a vigorous attack from the *Enquirer* against the constitutionality of a national bank. Experience had taught

[41] *Richmond Enquirer*, January 9, 1817; *Ibid.*, May 30, 1817; *Ibid.*, December 11, 1817; *Ibid.*, February 4, 1818.

[42] *Ibid.*, May 19, 1818; *Ibid.*, August 18, 1818.

Ritchie that it could not be relied upon to equalize exchange or to establish a uniform circulating medium. He now considered these things obtainable only through the use of specie paying state banks. Adam Smith and the English reviewers had made it plain to him that a uniform circulating medium must be either hard money or convertible paper. As it was then organized the Bank of the United States was simply a sluice through which metallic money flowed from our country to foreign countries.[43] With a restoration of peace in South America, a retrenchment in our trade with the Indies, and an end to speculating and wild financiering in the West, he felt that specie would again become abundant and that the state banks would then accomplish all the ends for which the federal bank had been incorporated.[44]

Though he disapproved of the use of force by Ohio to collect a tax from the branch of the federal bank located at Chillicothe, after the Supreme Court of the United States had ruled the tax unconstitutional, Ritchie protested against the contention that Ohio in so doing had been guilty of rebellion. He would have given a state as much latitude in resisting a "deliberate and dangerous" breach of the constitution when made by the judiciary as when made by the executive or legislative departments of the government. Moreover, he insisted that the duty to "interpose for arresting the progress of the evil" was as great and as imperative in one case as in the other. The striking similarity of these arguments to those made by Judge Spencer Roane on the same subject is apparent. But, as in his advice to the New England states, when they had on sundry occasions threatened secession and resistance to federal laws, Ritchie now pointed Ohio to the example of Virginia in 1798 and suggested also that she return to the federal government the money which she had taken from the branch bank.[45]

Crawford's defence of the federal bank and his vigorous

[43] *Richmond Enquirer*, August 13, 1819.

[44] *Ibid.*, October 30, 1818; *Ibid.*, June 4, 1819; *Ibid.*, August 17, 1819.

[45] *Richmond Enquirer*, October 15, 1819; *Ibid.*, November 16, 1819.

assault upon the state banks, as set forth in his "Currency Report" of 1820, was not convincing to Ritchie. Admitting the necessity, for the sake of argument, of a federal bank he now insisted that a constitutional amendment was necessary before it could have a legal existence and that the state banks should be maintained to prevent it from acquiring a monopoly of the banking business. The following extract from an editorial on Crawford's Report would make interesting reading for a modern "trust-buster": "All corporate bodies, and particularly those which are licensed to exact contributions from the public, are not only objectionable in themselves on account of the temptations which they constantly hold out to go beyond the object of their original creation, but because the exclusive privileges with which they are clothed are encroachments upon the common rights of the people and contrary to the avowed principles of republican government.[46]

The particularistic reaction completely revolutionized Ritchie's ideas regarding the proper use of a protective tariff. In 1807 he had favored it as the proper means of making the United States an independent and self-sufficing country; later, when New England had appealed for protection for her infant industries against the flood of importations which Great Britain poured into our country and when both Jefferson and Madison had favored granting them relief, Ritchie had said little or nothing on the subject, but in the proposed tariff of 1820 he saw an unjust, unnatural, and unnecessary effort to foster manufactures at the expense of commerce and agriculture. He believed that a redundancy of population and capital would eventually make the United States a manufacturing country, but he insisted that the change should be allowed to come about naturally and not as the result of intervention on the part of the government. He grasped clearly the principles of the American System, but feared that a protective tariff would bring low prices for raw materials, a monopoly capable of regulating all prices,

[46] *Ibid.*, March 21, 1820.

and retaliatory legislation designed to exclude our surplus flour, tobacco, cotton, rice, and lumber from foreign markets. He traced the causes of the panic of 1819 to that world-wide craze for speculation, which had carried distress and panic to Birmingham and the Valley of Deville and not to an insufficient protection for American manufacturers. In answer to the argument that agriculture and commerce had always received the fostering care of the federal government and that manufactures should not, therefore, be neglected, he showed clearly what the American farmer of today does not understand, that protective duties on articles produced chiefly for exportation are in no wise protective. Furthermore he justified the custom of placing the coast-wise trade in the hands of Americans as a means of national security and of building up a navy.[47]

That callousness to the iniquities of negro slavery, which came from the influences of a black "mammy" and from witnessing from childhood the sale of "likely negroes" to replenish the family exchequer was not the only, if indeed it was the chief cause of Ritchie's desire for the preservation of negro slavery in the proposed state of Missouri. Slavery in Missouri as well as the material interests of the sea-board sections of the old South, had become involved in the particularistic reaction, and was consequently a subject to be settled by a sovereign state. Ritchie thought it a mis-nomer to deny to a sovereign people the right to determine their own institutions. To exclude slavery from the state of Missouri without the consent of her people was more; it was a breach of faith and confiscation. In the treaty for the purchase of Louisiana the United States had agreed to admit the inhabitants of that territory to the full rights of citizenship on an equality with those of the other states, and since making that treaty she had permitted her citizens to carry their negro slaves into the Missouri territory. He thus contended that they had every reason to expect protection in the

[47] *Richmond Enquirer*, April 28, 1820; *Ibid.*, May 2, 1820.

[48] *Ibid.*, December 21, 1819; *Ibid.*, January 20, 1820.

possession of their property.[48] In language which smacks of the Dred Scott Decision he repudiated the Ordinance of 1787 as unconstitutional and ridiculed the talk about the proposed attempt to forbid the "migration of servile persons" into Missouri after the year 1820. He did not profess to know the status of the negro slaves of the other states, but he was certain that those from Virginia, when they went beyond her borders, were "imported and exported." Ritchie also opposed the exclusion of negro slavery from Missouri on the ground of expediency. He was confident that the new state would need slaves to clear and cultivate her lands, and he welcomed their removal from the congested areas of the old states as a means of ameliorating the condition of those who remained in bondage. In a further continuation of agitation of the subject he saw a way for demagogues like Rufus King to reach the presidency and heard the death knell of the Union.[49]

The first suggestion of a compromise whereby Missouri was to be admitted as a slave state on the condition that the territory north and west of her boundary should remain free, threw Ritchie into a frenzy. He looked upon the proposition as an effort to subvert one of the great compromises of the constitution and predicted that persistence in such designs would destroy the federal government. The constitution aside, however, he considered such a compromise inexpedient and detrimental to the best interests of the South. It meant the exclusion of her people from the common territory which had been acquired by the common councels and the common treasury. If the South was denied access to the West on a basis of equality with the North, he saw that the time was not far distant when the latter section would raise up a hot-bed of manufactures and abolish the slave representation feature of the federal constitution. He therefore contended that the South's only security to keep the North from "lording it over her" lay in a strict adherence to the constitution, and gave solemn warning that she would not

[49] *Richmond Enquirer*, December 21, 1819; *Ibid.*, January 20, 1820.

abide by her votes when the constitution failed to guarantee her rights.[50]

In less than a week after this vehement utterance Ritchie published two letters "from a gentleman in Washington to his friend in Richmond." These letters made it evident that a national crisis was at hand and expressed the deepest regret that so many persons in both the North and the South viewed "disunion with so little repugnance." They also made it plain that the South, and Virginia in particular, could hope to gain nothing by disunion. The writer, who seems to have stood high in national councils, therefore urged the acceptance of the proposed compromise that the Union might be saved, that the ambitions of King and other aspirants to national honors might be thwarted, and that some little of the coveted territory might remain open to slavery.[51]

It is believed that these letters were potent factors in reconciling Virginia, but they had little effect upon Ritchie. He did reconsider his remarks which had been "penned under some degree of excitement" at the first suggestion of compromise, but reflection brought no regrets for making them or changes in their form. Rumor now had it that acceptance of the compromise was the sole condition of Monroe's re-election to the presidency, but Ritchie was willing to forego the honor to the South, if it came at the price of such a sacrifice.[52] When compromise finally came he could not re-echo the congratulations which the *National Intelligencer* extended to the country. Instead he had "no recollection of having ever taken a bitterer cup." The only consolation which he found in the whole proceeding was the fact that Virginia had given two-fifths of the total vote against the compromise and that only four of her twenty-one representatives in Congress had voted for it.[53] An intere-

[50] *Richmond Enquirer,* February 10, 12, 15, 1820.

[51] *Ibid.,* February 17, 1820.

[52] *Richmond Enquirer,* April 20, 1820. The articles on Monroe's re-election were written by George Hay, his son-in-law. See *William and Mary College Quarterly,* X., 15.

[53] *Richmond Enquirer,* March 7, 1820.

love for the Union kept his heart buoyant, however, and he soon advised all good citizens "to hold to the sheet anchor, the law of the land."[54]

As has been noted, the particularistic movement in Virginia found its best expression in Spencer Roane's protests against the nationalistic tendencies of the decisions of the federal Supreme Court. In the case of *Hunter* vs. *Martin, lessee,* Virginia's highest court had been reversed, and the state was subsequently commanded by a mandate from the federal court to carry into effect the decision of her local court. At once Roane raised a voice of protest through the medium of the *Enquirer.* Again when the federal court decided in favor of the Bank of the United States in the case of *McCullough* vs. *Maryland* he spoke through the same medium over the venerable name of Hampden. In each instance Ritchie commended his attacks and endorsed their contents. His language in introducing Hampden is characteristic. "Hear him for his cause," said he. "The Supreme Court of the United States is a tribunal of great and commanding authority, whose decisions, if not received as 'the law and the prophets' are always entitled to the deepest attention. To the presiding justice of that court, we are always ready to pay that tribute, which his great abilities deserve, but no tribunal, however high, no abilities, however splendid, ought to canonize the opinions which are advanced. We solemnly believe the opinion of the Supreme Court in the case of the bank to be fraught with alarming consequences; the federal constitution to be misinterpreted; and the rights of the states and of the people to be threatened with danger." It grieved Ritchie sorely to see Republican prints, the *National Intelligencer,* the *Charleston* (S. C.) *Patriot,* and the *Kentucky Reporter* commend Marshall's decisions.[55]

The opinion of the federal court in the case *Cohens* vs. *Virginia,* reached the acme of endurance and brought forth Ritchie's severest criticism. He now denied that its juris-

[54] *Richmond Enquirer,* August 8, 1820; *Ibid.,* November 17, 1820.

[55] *Richmond Enquirer,* February 1, 1816; *Ibid.,* April 20, 1819; *Ibid.,* June 11, 1819.

diction extended to all cases in law and equity arising under the constitution and laws of the United States and was for restricting its jurisdiction to those cases which grew out of an exercise of the powers expressly delegated. To restrain the greedy spirit with which the judiciary was usurping the rights of the states, he now advocated the repeal of the Judiciary Act of 1789 and the consequent denial of authority in such cases as that of *Cohens* vs. *Virginia*. He believed that the Supreme Court should sit as a guardian of the rights of both the state and the federal governments. Inasmuch as it had failed in the performance of its constitutional functions, he would have abolished it and substituted in its stead an elective tribunal to be composed of tried and mature statesmen of the type of Jefferson and Madison. The state legislatures were to be given the power to elect the proposed tribunal.[56]

Meanwhile John Taylor's *Construction Construed,* the most valuable of his sundry contributions to the state rights literature, had been issued from Ritchie's press in Richmond. Strange as it may seem, considering their former relations, Ritchie wrote the preface for Colonel Taylor's masterpiece. This service called forth from Jefferson one of the "most gratifying compliments which the editor of the *Enquirer* ever received from the pen of any man."[57] In a ringing appeal, even more earnest than that with which he had introduced Hampden, he commended *Construction Construed* to the readers of the *Enquirer* as a breath of political life from the fathers. Ritchie sincerely believed that Taylor's work would do much to prevent the evils of centralization on the one side, and of decentralization on the other. As such a service would be instrumental in perpetuating "the grandest and most beautiful experiment ever known in the history of government," he pronounced its author the greatest benefactor of his day.[58]

[56] *Richmond Enquirer,* January 22, 1822.

[57] *Richmond Enquirer,* January 17, 1845.

[58] *Ibid.,* November 17, 1820.

Soon the *National Intelligencer* and other nationalistic prints, accustomed to the former liberalism of the Virginia dynasty, tried to make it appear that there were two parties in Virginia, one led by Jefferson, the other by Roane, Taylor and Ritchie. As they sympathized with the former, they spoke with contempt of the "new lights," the "new school," the "new party," and the "Richmond Junto," which it was claimed distributed the political spoils of the nation from its divan.[59] But there is every evidence that Ritchie knew his ground better than his critics and that his love for the Union and the constitution was as genuine and as patriotic as was theirs. Accordingly, it was a source of no little satisfaction to him to be able to tell the world authoritatively that the authors of the Virginia doctrines were in full accord with the particularistic movement.[60] Nevertheless there was much in the condition of affairs that grieved him. In the coma which had enveloped the minds of the people, in the temptations which were blinding the servants of the country, in the apathy of the press, which had long ceased to be a sentinel on the watch-tower of liberty, he saw grave danger to the republic and the source of the ridicule which was being heaped upon Virginia.[61]

Had not Monroe's veto of 1822 of the bill authorizing the President to cause toll-houses, gates, and turnpikes to be constructed along the Cumberland road been followed by that obnoxious doctrine, of his "Views on the Subject of Internal Improvements," which asserted the power of Congress to raise and appropriate money for "purposes of common defense and general, not local, national, not state benefit," the Virginia party could have boasted of a triumph. The veto message of 1822 was, to their minds, a distinct improvement upon that of 1817. Instead, however, of marking a complete triumph, it simply marked the parting of the ways in the Republican party and the passing of the Era of Good

[59] *Richmond Enquirer*, September 4, 1821; *Ibid.*, November 16, 1821.

[60] *Jefferson Papers*, Series I., Vol. 14, No. 215; *Richmond Enquirer*, July 17, 1821; *Ibid.*, August 3, 1821.

[61] *Richmond Enquirer*, November 16, 1821; *Ibid.*, November 27, 1820.

JUDGE SPENCER ROANE
OF
COURT OF APPEALS OF VIRGINIA

Feeling.[62] Henceforth one faction tended more and more to nationalism, following the ideas set forth in Monroe's "Views," and the other followed the ways of particularism as set forth in his veto message and the writings of John Taylor and Spencer Roane. The former faction in due time became the National-Republican party, and the latter became the National-Democratic party, which thus claimed to inherit the Jeffersonian traditions.

The efforts of the crowned heads of Europe to crush out liberalism at home and the rumors of their plans for the reconquest of Spanish America came as a challenge to all our theories and experiences. Already Ritchie had pronounced the attempt of the allies to put down revolution in Italy and Spain a blow at democratic government and not what it was claimed to be, an effort to preserve the "order and peace" of Europe. Moreover, he saw in the noiseless tread with which Russia was extending her possessions into and beyond the Oregon territory, a direct menace to our future possibilities as a nation. He ridiculed the idea that Russia could, by the use of a gate four thousand miles wide, exclude other nations from the northern portions of the Pacific ocean,[63] where our fishing and commercial interests were already gaining a foot-hold. He hailed with delight the reports of a successful revolution in Mexico and Monroe's message of March 8, 1822, recommending to Congress the recognition of the independence of the South American republics. Recognition by the United States, he was confident, would be followed by recognition by Great Britain, whose commercial interests in South America were such that she could not afford to be outdone in efforts to win the good will of the revolting Spaniards.[64] He did not credit the rumor that Spain had temporarily ceded Cuba to Great Britain to keep France from claiming it as the price of putting down revolution in Spain. He insisted, however, that "if Great Britain

[62] *Richmond Enquirer*, May 31, 1822; *Ibid.*, January 24, 1824.

[63] *Richmond Enquirer*, April 23, 1822.

[64] *Ibid.*, March 12, 1822; *Ibid.*, June 7, 25, 1822.

did intend temporarily to occupy Cuba to keep France from getting it and to save it to Spain, then we should occupy it temporarily to keep it from falling to Great Britain permanently."[65] Later when the Greeks revolted against the oppressive rule of Turkey, he earnestly espoused their cause, commended those who volunteered to aid them, and became the secretary of a mass-meeting held in Richmond to send material aid and to adopt resolutions of sympathy for their cause.[66]

Notwithstanding the frequent approaches in his numerous editorials on foreign relations to the principles of the Monroe Doctrine, its formal announcement, as set forth in the President's message of December, 1823, came as a surprise to Ritchie. It is more than likely that he had not been informed of the abrupt turn which John Q. Adams had given to the plan for concerted action with Great Britain in opposing the alleged intentions of the continental powers to interfere in South America. The editorials of the *Enquirer* leave little doubt that he was informed of Jefferson's and Madison's approval of the plans for concerted action. In a light-hearted vein, possible only to one who was acquainted with the inner secrets of our diplomatic relations, he had repeatedly assured his countrymen that they had nothing to fear from the tyrants of Europe. As has been shown he had long considered Great Britain's commercial interests in South America as more important to her than the preservation of the Holy Alliance, but his predictions regarding the intentions of the continental powers in America must have had a better foundation than the belief that Great Britain would not aid them. His constitutional inability for adjusting himself to sudden changes in the policy of state did not, however, blind Ritchie to the superior advantages of the Monroe Doctrine as finally declared. After all it followed the injunctions of the Father of his Country and the previous course of national events. Thus a conservative like Ritchie could readily become its champion and defender.

[65] *Richmond Enquirer*, February 13, 15, 1823.

[66] *Ibid.*, January 15, 17, 31, 1824.

CHAPTER IV.

PRESIDENT MAKING.

Unlike the editor of the *National Intelligencer* and those other persons who believed Monroe perfect, Ritchie did not hail his re-election as a triumph for republicanism. With an eye upon "the bright suns which have already set" (probably Jefferson and Madison), he spoke of that event only with "reluctance and regret."[1] Except for the rumor that Martin Van Buren had attempted to use the federal patronage to destroy his political enemies who had voted to restrict the extension of negro slavery in Missouri, and that he was thus attempting to cement more closely the political ties between New York and the South, the presidential election of 1820 was as uninteresting as it was undisputed. Ritchie attributed these conditions to indifference on the part of the voters and to the absence of an opposition party, and not to any merits of statesmanship or to any popularity on the part of the President-elect. He observed also the absence of that zeal and enthusiasm which had accompanied the election and the successive re-elections of Jefferson and Madison, but his keen political insight scented in the existing calm the rapid approach of a "war of the giants," Adams, Crawford, Clinton, and King, for the succession.

From the very beginning Ritchie saw that the approaching political battle would be waged between men and sections and not, as in the past, between political parties with well-defined principles. Thus while their respective states were putting forward the claims of Adams, Crawford, Clinton, Clay, Jackson, and Lowndes, and while Pennsylvanians were "backing their friend," Calhoun, he refrained from expressing a preference for either and concerned himself

[1] *Richmond Enquirer*, June 23, 1820; *Ibid.*, November 7, 1820.

mainly with the solution of a plan to keep the election from the House of Representatives. Hoping that public opinion would meanwhile concentrate upon one or two candidates, he at first advised a two year's truce to be agreed upon among the political knights.[2] This wise council went unheeded, and he then proposed a national nominating convention, then not an entirely new idea, to be composed of delegates elected by the several state legislatures in caucus assembled or by the voters of each congressional district.[3] This suggestion was, however, too, revolutionary, and, as the necessity for concerted party action became more imperative, to keep the election from the House, Ritchie took up and endorsed Colonel John Taylor's proposed amendment to the constitution, which would have recommitted the election to the college of electors in case of a failure to elect at their first meetings.[4] But personal ambitions, sectional jealousies, and conservative indifference thwarted these patriotic reforms which, had they been caried out, would have saved our present legislators much worry.

In spite of his indifference, at this time amusing because so unnatural, a casual reading of the *Enquirer* for 1822 would convince one that, even thus early, Ritchie preferred Crawford to all others for the presidency, and that he felt reasonably confident of his ultimate success. Indeed, his effort at reform in the methods of naming the party candidates, though honestly and earnestly proposed, may have been, like many of Ritchie's proposed reforms, actuated also by a desire for political advantage. Crawford's candidacy had a following in all the states, and a political truce or national convention could not have been, under ordinary circumstances, detrimental to his interests. By a process of elimination Ritchie had also made it evident that his choice would not fall upon certain candidates. Calhoun's "d——d good natured friends" in Pennsylvania, among whom was

[2] *Richmond Enquirer*, January 10, 1822.

[3] *Ibid.*, July 23, 1822; *Ibid.*, August 3, 1822.

[4] *Ibid.*, October 7, 1823.

Walsh of the *Philadelphia Franklin Gazette,* had nauseated the people with a too frequent mention of their candidate's name; Jackson was never "seriously mentioned" by anyone; Clinton could not get the nomination of his own state, much less that of Ohio; and Lowndes was scarcely considered even in South Carolina.[5] Only Crawford, Adams, and Clay therefore remained, but the *Lynchburg Virginian* which supported Adams and maintained, with some semblance of truth, that he was the choice of Virginia, knew that Ritchie was waiting an opportune time to throw the *Enquirer,* like the sword of Brennus, into the political balances for Crawford. Considering Van Buren's activity for the same candidate, it was not difficult to make such inferences as that of the *Virginian,* after an assurance from Ritchie that there would be no difference between New York and Virginia on the question of the presidency. Thus he had made clear his position, and with it that of Virginia, without saying anything either directly or indirectly against either Adams or Clay. On the contrary each had been the subject of his frequent commendation.[6]

An incident of 1822, though small in itself, came near producing large results in the contest then waging for the presidency. That year Henry Clay visited Richmond as the representative of Kentucky in a boundary dispute with Virginia. The Assembly was in session at the time, and Spencer Roane, Ritchie's former choice for the presidency to succeed Monroe, had just died. The fact that Clay was now generally regarded as the favorite of the West for the presidency, Missouri and Kentucky having already nominated him for that office, made it an opportune time for him to renew the acquaintances of his early manhood and to talk with them of his chances for promotion. With characteristic weakness for those to the manor born, many Virginians now forgot the follies of the American System, which had not yet become

[5] *Richmond Enquirer,* March 26, 1822; *Ibid.,* July 30, 1822; *Ibid.,* August 3, 1822; *Ibid.,* October 4, 1822; *Ibid.,* December 24, 1822.

[6] *Ibid.,* July 22, 1822; *Ibid.,* November 12, 29, 1822.

odious, and looked with favor upon the political prospect of "the mill boy of the slashes." Together he and Ritchie promenaded the long hall of the Eagle Hotel and talked of bygone days and of their political differences. Clay was certain that he himself had not departed from the Virginia doctrines, and assured Ritchie that his preference for a national bank was due mainly to a desire to relieve Kentucky from the curse of the state banks. This was certainly an argument which appealed to both Ritchie and to Dr. Brockenbrough. He also assured him that when "he (Ritchie) had crossed the mountains, and traveled the miserable roads, in all seasons of the year, as he was compelled to do on his way to Washington," he, too, would excuse in some degree his anxiety to claim for the federal government the power to prosecute internal improvements.[7] Though unable to make a convert of Ritchie who would not have objected to him for the vice-presidency, Clay had from this day hence many friends in Richmond who would have liked to see him President.

Shortly after Clay's visit to Richmond, Ritchie published in the *Enquirer* a letter from Washington, together with comments on the same, which gave a comprehensive view of the political situation at that time, and indicated the lines along which the approaching contest was to be waged. Only three candidates, Adams, Crawford, and Clay, were then considered as possibilities. Of these it was expected that Adams would carry the New England states; Clay the West, including Ohio, Indiana, Illinois, Missouri, Kentucky, and a part of Tennessee and Louisiana; and that Crawford would get the South, except possibly South Carolina and Georgia. Thus it was evident to Ritchie and his correspondent that the successful candidate would have to secure the votes of New York, Pennsylvania, and New Jersey, the acknowledged battle ground of the contest. Accordingly J. C. Calhoun, who stood as the sole barrier to any effort to unite this section in support of Crawford, became an object of attack and hatred.

[7] *Richmond Enquirer,* September 10, 1852.

On the contrary, Van Buren and his fellow spoilsmen who were doing their best to secure the election of Crawford, were hailed as statesmen and patriots.[8]

These conditions brought forth from Ritchie interesting and instructive estimates of the respective merits of the candidates. It could not be denied that Adams had many friends in both Virginia and North Carolina, who thought that the best interests of the Union, his acknowledged abilities as a cabinet officer, and his sterling character, which removed wrong doing from him, entitled their favorite to the presidency. James Barbour, a Senator in Congress from Virginia, was known to be friendly to his candidacy; John Taylor of Carolina was in doubt; and the *Lynchburg Virginian* insisted that Jefferson desired the election of Adams.[9] Adams' famous letter to General Smyth of Virginia, written especially for that meridian, convinced many of the old school and some of the more charitable of the new school that its author was a true friend of the doctrines of '98. But Ritchie agreed with those who argued that mere intellectual achievements and a sterling character did not necessarily make a statesman. Like them he also feared that Adams, if clothed with power, would develop the same irritable temper as that displayed by his father, and that he would eventually return to the nationalistic tendencies of the section which was most active in urging his candidacy.[10]

Ritchie saw in Clay a genius in the mastery of men, but not what his friends professed to see, a presidential possibility able to unite the warring sections and to be the President of the whole country. In spite of the fact that he was a native Virginian, a most valuable asset when Virginians estimate the merits of any man, Ritchie saw that Clay's pliancy and laxity in matters of administration as well as matters of morals would make him an unsafe repository of great powers. Despite the claims of the *Petersburg Intelli-*

[8] *Richmond Enquirer*, January 28, 1823; *Ibid.*, February 13, 1823.
[9] *Ibid.*, August 5, 1823.
[10] *Ibid.*, January 28, 1823; *Ibid.*, August 5, 1823.

gencer, he also mistrusted his nationalistic leanings and his loyalty to Monroe's administration.[11]

It was plain that Ritchie now regarded Virginia as practically pledged to support Crawford's candidacy. Gratitude alone necessitated such a course, when it involved the claims of a candidate who was a native Virginian and a supporter of Monroe's candidacy in 1816 and again in 1820.[12] It was true that Crawford had made mistakes as Secretary of the Treasury; he had favored John Adams in 1798; and he had even stood for the recharter of the Bank of the United States. Notwithstanding all these objections his escutcheon showed fewer blots than that of any of his rivals, and his principles were now more in accord with those of the older school of politicians. He possessed the first qualities of a statesman: judgment and good sense; he was bound down by no formal etiquette; and experience had brought its lessons in diplomacy, legislation, and administration.

Henceforth there was no mistaking Ritchie's attitude toward Crawford's candidacy. Rumors of the influence of and plans of "the Richmond party" and of "the Richmond Junto" were again revived, and Ritchie's friendship for Van Buren became a subject of comment.[13] The importance of the Albany influence and the Richmond influence were doubtless exaggerated. John Hampden Pleasants, then editor of the *Lynchburg Virginian,* estimated the latter at its true value. He would not admit that there was in Richmond, as in Albany, a political club or junto whose power and purposes extended to the whole country and whose opinions and wishes could suplant those of the whole people. He did not deny, however, that there was in the city of Richmond a body of men distinguished by talents, eminent in service, and possessed of "a great degree of confidence in the power and importance of Virginia" which could, by constituting itself a

[11] *Richmond Enquirer,* January 28, 1823; *Ibid.,* August 26, 1823.

[12] *Stevenson MSS.* George M. Shepherd to A. Stevenson, April 20, 1824.

[13] *Richmond Enquirer,* March 7, 1823; *Ibid.,* July 4, 1823.

central committee of correspondence, practically shape the political sentiment of the state.[14] Pleasants might have added that Thomas Ritchie was the tried and trusted secretary of that central committee and the inspired genius of the "body of men" so distinguished for talents and eminent for services.

Like the "machine men" of today Ritchie disclaimed affiliation with the organization. Serenely and blissfully he pronounced the talk about the Richmond Junto "mere cant." He continued to sing the praises of W. H. Crawford, and at times went out of his way to praise "the little Magician."[15] Despairing of success in his attempts to unite the party upon one candidate by means of a truce or a nominating convention, it became evident quite early in 1823 that he was willing to wager the success of his favorite upon the outcome of a congressional caucus and upon the possibility of uniting Pennsylvania, New York, and Virginia to control it.[16] After the Republicans of New York, under the direction of Van Buren, had endorsed the congressional caucus, Ritchie, and even John Taylor, found less objection than formerly to that method of nominating candidates for the presidency.[17] Indeed, the proposed nominating convention now became impracticable, and, when the Assembly met in December, 1823, a legislative caucus in Virginia endorsed the action of the Republicans in New York and began active steps to further Crawford's candidacy.[18]

With the methods and means thus agreed upon, Ritchie's chief interest centered in the efforts being made to put Calhoun out of the race that Pennsylvania might be left free to act in conjunction with New York and Virginia. Of the ultimate outcome he had no doubt. As he saw it, Calhoun

[14] *Richmond Enquirer*, May 6, 1823.

[15] *Ibid.*, July 4, 1823; *Ibid.*, September 12, 1823.

[16] *Ibid.*, October 7, 1823.

[17] *Ibid.*, January 6, 1824; *Van Buren MSS.*, John Taylor to Van Buren, May 12, 1823.

[18] *Richmond Enquirer*, January 29, 1824; *Ibid.*, February 12, 1824.

was the most unpopular of all the candidates in Virginia; he had not a single friend in the Assembly; and he could not poll three hundred votes in the whole state.[19] It seemed folly, certainly poor politics, to continue before the public as a candidate for the presidency in a state which was the acknowledged mother of Presidents.

Though largely a New York and Virginia affair, the congressional caucus which met on February 14, 1824, and nominated Crawford for the presidency and Gallatin for the vice-presidency was a sad disappointment to Ritchie. His favorite had won a political victory which was a positive burden, and the bribe extended to Pennsylvania in the nomination of one of her favorite sons for the second place was ignored with contempt. Few of Pennsylvania's representatives had attended the caucus, and Crawford's rivals continued in the race as if no nomination had been made. Ritchie now denounced the conduct of the "fourteen deserters" from Pennsylvania and of all those who were unwilling to agree upon a single candidate for the presidency. Nevertheless he did not despair. In a few days after the nomination of Crawford the Republicans of Virginia placed an electoral ticket in the field committed to his candidacy, and Ritchie reminded his readers that all congressional caucuses had been attended by small minorities. In that of 1808 only eighty-nine members were present, in that of 1812 only eighty-two, and in that of 1816 only one hundred and nineteen. Moreover, he was certain that the sixty-six members who had attended the caucus of 1824 did not represent Crawford's strength in the country or even in Congress.[20]

There was, however, one of those surprises peculiar to American politics in store for the New Yorkers and the Virginians. Pennsylvania, upon which they staked so much, now deserted Calhoun and enlisted under the leadership of Andrew Jackson. Though he had noted with alarm the increase of Jackson's strength in the West and even in Penn-

[19] *Richmond Enquirer*, October 3, 1823; *Ibid.*, December 11, 1823.
[20] *Ibid.*, February 19, 24, 1824.

sylvania, after the caucus had become an issue, and had revised his list of presidential possibilities by substituting Jackson's name for that of Clay,[21] Ritchie had fully expected Pennsylvania to acquiesce in the action of the congressional caucus. Her failure to do so left him at sea without chart or compass. It meant simply that Crawford had missed the presidency and that Calhoun's persistency and its consequent effect upon the course of Pennsylvania had made for him two political enemies, Van Buren and Ritchie, who were henceforth to play a leading role in keeping him from the goal of his greatest ambition.

In view of his previous criticism and of the subsequent relations between himself and Jackson, Ritchie's estimates of the gladiator who had now entered the political arena are of interest. He had always conceded to Jackson the noblest qualities of patriotism and the best of intentions, but he now feared that his fiery temper and impetuous spirit would unfit him for the position of chief executive of a great nation. He saw clearly that a man of Jackson's temperament, experiences, and education would be exposed to the influence of men of superior abilities in statesmanship, who would devote themselves to his person and thus obtain his confidence, possibly to abuse it. They would become "the power behind the throne." It was true that the impetuosity of his temper would at times stand for independence, but it would more frequently carry him beyond the bounds of authority and reason.[22] Ritchie was willing, however, to bow to the will of the majority. His reluctance in doing so might have been overcome, had he known that he himself was eventually to become a power behind the throne.

As the mysteries of the "A. B." plot, over which signature Ninian Edwards had accused Crawford of a corrupt use of the federal moneys, thickened, and as the rumors of Crawford's failing health became more disconcerting, efforts were made to induce the Richmond Junto and the Albany Regency

[21] *Richmond Enquirer*, February 21, 26, 1824.

[22] *Ibid.*

to abandon his candidacy. Had the members of each been able to agree upon a second choice, the efforts would probably have been successful. But these close political corporations had come to know that in union and organization there is strength even in defeat.[23] Accordingly Ritchie set himself firmly against all attempts "to blow up" Crawford. At the same time the central committee of the Republican party in Virginia, the official name of the Junto,[24] issued an address in language which showed that its interest in Crawford was rapidly ripening into sentiment. To dispel all rumors of discord the central committee also endorsed the candidacy of Gallatin for the vice-presidency.[25]

The conflicting rumors of a combination between Jackson and Calhoun and between Adams and Calhoun made an alliance between the friends of Crawford and Clay both tempting and desirable to the politicians of Virginia.[26] Pennsylvania's course in supporting Jackson had rendered Gallatin a poor political asset. Indeed, he had never been popular in Virginia since the days of the Quids. As has been seen, Clay had already won a place in the hearts of the Junto, but he, unlike Calhoun, was unwilling to play a second fiddle and could not be approached upon the subject of the vice-presidency. Accordingly, the Junto decided to force it upon him, hoping that circumstances would bring about acquiescence. Since both Clay and Crawford were native Virginians, and Gallatin had simplified the situation by withdrawing from the contest, it was deemed best for New York to place Clay in nomination for the second place.[27] On Sep-

[23] *Richmond Enquirer*, June 18, 1824.

[24] The members of the Central Committee at this time were: John W. Green, P. N. Nicholas, John Robertson, Peter V. Daniel, Jerman Baker, Andrew Stevenson, Thomas Ritchie, William Munford, and Jacqueline B. Harvie.

[25] *Ibid.*, June 15, 1824.

[26] Such a combination had been suggested in April, 1824. See *Stevenson MSS.*, April 4, 1824, also the *Richmond Enquirer*, July 30, 1824.

[27] *Van Buren MSS.*, P. N. Nicholas to Van Buren, October 19, and 31, 1824.

tember 4, 1824, C. W. Gooch, now joint editor with Ritchie of the *Enquirer,* wrote Van Buren as follows:

"Mr. Clay's friends in Virginia are anxious that he should be taken up in this manner, (by New York . . .) It will unite us most effectively. As to consulting Mr. Clay it is injudicious. Let him not be consulted, and the force of circumstances must urge him into an acquiescence. And this will be done, too, without hazard or compromitment. When New York elects electors favorable to Mr. Crawford her Legislature ought to nominate Mr. Clay as vice-president."[28] Gales and Seaton of the *National Intelligencer* were in full accord with the plans of the Virginia politicians and wrote Van Buren endorsing them.[29]

These belated efforts to save Crawford were of no avail, but defeat did not come as a surprise to the editor of the *Enquirer*. As Jackson had received a plurality of both the electoral and the popular votes, Ritchie readily conceded his final election, but, strange as it may seem, he now assumed a position not unlike that later taken by the Whigs. Virginia was to be found henceforth in the opposition, doing all she could to protect the whole country against the sordid, selfish, and timid trimmers and time-servers who were creeping in among the courtiers and sycophants of this "era of good feeling and bad principles."[30] He urged the selection of strong men to the United States Senate, where the Whig party later entrenched itself, men who would oppose the evils which were expected to flow from Jackson's administration, and who would give character and dignity to the government. He thought Littleton W. Tazewell too nationalistic to be entrusted with such a commission.[31]

John Hampden Pleasants considered the occasion of Crawford's defeat a suitable time to write Ritchie's obituary. His tribute to the memory of his rival editor is a fair

[28] *Van Buren MSS.*.

[29] *Richmond Enquirer,* October 19, 1824.

[30] *Ibid.,* December 16, 1824.

[31] *Ibid.,* December 9, 1824.

example of the editorial sparring of the day. This fact and the subtle references which it contains are sufficient justifications for publishing it here in full:

"Farewell my friends, farewell my foes,
"My peace to these, my love to those!"

"Death of Thomas Ritchie.

"A great man has fallen in Israel! It becomes our painful duty to announce to the public the death of Thomas Ritchie, Esq., Senior Editor of the *Enquirer*. This great event toook place on Sunday evening last, about nine o'clock, P. M. The following is a brief but authentic narrative of the causes and progress of the malady, which terminated in this melancholy catastrophe.

"For some months Mr. Ritchie had been in a drooping and languishing condition. This was first observed by his friends, soon after the 14th, February, last, when the Congressional Caucus was held in the city of Washington. Mr. Ritchie was an ardent patriot, and the abortion of a measure, upon which he supposed the salvation of the country depended, preyed upon his spirits, wasted his strength, and sapped the foundation of his constitution. Like the celebrated Lucius Carey, after the commencement of the great Civil War between Charles the 1st and his Parliament, he was never seen to smile more; or if he smiled, it was the melancholy and unmeaning smile of mental abstraction. The impending fate of the Republic was the constant tenant of his thoughts, and the unceasing theme of his tongue. Latterly he embraced the opinion 'the people were their own worst enemies,' and, in their defeat of the Caucus, he saw evidences of the truth of the death, and the harbingers of the final overthrow of the Constitution. The mournful exclamation, 'O my country!' burst frequently from his lips, in tones so dolorous, as proved that it came from the heart. His appearance indicated the effect that his patriotic solicitude had upon his health, and his 'mortal coil' shrunk and attenuated to the most lilliputian dimensions. He had taken up an odd and whimsical notion, not unlike that of the Egyptian astronomer described by Rasselas, who was firmly impressed with the idea that his personal superintendence was required to hold the sun and the stars in their spheres, and make them discharge their diurnal duties to the world which they lighted up. Mr. Ritchie was no less confident that his private superintendence was essential to confine the sun and planets of our system within their orbits. We regret to say that this honest, but whimsical opinion, embittered his last moments and occupied much of his last thoughts which ought to have been devoted to God, and the concerns of his soul. 'What will my country—What will the world do without me?' was the absorbing reflection, when he saw the gradual approach of death. It was in vain that his friends reasoned upon the vanity of such an idea—in vain they reminded him that the order and affairs of the world depended not upon the life of a single individual, and that even the death of Washington had not impeded the prosperous march of the Republic—the poor gentleman was in no condition to hear reason. Don Quixote, on his death bed, recanted the errors of chivalry, but Mr. Ritchie, on his, clung to his mistake with fond and increasing tenacity. His disordered imagination anticipated all the horrors of anarchy when the pervading influence of the *Enquirer* should be extinguished in his death. The delirium conjured up the most appalling and opposite fancies. At one moment he saw the States losing all subordination, disorganizing the Union, and setting up separate and independent governments—at another the general government absorbing all power, and 'rushing into consolidation.' 'State rights,' 'the sovereignity of the people,' 'the integrity of the Constitution,' 'the doctrines of '98,' 'Madison's report,' all were anhilated in this general 'wreck of matter and crush of worlds.' All this he predicted would come to pass after his death.

"With such stupenduous fancies brooding incessantly in his mind, it is no wonder that he made rapid advance to the gates of death. During the last days of his illness some of his opinions underwent the most extravagant changes. At one time he was extremely alarmed at the idea of the Presidents being chosen by the House of Representatives. He dreaded the recurrence of such another scene as that between Jefferson and Burr, and was not sure that it would lead to a dissolution of the Union. To prevent this he strenuously advocated the Caucus, and the nomination of Crawford; but when it became certain that Mr. Crawford could not be elected by the people, all his efforts were directed to prevent them from making any choice. He was now as solicitous that the election devolve on Congress, as he was before, that it should be made by the people. Perhaps it would not be difficult to prove this, that all he wanted was the election of his man—that it was Mr. Crawford he wished to serve. But let us tread lightly on the ashes of the dead, and under the influence of the human maxim, '*de mortuis, nihil nisi bonum,*' let charity hide what reason would discover.

"For several days Mr. Ritchie was kept alive by the stimulus of anxiety. To hear from New York, North Carolina, and Ohio was his last wish. His friends began to hope that cheering news from these States might revive him, and even restore him to health again. Vain hope! and evanescence as vain. On Saturday night Mr. Van Buren wrote that all 'except honor' and four electors were lost in New York. On Sunday night it was ascertained that North Carolina had abjured the Caucus. It seemed that the spirit of Mr. Ritchie only lingered to carry these disastrous tidings to Heaven. It fled immediately upon their annunciation, refusing, like Patrick Coutts, to wait for the news from Ohio.

'The evil that men do lives after them,
The good is often interred with their bones.'

So let it not be with Mr. Ritchie. We have shown that he fell a victim to his patriotism. Let that be remembered when his transgressions are forgotten. For fifteen years he had ruled public opinion in Virginia, and in all that time he had never dissented from the majority. He was so good a Republican that he refused to express any opinion, to advocate any measure, before he had clearly discovered on whose side of the question public opinion was. His own sentiments were cheerfully sacrificed to those of the majority. Where is the man, living or dead, who has given stronger devotion than this to the 'will of the people' or paid greater respect to the 'omnipotence of public opinion!' "

When the election of the President was taken to the House of Representatives, Ritchie again conceded Jackson's election, but continued to entertain a hope for Crawford. On January 10, 1825, he wrote his brother Archibald: "Crawford's cause is almost hopeless. I had a letter from a Western Senator two days ago, who writes me that C. has many friends among the Western Delegation, but that they can not think of going for him apparently against the sense of their own people, unless they see New York leading the way. That state and his other Atlantic states will give him 1/3d of the Union—and thus excuse themselves to their people for voting for *him*:—but even in the event of N. Y.'s going for him, there is so much doubt of the Western Representatives imitating their example. He adds that 8 western states may otherwise be set down for Jackson, Cooke of Illinois being for Adams.

"What a desperate choice would our Reps. have to take between Jackson and Adams. I almost pity them for being obliged to vote. The elective power is in such a case a curse instead of a blessing. It is said this morning that our Va. members will stick to Crawford to the very last extremity, and perhaps at last not vote for either Jackson or Adams. The friends of the last are very sanguine. But for my part I think there is no certainty about the matter. The members seldom write to me. They are cautious, shy as a parcel of mice. Their present situation is certainly one of great delicacy & responsibility."[32]

Although Jefferson and a majority of the politicians of the old school preferred Adams to Jackson for the presidency, the Junto took Clay as a second choice. Ritchie shared the opinion of the Junto, was not hostile to Adams, and thought Jackson justly entitled to the place.[33] It is strange, therefore, that the final selection of Adams encoun-

[32] *Ritchie MSS.*

[33] *Richmond Enquirer*, January 29, 1835; *Ibid.*, March 10, 1827; *Ibid.*, December 20, 1828; *Ibid.*, September 19, 1828; *Richmond Whig*, March 21, 1829; Giles, *Political Miscellanies*, pp. 165, 166.

tered opposition in Virginia. Though inclined to nip the bait themselves when prepared by Van Buren, the Virginians were yet opposed to anything that savored of corruption or bargaining. That was why the letter which arrived in Richmond on the evening of January 29, 1825, telling of the alleged bargain between Clay and Adams whereby the latter was to become President and the former the heir apparent, created such a sensation. The effect is best described in the following brief note from Betsy Coles to her brother, Andrew Stevenson, then a representative in Congress: "The good people are run mad here about the presidential election. I was with some of our great men at Dr. Brockenbrough's the other night and found them all universally denouncing Clay and Adams. They (Mr. Nicholas, Dr. & Judge S., Rone, Campbell, etc., etc.) said that they would take Jackson and any body now in preference to Adams."[34]

Ritchie shared the indignation and alarm of his countrymen and repudiated the "corrupt and vile bargain" even more quickly than they. It seemed to him an effort to parcel out the empire between Pompey and Cæsar. He at once suspended all friendly intercourse with Clay, who had thus treacherously betrayed the South. From this time to March 4, 1837, when Van Buren was inaugurated, they did not meet, and Ritchie was most relentless and effective in keeping him from the goal of his ambition, the presidency. Though he announced it as his intention to judge the new administration solely upon its merits,[35] there can be no doubt that the guns prepared for Jackson were now turned upon Adams, and that Betsy Coles spoke for Ritchie also when she said that the Junto was willing to "take Jackson and any body now in preference to Adams."[36]

Disappointed and disgusted the *Enquirer* abandoned temporarily the field of politics and devoted itself to local affairs.

[34] *Stevenson MSS.*, February 3, 1825.

[35] *Richmond Enquirer*, February 8, 1825; *Ibid.*, May 24, 1825.

[36] Giles, *Political Miscellanies*, p. 165.

Since the debates on the admission of Missouri the subject of negro slavery had been an absorbing one. To those who contend that the abolition movement began about 1830, Ritchie's remarks of 1825 on that subject may be interesting and even instructive. He had long tried to quiet those "vain glorious knights of the quill" at the North, who persisted in discussing a subject "of all others the most interesting and delicate to the people of the South." At the same time he had warned the "officious and facetious" individuals of the former section that the evils of negro slavery were to them largely dreams and imaginations. He readily acknowledged, however, its real evils and confessed his willingness to be entirely free from "the curse." But, like the true southerner of a later period, he was unwilling, even now, to trust the abolition of negro slavery to inexperienced hands—to persons who could not follow the innumerable fibers by which it was attached to and interwoven with the people. At this time, as later, the slavery problem presented also a negro problem which Ritchie saw clearly. Regardless of his disapproval of slavery and of his fears regarding the presence of the negro, he was now unwilling to sanction a violation of the constitution by accepting King's resolution which provided for the use of the funds arising from the sale of the public lands to aid in abolishing slavery by purchasing the negroes and deporting them.

Although it involved the subject of negro slavery, Ritchie believed that good would come from the proposed Panama Congress. He could not defend Georgia in her dispute with the federal government about the removal of the Indians. But his chief interest centered in the internal development and in the educational progress of Virginia. To the former end he considered free commercial intercourse with the West Indies imperative, and expressed grave fear lest Great Britain should monopolize our western trade thence by diverting it to free ports in Canada.[37] With remarkable en-

[37] *Richmond Enquirer*, May 30, 1827.

thusiasm and foresight he set forth the advantages of "railroads and steam moving carriages," and had the boldness to suggest that they would in time supersede canals and canal-boats. He felt that Virginia could regain her place of prestige in the Union only by maintaining and strengthening the moral force and tone of her citizens. Accordingly he made an earnest plea for the proposed state university, which he expected to become the sheet anchor of her intelligence and her morals. It mattered not that its professors were to be foreigners; mind was of no country; and science had neither latitude nor longitude.[38]

Adams' first annual message to Congress set the ball of political revolution again in motion and recalled the editor of the *Enquirer* to a place on the watch tower of our national liberties. Henceforth Adams was to be fought in the open. Where prudence had dictated silence he had characteristically espoused broad principles of national power. Not only had he urged the construction of roads and canals, but, in his enlarged view of internal improvements, he included the establishment of a national university, the support of observatories, "light-houses of the skies," and the exploration of the interior of the United States and of the northwest coast. He urged also the enactment of laws for the promotion of agriculture, commerce and manufactures, the "encouragement of the mechanic and of the elegant arts, the advancement of literature, and the progress of the sciences, ornamental and profound." This was all to be done to promote the "general welfare."

Ritchie demanded at once to know where Clay and James Barbour were when the President penned that part of the message which related to the general welfare. He was never more serious in making any inquiry. Even a casual reading of the *Enquirer* and of his correspondence for this period shows that he was not playing politics and that he was actuated by a patriotic desire to preserve the balance be-

[38] *Richmond Enquirer*, October 11, 1825.

tween the centralizing and the decentralizing forces in our government. In the words of the celebrated jurist, Edmund Pendleton, he raised the cry, "The Danger Not Over;" he also implored Jefferson and Madison to interpose their efforts to arrest the tendencies toward consolidation; and in his zeal for a return to original principles, he republished the Journal and the Proceedings of the Constitutional Convention of 1787.[39] There is no mistaking the sentiment of the language to his brother Archibald when he said: "I have stood by Virginia like an affectionate son & an honest man. I stand by her at this moment when I am humbly attempting to defend the constitution against the heresies of J. Q. A."[40]

Though his zeal and methods did not command the approval of the *Albany Argus,* the political organ of the Van Buren party, they doubtless had the sanction of all those patriots who understood the original nature of the federal government and desired to preserve it to avoid the evils of despotism on one extreme and of democracy on the other. His able presentation of the theory of the division of power in our government was the inspiring source of the numerous resolutions which Virginia and other states now began to adopt on the subject of federal relations. They came to be called abstractions and, because of the political uses which were later made of them, doubtless did much to cheapen the theory of state sovereignty. But they had their origin in that great reaction toward particularism which began about 1816 and ended in civil war.

In view of the large part which the West has played in our national history, the following extract from a letter by Jefferson to Ritchie, written at this crisis when it seemed that Clay had betrayed the country, is of interest:

"I fear with you all the evils which the present lowering aspect of our political horizon so ominously portends. That at some future day, which I hope to be very distant, the free principles of our government might change, with the changes of circumstances, was to be ex-

[39] *Richmond Enquirer,* December 8, 10, 24, 1825; *Ibid.,* September 11, 1825; *Writings of James Madison* (Ford Ed.) IX., 231.

[40] *Ritchie MSS.* (No date.)

pected; but I certainly did not expect that they would not *overlive* the generation which established them. And what is still less expected was that my favorite western country was to be made the instrument of that change. I have ever and fondly cherished the interests of that country, relying upon it as a barrier against the degeneracy of public opinion from our original and free principles. But the bait of local interests, artfully prepared for their palates, has decoyed them from their kindred attachments to alliances alien to them. Yet though I have little hope that the torrent of consolidation can be withstood, I shall not be for giving up the ship without efforts to save her. She lived well through the first squall and may weather the present one."[41]

It was indeed a crisis, and the politicians of Virginia bestirred themselves to avert it. First they sought a "real coadjutor of Tazewell" to represent the state in the federal Senate. The resignation of James Barbour to accept a place in the new cabinet presented an opportunity for redemption. But Virginia was not equal to the occasion. She had no better material to offer for leaders than William B. Giles, John Randolph, John Floyd, and Henry St. George Tucker. Of these, Giles had one foot in the grave and was too hostile to Jackson to be an effective co-worker with him; Floyd had also seen his best days and had little following except in the western counties; and Tucker was a nationalist. Thus the choice fell upon Randolph, who was unfitted by temperament and habits for leadership and who, despite the length of his service, was not popular even at his home.[42]

Though the columns of the *Enquirer* did not betray him, Ritchie had opposed in vain the election of Randolph to the Senate. He preferred Giles, but local conditions were such as to render it inexpedient to express a preference. His activity in the presidential election of 1824 and his strict construction doctrines had neutralized temporarily his popularity in the western counties so that John Hampden Pleasants was about to succeed in ousting him from the office of public printer by organizing the representatives of the western counties in the Assembly against him. The following extract from a letter to his brother gives an adequate de-

[41] *Richmond Enquirer*, September 11, 1827.

[42] *Ritchie MSS.* Thomas Ritchie to Col. A. Ritchie, (no date); *Richmond Enquirer*, December 10, 1825.

scription of the situation as well as an index to the true Ritchie:

"The Legislature has been in a sort of hurly-burly since it met. There are many new members; many young ones; many whom I never saw and who never saw me; several from the West have come not very well inclined to take my part, because they were for Tucker and I was for Giles. They were for Roads and Canals at all events, and I only when the Constitution should be amended to authorize them; and what with these causes, and what with the offence I had given to some about the Yorktown bill and to others about the William & Mary College bill & &; and what with the votes my opponent got by his personal friends & legislative acquaintances and some who felt for his poverty, and the Adams & Clay men, and what with the 10 or 12 ( ) votes he got, he received the vote you have seen. Not content with that, some of his friends are trying to strike at me in other ways. A young member from Harrison (son of John G. Jackson) who nominated Tucker first and J. H. Pleasants next, has proposed a Resolution to let out the Public Printing to the lowest job. Meantime they are circulating every description of *lie* against me; that it is the most lucrative office in the Commonwealth, when the net profits do not exceed $1,200, of which I only receive *one third* (the rest is divided among printers whom I have *interested* in the work to have it well and properly done, and as well or as properly, it has never yet been done). They say that it is a ( ) when I read the proof-sheets, and turn out at almost all hours, day & night, to see their work; when I read over yesterday, most carefully, equal to 50 pages in octavo of the public work. They say that I employ a printer to do the work at most inadequate wages, and skim the cream myself; when it is a fact that Shepherd, the best printer in the Commonwealth, and equal to any in the Union, receives a salary of $850, besides being as much interested in the profits as I am, that is just one third. When I proposed three years ago to resign Shepherd would not let me. He was pleased to say such had been my liberality he could not consent to lose me. But they will not lie me down. I have weathered too many a storm to care for *this*. If they put out the work to the lowest bid, be it so. They have the right to do it; and they may at their own risk try a project, which did the work at Washington so badly & so slowly that Congress had to abandon the system & employ a Public Printer. Let the thing go as it will, I shall not bow my spirit before the proudest of them. I am as honest as any of my opponents, and as independent and as unbending. They calumniate me as a Dictator, as possessing too undue an influence in the Commonwealth (this is what that foolish fellow, the editor of the *Whig*, charged upon me last Tuesday), but I laugh the imputation to scorn. It is a poor compliment to the citizens of Virginia to raise my influence at their expense. It is false as it is malignant. It is a leaf from the Richmond letters, and I will not stoop to answer it."[43]

Triumphant at home, Ritchie again turned his attention to national politics. Virginia was now to present a united

[43] *Ritchie MSS.*

front both at home and in the national councils. To the first end he sought to conciliate the inhabitants of the western counties, where Adams was strong, by supporting the movement for reforms in the state constitution and by substituting state for federal aid in completing their proposed internal improvements. When Hezekiah Niles reminded Ritchie that Virginia had requested aid from the federal government in 1815 to extend the National Road, and suggested that the inhabitants of the western counties, in continuing to look to that source for aid, were acting in keeping with the best and the latest traditions of the state, Ritchie insisted that the resolutions of 1815 had been adopted without due deliberation and that no one had ever thought of regarding them as a "life precedent."[44] To accomplish the second end he urged that the state stand by and reiterate its resolutions on federal relations and that she place her ablest men in public life. Though not a resident of the district, Giles was put forward to succeed Randolph in the House. His defeat was followed by the publication of his "Political Disquisitions" and another futile attempt to reach Congress by contesting the re-election of W. S. Archer.[45] Notwithstanding the opinions of the *National Intelligencer* to the contrary, Ritchie, unlike "men of principle in proportion to their own interest," knew that Virginia would never be bribed by any appropriations to works of internal improvement within her boundaries.[46]

Meanwhile the bitterness which John Randolph, in his moments of hysteria, was injecting into the political caldron had so agitated the anti-administration forces as to make it possible for Van Buren, with his gentle touch, to organize a working opposition and to launch Jackson's candidacy for the presidency. It was the best way to get rid of him and to destroy the power and influence of Adams and Clay, and for

[44] *Richmond Enquirer*, June 23, 1826.

[45] *Ibid.*, January 21, 1826; *Ibid.*, March 11, 1826; *Ibid.*, August 29, 1826; *Ibid.*, October 13, 1826.

[46] *Ibid.*

that reason Van Buren's more disinterested efforts received the hearty endorsement of such leaders as Randolph, Tazewell, and Calhoun. Under the direction of Randolph the campaign for Jackson's re-election was accordingly launched from some of the most strategic points in Virginia on July 4, 1826. Both Calhoun and Van Buren now became popular heroes, and the ambitions of the former to reach the presidency as the heir to the "Old Hero's" popularity found indulgence in the columns of the *Enquirer*.[47] His desire for unity and accord, as the only possible means of overthrowing the federalistic regime, led Ritchie even to condemn Randolph's attacks upon the North.[48]

Though in sympathy with anything that would unite the opposition and defeat Adams, Ritchie had accepted Jackson's candidacy with reluctance. Consequently he and others of the Junto had not been readily admitted to the secrets of the little magician and his political henchmen. As early as October, 1826, P. N. Nicholas, one of Ritchie's closest friends, wrote to Van Buren for information regarding "the views of those with whom we would co-operate in the other states," and assured him that there were "some of us who are discreet enough to be confided in"[49] At the same time he informed him of the continued hostility to Jackson in Virginia, but was careful to assure him that Adams was even more unpopular. In due time the administration came to the rescue of those desirous of winning Ritchie. By uniting its strength with those Republicans of the Assembly who could not endorse Randolph's record in the United States Senate, it brought about his defeat for a re-election and secured the election of John Tyler, who had favored Adams for the presidency in 1825 and who was at the time of his election to the Senate on friendly terms with Clay.[50] Con-

[47] *Richmond Enquirer*, February 14, 1826; *Ibid.*, April 28, 1826; *Ibid.*, July 4, 1826.

[48] *Ibid.*, August 18, 1826.

[49] *Van Buren MSS.* P. N. Nicholas to Van Buren.

[50] *Richmond Enquirer*, February 13, 1827.

sidering the active part taken by Randolph in promoting Jackson's candidacy and in attacking the administration, Tyler's election to the Senate was an anti-Jackson victory. But it was one of those victories which act as a boomerang. Incensed at the tactics by which it had been accomplished, Ritchie now rallied to the Jackson banner, determined to put down Adams and Clay, to retrieve the injustice done the "Old Hero" by the "corrupt bargain," and to avenge Virginia's apostle of republicanism.[51]

Van Buren did not delay in extending a ready welcome to his new political ally. In a letter dated January 13, 1827, he outlined the plans of and reasons for a political alliance between "the planters of the South and the plain Republicans of the North," which continued to be the basis of their alliance until 1860. The proposed union was to be accomplished through a national convention, by which means Van Buren felt that the "Old Republican Party" could be reorganized in such a way as to combine Jackson's personal popularity with the attachment of his followers for a particular party. Such a development would then permit a substitution of party principles for sectional and personal preferences. Van Buren's experiences in New York had taught him to regard political combinations as unavoidable, and he now considered that between the "planters of the South and the plain Republicans of the North" as the most practicable and desirable for national purposes. The Republicans had once won victory by it, and he saw no reason why they could not do so again. "It would take longer than our lives (even if it were practicable)," said he, "to create new party feelings to keep those masses together. If the old ones are suppressed, geographical divisions founded on local interests or what is more, prejudices between free and slave-holding states will inevitably take their place. Party attachments in former times furnished a complete antidote for sectional prejudices by producing counteracting feelings. It was not until that pre-

[51] *Richmond Enquirer*, January 16, 1827.

judice had been broken down that the clamour against Southern Influence and African Slavery could be made effectual in the North." He also called Ritchie's attention to the fact that in former times "attacks upon Southern Republicans were regarded by those of the North as assaults upon their political brethren and resented accordingly," and that this "all powerful sympathy had been weakened, if not destroyed, by the amalgamating policy of Mr. Monroe." This important, if not epoch making letter, marked the first application of the methods of the local spoilsmen to national politics and consummated a political alliance of long standing between the North and the South. It had been written at the instigation of Calhoun and of Ingham of Pennsylvania, for the former of whom it carried a dagger, and closed with the assurance that Ritchie could render great service to the cause.

In less than one month after his initiation to the secrets of the politicians "higher up," but not before he had committed the *Enquirer* irrevocably to Jackson's candidacy, Tazewell wrote to Ritchie that he and Van Buren had discussed "the propriety, nay necessity, of establishing a journal in the city (Washington) which should be a suitable organ of the views and opinions of the opposition in Congress both now and hereafter." They had each concurred in the wish that Ritchie should be the editor of the proposed paper "in preference to any other editor in the United States." No pledges or conditions were exacted, and he was also informed that the election of General Jackson was only a secondary desire with them. On the other hand, said Tazewell, "our great wish is to inculcate and to keep alive by frequent repetition and argument, the great principles of the Republican party, as they were manifested and expressed prior to 1801. To support those who support them, and to oppose those who oppose them."

In this remarkable letter, marking as it did the beginning of the partisan press and the influence of the party organ, Tazewell betrayed the prevailing distrust of the southern politicians for Van Buren and gave evidence of a desire, which later manifested itself more strikingly, to rule or ruin the Republican party. "For my part," said he, "I look forward beyond the 4th of March, 1829. Should we be defeated then, it would be necessary to take a new departure. Should we then succeed (of which I have no doubt) it is possible, nay probable, that our party will soon be in danger of separating from the very fact of its overwhelming force and unmanageable numbers. Then will arise a new crisis, for the occurrence of which timely preparation should be made; & I feel solicitous that a Southern Editor should have acquired and established the reputation of the proposed Journal before that day arrives. What may be Mr. Van Buren's views upon this point of the subject I know not, nor does he know mine. In your reply, therefore, to this letter (which I shall be compelled to show him) you will not of course notice this.

"Many reasons exist why this communication should be considered by you as strictly *confidential* for the present at least."[52]

It would be difficult to estimate the results of Ritchie's refusal to accept this offer. He gave as his reasons for declining his doubtful qualifications for such a position and his attachment to Virginia. He preferred to rely for support upon "a generous people than to be dependent in any manner upon the favor of a Clique, however respectable, or to the control which might be required over the Government Press." So far as he was personally concerned, this opportunity may have been the tide which, had it been seized, would have led to even greater national fame and greatness than that later attained by Francis P. Blair, Duff Green, or any of the other great editors of the Jacksonian era. It was the only opportunity which came to Ritchie in the prime of his life to enter national politics. After the presidential election of 1828 that door was practically closed, because Jackson could not forget the attitude of the *Enquirer* in 1819

[52] This letter is the property of Mrs. Geo. E. Harrison, of Brandon, Virginia.

and in 1824. Besides, Ritchie's conciliatory nature and conservative tendencies revolted against his abrupt and uncompromising disposition. Had he entered the national arena before Jackson, it is not probable that he would have been dislodged, as was Duff Green. Instead, he would have remained as a co-worker with Van Buren in maintaining a balance for the eccentric head of the government.

It is equally difficult to estimate the effects of Ritchie's refusal upon the course of national politics. In the first place, it left the way open to Francis P. Blair, who was more nationalistic in his views and less soundly versed in the federalistic theories of statecraft. In their fight for political preferment Jefferson and Madison had revived the original and true conception of the nature of the federal government. It is true they later followed its practical problems into the haunts of nationalism and centralization. But it is also true that they sympathized with the great reaction to particularism, which, in conjunction with an awakened democracy, had made the Jacksonian era possible. As the authoratative spokesman of the Virginia doctrines, Ritchie's opportunity to be a power in directing the ship of state safely between the shoals of democracy and of nationalism had come and gone forever. As the spokesman of a great party he might have retarded the relegation of the Virginia doctrines to the junk pile of "abstractions" and sustained the influence of the Border as a leaven for the decentralizing forces which were now working at the South and for the centralizing tendencies at the North. The effect upon the body politic, whether to defer a resort to arms or to render that final arbiter unnecessary, lies only in the field of conjecture.

Nevertheless Virginia was to remain for a long time the connecting link between the North and the South in the political alliance which Van Buren had already formulated. Under the circumstances political success seemed assured, and the Virginians were eager for the fray. Under the leadership of Tazewell, Andrew Stevenson, John Randolph, and John Floyd in national, and Ritchie, Geo. C. Dromgoole,

Wm. C. Goode, John Y. Mason, and W. C. Rives in local affairs, they began to play the political game as it had never been played before in the Old Dominion. They had thus fallen easy victims to the spoils system and to its methods. To their own and the great detriment of those who came after them, Virginia has followed, with few important interruptions, the lead of New York ever since, even to the point in recent times of dependence upon Tammany. Thus State sovereignty received its most vital blow at a time when it seemed most buoyant and when the attraction of the flesh pots was most tempting.

Only a few of the anti-administration leaders in Virginia held aloof from the movement inaugurated by Van Buren, Tazewell, and John Randolph to make Jackson President and to bury their minor differences for the accomplishment of that end. Like John Tyler, those who hesitated to join it were friendly to Clay, but could not endorse Adams.[53] The others looked eagerly to the time when Jackson would "reign but not rule" in the White House, and they would again enjoy the spoils of office. Under the circumstances federal relations ceased to be a subject of serious consideration, though the demands of the North had become more pressing and her power more menacing. It was a time only for conciliation and union among the opposition forces. Accordingly every effort was made to convert Tyler and those similarly disposed into Jackson men; Van Buren's plan to depose Gales and Seaton, editors of the *National Intelligencer,* by depriving them of the public printing, and to entrench Duff Green, editor of the *United States Telegraph,* in their place by giving the public printing to him, was praised by Ritchie as a patriotic effort "to regulate and purify" the press. Meanwhile the petulant and irritable Giles, to avert the danger of a worse calamity, was placed in the governor's chair; McDuffie was given a hearty welcome to Richmond at the same time that Van Buren and his friend Cambreleng were wel-

[53] *Richmond Enquirer,* March 6, 1827.

comed to the Southland; and the talk about the ambitions of the little magician to reach the vice-presidency and ultimately the presidency as the political heir of Jackson was pronounced a "vile trick" to sow discord between Van Buren and his "friend" Calhoun.[54]

Assaults from the *Richmond Whig* and other nationalistic organs exposing his inconsistency in supporting Jackson for the presidency, did not dampen Ritchie's enthusiasm for the northern alliance and its program. He not only endorsed its methods but in some instances fathered them. With the avidity of a partisan he now drank toasts to Henry Clay, "the base Judean," who had thrown "a pearl (the presidency) away, richer than all his tribe," for a mess of pottage. At the same time he praised both Van Buren and Calhoun, and did not believe that there was in all New England "a more able and respectable editor than Mr. Hill of the *New Hampshire Patriot,*" or in the whole West a "more powerful editor than Mr. Kendall of the *Kentucky Argus,*" who later became members of the "Kitchen Cabinet." He also became most vehement in his denial of the existence of a Junto in Richmond, which thwarted all efforts at reform and distributed from its Divan all patronage both local and federal. The results of the elections of 1827 in New York and Pennsylvania were hailed by him as the death knell of the administration.[55] As he saw it there was just one question to be settled in the coming presidential election, viz: "shall the voice of this country call him (Andrew Jackson) forth for four years—for four years only will he serve" or "shall it continue J. Q. A. for another four years, with a reversion to his present Secretary of State for another eight years after him?" He thought it much better to take a military chieftain "badly bred and with an impetuous temper" than to

[54] *Richmond Enquirer*, March 20, 1827; *Ibid.*, February 22, 1827; Foote, *Casket of Reminiscences*, p. 24; *Richmond Enquirer*, June 12, 1827.

[55] *Richmond Enquirer,* November 13, 1827; *Ibid.*, December 11, 1827.

continue a "vicious and corrupt" administration conceived in political bargaining and reared in the school of nationalism.[56] The *National Intelligencer* now spoke of him as the "sovereign dictator of the political opinions of Virginia," and lamented the condition which made it possible for a great people to "be led about by a weak and wicked editor."[57]

After the meeting of the Harrisburg Convention the tariff played the important part in the work of president making. As the spokesman of Virginia, standing as she did midway between the pro-tariff and the anti-tariff strongholds, Ritchie had a difficult position. As might be expected, he took a conciliatory attitude hoping that the South would follow the lead of Virginia. Nevertheless he endorsed the plan to make his friend, Andrew Stevenson, Speaker of the House of Representatives in an effort to control all tariff legislation by placing the appointment of the committees in the hands of a southerner. At the same time he took pains to assure the whole country that Governor Giles' radical message on the subject of federal relations did not voice the sentiment of Virginia, and to warn both South Carolina and Georgia against taking steps hostile to the Union either on account of the tariff or the Indians.[58] Although he distrusted their friends in South Carolina he now regarded the northern alliance as the more important. Accordingly he frankly admitted the legality of the tariff but urged only its inexpediency.[59] When the Carolinians began to calculate the value of their alliance with the North and to threaten the opposition program with disruption, Ritchie visited the Albany Regency in its divan on a political mission and later suggested to Van Buren, by letter, that his elevation to the governorship of New York had opened up to him "another destiny under the general government."[60]

[56] *Richmond Enquirer*, October 26, 1827.

[57] *Ibid.*, June 26, 1827.

[58] *Ibid.*, February 26, 1828; *Ibid.*, March 4, 1828.

[59] *Ibid.*, November 16, 1827.

[60] *Van Buren MSS.* Ritchie to Van Buren, March 11, 1828.

Unlike many Virginians the South Carolinians regarded the Tariff Bill of 1828 as of more vital concern than the "manufacture of a President of the United States." Few of the rank and file of the party there, as elsewhere, understood the object of the political alliance with New York. The "Bill of Abominations" was a direct menace to their material well being and called forth vigorous, and in some instances, hostile protests. In ten days after its passage the whole state was aflame and talk of secession was rampant. They were not willing to stand by and see their rights and interests bartered away as the price of promotion for a favorite son, and were thus on the verge of passing from the control of their leaders. But Calhoun was reluctant to give up his political friends, both in Virginia and in New York, and set himself to the task of converting the threatened revolution and revolt of his countrymen into an orderly and conservative resistance. The famous Exposition which he worked out in the summer of 1828 was the result of these efforts.

To a patriot concerned only temporarily with the task of president making and the duty of humiliating Adams and Clay, the conditions in South Carolina became alarming. In an effort to find campaign material the *National Intelligencer,* and other administration prints, charged the South Carolinians with disloyalty and insinuated that the Virginians were parties to their treasonable designs. In this new issue Ritchie saw a real danger to Jackson's chances of reaching the presidency. Accordingly he addressed letters to Calhoun, Stevenson, and his cousin, Richard E. Parker, to determine their attitude toward the Union. On July 18th he published Calhoun's reply, which expressed loyalty to both Jackson and the Union and the belief that South Carolina would remain "within the bounds of moderation" in her opposition to the tariff.[61] Later he pronounced Stevenson and Parker sound on authoritative information, and denied that

[61] *Richmond Enquirer,* July 18, 1828; *Ibid.,* August 15, 1828.

Giles had been disloyal, as charged, in 1798.[62] Meanwhile he threatened the New Yorkers with a loss of their political friends in the South, if the tariff evils were not remedied, and conseled the Carolinians to use moderation in their opposition to the tariff. He would have had Virginia stand where she stood in 1798 for both the letter and the spirit of the constitution, which would have admitted of a liberal compromise. Should she fail in her efforts it would then be time for the South to resort to non-consumption of articles produced at the North, and to raising her own hogs, horses, and mules. He was confident that other steps would be unnecessary, because he already detected a movement on the part of the anti-tariff interests in Maine, New York, Massachusetts, and the West to prevent the Bill of Abominations from becoming operative.[63]

The subject of internal improvements was of almost as much concern to Ritchie as the tariff. Locally it was a much more important issue in the campaign. Operating under the General Survey Act, Adams was at that time trying to melt down the political scruples of the Virginians "in the crucible of mercenary interests" by a systematic use of "political engineering and topographical arguments;" the Baltimore and Ohio Railroad Company and the Chesapeake and Ohio Canal Company had secured charters and were inaugurating systems intended to make western Virginia tributary to Baltimore and Philadelphia; and New York and Pennslvania had already outstripped Virginia in the race to tap the granary of the nation, the Ohio Valley. Disguise it as they would, Jackson's chief strength lay in the western counties which were most interested in all these movements. Accordingly Ritchie now said little about the constitutionality of federal appropriations to works of internal improvement.[64] He lost no opportunity, however, to urge the state to greater activity in the construction of roads and canals, and again renewed

[62] *Richmond* Enquirer, July 29, 1828; *Ibid.*, August 12, 1828.

[63] *Ibid.*, June 27, 1828; *Ibid.*, July 8, 1828.

[64] *Ibid.*, March 1, 1828; *Ibid.*, May 30, 1828.

his assurances that Virginia could not be bribed into accepting the American System by Adams' topographical arguments or by an occasional appropriation to the proposed Dismal Swamp's Canal or to the National Road.

Meanwhile the work of the campaign within the state was proceeding with interest. From the very beginning the administration entertained hope of carrying it. Ex-Governor James Pleasants, probably the most beloved and popular man then in active politics in Virginia, was talked of as a proper running mate for Adams; both Madison and Monroe were placed on the Adams Electoral Ticket; although he had not voted in twenty years, John Marshall was induced to come forward and register a protest against the unjust assaults which were being made upon the administration;[65] and it was everywhere argued that the election of John Tyler to the federal Senate and of Wm. B. Giles to the governorship pointed to the triumph of Adams in the general election.

Considering his interest in the contest, Ritchie's indifference to the plans and the activities of the administration to carry Virginia must have been founded upon absolute confidence in his position. Before they declined to permit the use of their names upon the Adams Electoral Ticket he pronounced the attempt to drag Madison and Monroe into the campaign an insult to them and a disgrace to Virginia. Whatever their previous attitude may have been, he was now certain that neither Giles nor Tyler was opposed to the election of Jackson. The other claims of the opposition went unnoticed, and the *Enquirer* continued to devote itself to the larger aspects of the campaign. He was greatly alarmed lest the anti-Masons would combine with the administration and carry New York, Ohio, and Kentucky. Thurlow Weed's frequent visits to Washington and the influence of his subsidized press in western New York were factors, the influence of which he could not calculate. On the other hand he lost

[65] *Richmond Enquirer*, August 21, 1827; *Ibid.*, December 18, 1827; *Ibid.*, January 12, 1828; *Ibid.*, March 4, 21, 1828; *Ibid.*, April 4, 1828; May 13, 1828.

no opportunity to enlist Crawford's followers under Jackson's banner. To this end he quoted from a letter from Crawford endorsing the candidacy of Jackson.

Jackson's election was no surprise to Ritchie who, like Benton, viewed it as "a triumph of democratic principles, and an assertion of the people's right to govern themselves." The efforts to effect it had, as if by magic, lifted him from the groove of safe precedent and prepared him for valiant service in the cause of a new democracy. The interest of the cause had eclipsed the unattractive personality of the untrained, self-willed, and passionate frontiersman who had led the Republican hosts to victory. It was therefore a feeling of pure patriotism (he never asked for an office) which later induced him to join that motley army of office-seekers, personal friends, and sight-seers who flocked to Washington to see the "Old Hero" take the oath which made him President of the United States and ushered in a new era in our national life.

CHAPTER V.

REFORM AND NULLIFICATION.

Immediately following the presidential election of 1828 the partnership which had existed between Ritchie and C. W. Gooch since March, 1820, as joint editors of the *Enquirer*, was dissolved, and with his tried and trusted friend, John L. Cooke, as a co-laborer, Ritchie entered upon a period of greater and more effective usefulness in both local and national affairs. A planter owning several large estates in eastern Virginia, Gooch had, like others of his class, consistently opposed all efforts at reform in the statutes and fundamental laws of the state, and in so doing had developed opinions radically different from those entertained by his colleague. The common courtesy of its editors for each other had thus prevented the *Enquirer* from taking an active part in the movement about to culminate in a constitutional convention and had confined it almost entirely to a discussion of national affairs. With the enthusiasm and spirit of a Jacksonian Democrat and with a patriotic sympathy for the ideals and movements which had made possible the political revolution of 1828, Ritchie now cast his lot with the reformers to the great chagrin and alarm of the plantation aristocracy.[1] The effect of his course in both local and national politics, in keeping western Virginia true to the principles of Jacksonian Democracy, and permeating the whole Union with a feeling of patriotism, has not been understood or appreciated even to this day. It was a factor to be reckoned with in Democratic councils down to 1860, in producing a Union sentiment in eastern Virginia, and in keeping western Virginia loyal to the federal government during the greatest crisis of our history.

[1] *Richmond Enquirer*, November 7, 1828; *Ibid.*, July 25, 1854.

Had not the election of Adams diverted attention from local to national issues and had not the indiscretion of Giles created discord within the Democratic-Republican party of the state, the reform movement, set in motion by the banking interests of western Virginia in 1816, would doubtless have prevailed before 1828. It came near succeeding in 1825. Fortunately for Ritchie, success came at a time when he was free to throw his whole force in the direction of his inclinations. Accordingly, he united with the westerners in their plans for controlling the organization of the convention. Actuated by a desire to clinch the main point at issue, they demanded the white basis of representation, which would have given equal numbers of delegates for equal numbers of voters or equal numbers of the white population. On the other hand the easterners desired a mixed basis which would have considered property as well as population as a basis of representation in the proposed convention.

With the fearlessness of a true reformer, Ritchie repeatedly warned the lowlanders that both necessity and principle required acquiescence in the demands of the westerners. Great and peculiar as were their property interests he felt that the slaveholders could not now afford to look beyond the great general principles which lay at the basis of all representative government. He therefore found no excuse for their desire to give a free man in a large county less power in the government than a free man who lived in a small county, to make the vote of a man who lived in Shenandoah count for only one-twelfth as much as that of the man who lived in Warwick, and to maintain an oligarchy under the guise of a democracy. If its work was to be permanent, if representative government was not to become mockery, and if the integrity and influence of the Commonwealth was to be maintained, he saw and urged the necessity of organizing the proposed convention on a basis of equal and just representation.[2] It is thus evident that he had little sympathy with

[2] *Richmond Enquirer*, January 22, 1829.

the new theories regarding the rights and privileges of minorities in government, which were becoming popular in the older sections of the South and extending themselves, through Calhoun's influence, into the national councils. On the contrary he remained loyal to the Jeffersonian teachings which had endorsed and made popular the rule of the majority. There was, therefore, small place in his idea of the proper comity betwen the states or even the sections for an exercise of local sovereignty which could assert its latent possibilities as the dictates of its interest demanded.

Although defeated in his plans for the organization of the proposed convention, Ritchie continued dauntless in the cause of reform. While the election of delegates was in progress he concerned himself especially with the movement to extend the suffrage to the non-freeholders. They paid a large tax upon personal property; labored upon the public highways; bore arms in times of war; maintained the militia in times of peace; and he saw no reason why they should not exercise the right of suffrage. He was certain that their services to the body politic were ample evidence of a permanent common interest with an attachment to the community and that their duties were in no way commensurate with their rights and privileges. He also thought it contrary to the Bill of Rights to exclude them from the electorate, and suggested that they petition the constitutional convention for a redress of grievances.[3]

Although his proposed reforms were far reaching, at times tolerating the idea of woman suffrage,[4] Ritchie thought the time inopportune for a consideration of any plans for the abolition of negro slavery. Accordingly he disapproved of the attempts of the westerners to inject that subject into the discussions regarding the proposed convention. He knew that "this sting can scarcely be touched without jarring the body politic," and warned all that its discussion would "instantly

[3] *Richmond Enquirer*, February 14, 1829; *Ibid.*, October 15, 1829.
[4] *Ibid.*, October 20, 1829.

inflame the minds of the eastern members, prove a source of discord, and distract the deliberations of that assembly more than all other points of required concession."[5]

Nevertheless Ritchie did not give up on the main issues involved and continued to excoriate the slaveholding aristocracy in the name of justice and of progress. His abruptness in breaking through the crust of custom and the sanctity of privilege with which the aristocrats clothed their long established and timidly questioned right to rule, caused many to pity him and others to wish for the destruction of his press. Those whom he was trying to aid hardly appreciated his situation sufficiently to be helpful. They did, however, rush to his aid with subscriptions, raising the total number of those taking the *Enquirer* to 5,000, and increasing that number at the rate of three daily during the month of July, 1829, and thus making it possible for Ritchie to win his way to the hearts of the westerners. Encouraged by these evidences of approval and buoyant with the spirit of the times he, in the face of the hostile east, enlarged the size of his paper, purchased new type, confessed his former errors in neglecting the interests of the people, and recommitted himself to the cause of reform.

Amid the talk of dismemberment and the counter attacks of the easterners and the westerners in that memorable convention which met in Richmond in October, 1829, Ritchie continued to demand reforms. His demands became even insistent and impetuous. After weeks of debate and fruitless effort in which the respective rights of a majority and a minority in government were clearly and forcefully set forth by such debaters as Benjamin W. Leigh, Abel P. Upshur, Chapman Johnson, John Tyler, Littleton W. Tazewell, John Randolph, and W. B. Giles on one side, and Philip Doddridge, C. F. Mercer, Briscoe G. Baldwin, Judge Lewis Summers, and Alexander Campbell on the other, with two ex-presidents, Madison and Monroe, and the Chief Justice of

[5] *Richmond Enquirer*, July 24, 1829.

the United States, John Marshall, as referees, the eastern aristocrats suddenly awoke to the fact that their antagonists' most trusted sentinel was located in Richmond in the office of the *Enquirer*. When they handed down their ultimatum the most that he would concede was compromise. Accordingly a movement was set on foot to destroy the *Enquirer* by establishing a pro-eastern and a pro-slavery press in Richmond. The best description of this incident, together with the attending circumstances, is found in the following extracts of a not wholly disinterested letter written some years later by C. W. Gooch to Van Buren:

"I have been to Mr. Ritchie and his family—a *friend*—a *brother*—a *child*—a *Father*—a *Benefactor*. He knows it—he feels it! On several occasions I have had the bread of his five children in my hands! During the session of our Convention, the whole of Eastern Virginia (including some of his nearest relations) were exasperated at his course. They were determined to destroy him and his press. Deputies from many counties came to Richmond; the Members of the Convention and of the Legislature and others had Meeetings or Caucuses—they understood one another—and appointed a large Committee of *Management* to get up a press they could support. That Committee had several meetings to select an Editor. *My name* was promptly brought forward; but two personal friends told the meeting that they would vouch for my declining any offer they could make; that I stood peculiarly related to the *Enquirer;* the Editor of that paper was my *friend*, and owed me $10,000, (*which he has since paid*) for my interest in the paper—that independent as I was, and this debt over Mr. R's head & my intimacy & good feeling with him & his family, it was impossible for me to think of the proposition; and, the more especially, since I had quitted the paper but a short time & could take it back & control it, if I thought proper. They then looked out for another; but they could not agree upon any man; and insisted that my friends should make the proposition, and assure me that within ten days, $10,000 should be paid me in money, the price for 2,000 subscriptions; that they would contribute original matter and make such exertions as should insure unprecedent success to the paper. These propositions were accordingly submitted to me. I could give but one answer. *No.* But seeing the course things *must take* in the Convention, and that the excitement about the *white basis* would soon subside, I gladly seized the opportunity of preventng the enlistment & pledged devotion of more than half the State, in a crusade against the Enquirer, and the more especially when I saw that *Calhounism* was the next great object of the leaders in this business. Under these circumstances I asked 8 or 10 days to think of the matter & make my decision; going at once to Mr. Ritchie & telling him to quiet his alarms, repeating all the circumstances (but names) and informing him what was my predetermined decision, & my motives for delay. Mr. R. was truly alarmed, but my frank declarations transscribed him into a moving shadow over the room. His tears witnessed the sincerity of his declarations when he said if I would not embark in such a scheme, he *defied* any other man. It was a critical time in the fortunes of his paper. The eighth or ninth day after, when Gordon's compromise had been adopted in the Convention, and the minds of men had been freed of an excitement of which I partook like others, since my property was likely to be taxed by men who had no *property*, etc.—when I saw the calm so rapidly succeeding the tempest, I made my decision in form, and communicated with the Committee. I protested against throwing the *Enquirer* over board, because Mr. Ritchie was in favor of the white basis; that it was a paper more devoted to federal politics than any thing else; that upon almost every other point *that far* he had gone wth *lower Virginia*—that the Convention would soon adjourn with a Constitution which the people would ratify, & that we should be thrown back upon federal politics in all our political movements—and that in these respects I was not aware of any difference in mine and Mr. R's opinions. I explained the personal relationship and connection between us, and the impropriety at *that time* of setting up a new paper. But, that when Mr. Ritchie did not support the Administration of Gen. Jackson as he ought; whenever he showed a leaning to either Clay or Calhoun, or to their opposite policies, then I would embark under such flattering offers, and apply myself again to what I knew to be the most slavish, the most disagreeable, nay, revolting employments. The *Managers* in this Matter, including my personal friends, were then covertly and are now ardent Calhoun Men & Nullifiers. To such men my answer was *decisive.* In the meantime the friends of the Administration had become satisfied with the Compromise in the Convention, & their ardor for a new paper had cooled down. As you may suppose, the subject was dropped for a time. I had anticipated this result. The little Calhoun party, however, being thus foiled rallied after a while upon their own supposed strength, and set up the *Jeffersonian Republican*, which found a circulation only on the south side of the James River & in some of the Calhoun States. It proved a losing business, tho' it struggled on to this winter when the Coalition between Clay & Calhoun caused its amalgamation with the *Whig.* The hostility to the *Enquirer* has been kept up, and has increased so much that Mr. R. was near being ousted as public printer. His enemies are confident of success at the next Session, & I fear will succeed. Many of the cordial friends of the Administration voted against him on account of the milk & water course he pursues. He was, in fact, only saved by the Clay men and old federalists who are afraid of Nullification."[6]

Ritchie emerged from the exasperating and initimidating experiences of the constitutional convention stronger than when he entered it. Threats to dismember the Commonwealth and attempts to destroy his press caused him to modify his attitude toward and his "rash" statements about the lowlanders and to endorse the compromise which they pro-

[6] *Van Buren MSS.*

posed as a settlement of the differences between the sections about representation. Nevertheless his heart continued to overflow with sympathy for the "men beyond the mountains," whom he was ever ready to admit on a basis of equality to a share in the common traditions and achievements of the Old Dominion.[7] His reluctance in accepting the constitution of 1830 was ample proof that intimidation had not produced conviction. Now that the slaveholders had won without establishing an independent press, he continued as their spokesman, but was henceforth the acknowledged leader of the Jacksonian Democrats of the uplands.

Meanwhile national politics had assumed an alarming aspect. The tariff agitation of 1827 and the passage of the act of 1828 had inflamed the South to the point of conflagration. John Randolph continued to hold high the standard of revolt; Dr. Cooper, the apostle of the Manchester doctrines of *laissez-faire* and free trade, was calculating the value of the Union; agricultural societies met to protest and threaten; and the South Carolina delegation were on the point of vacating their seats in the federal Congress. It was not evident how far Calhoun's desires to be the leader of his section would carry him into the paths of Nullification or when the keen appetite of the protectionists would be satisfied. It was evident though that a reaction against Adams' vain but not unpopular attempt to erect "light-houses of the skies" and to lay low the mountains by a liberal interpretation of the constitution was at hand, but it was equally evident that every step of the movement would be fought most stubbornly by that arch strategist, Henry Clay.

Though sympathizing most heartily with the strict construction program, Ritchie saw danger ahead for the new administration. That danger lay within the party, and history had taught him that internal discord was fatal to vigorous party life. A time for conciliation and compromise had thus arrived. Accordingly he advocated a return to the Vir-

[7] *Richmond Enquirer*, December 3, 1829.

ginia doctrines of '98 as a happy and constitutional mean between the unconstitutional tendencies toward nationalism at the North and the equally unconstitutional tendencies toward Nullification in South Carolina. Either tendency admitted of no compromise and thus vitiated both the spirit and the letter of the federal compact which was itself a bundle of compromises. He lamented the fact that the sections had gone so far adrift in their contest for material gain and political advantage as to lose sight of the spirit and nature of the federal government. With a view to recalling his countrymen to original principles he therefore embarked upon a campaign of education. To this end Edmund Pendleton's famous essay, written in 1801 after the Jeffersonian triumph, and entitled "The Danger not Over," was republished in the *Enquirer*;[8] protests were made against the attempts to place the federal Senate in control of the opposition; and a movement was launched for a federal convention to aid in recalling the country to original principles and in settling by compromise the questions involved in the application of the federal constitution.[9]

Like the elder statesmen of Virginia and elsewhere, Ritchie, despite his avowals of 1828, had no exalted opinion of Jackson's ability as a statesman and a constructive leader. Least of all did he consider him a conciliator and a compromiser. He had accepted the Old General's candidacy in the hope that his popularity would blast the ambitions of those engaged in the "corrupt bargain" and make it possible for wiser heads to restore the government of the fathers. For himself he had already undertaken in a most patriotic spirit what he conceived to be his part in this noble work. Considering the contemplated revival of the power and influence of the states it is not strange that he had elected to perform his services at Richmond instead of going to Washington. His first duty had ever been to Virginia, and he now considered her leadership necessary to make the political revolution of

[8] *Richmond Enquirer*, December 6, 1828.

[9] *Ibid.*, December 18, 22, 1828.

1828 effective. She was allied to the West by the strongest ties of interest, and her relations with the South were such as to call for all the "prudence of the head" and all the "energies of the heart." Therefore he did not see why a free and vigorous press in Virginia could not aid materially in curbing the ambition of the former and in restraining the ardent and centrifugal forces of the latter, while it at the same time opposed the encroaching domination of the North and the East.[10]

Ritchie's position was clearly evident from his attitude toward and advice to the newly elected President. Though willing to entrust the patriotic duty to other and younger heads, he urged the necessity of a press in Washington that would dare to "speak the truth to the Court and to the People." Familiar with what he considered the "Old Hero's" besetting weaknesses he also made bold to advise that he devote his whole energies to the services of his country, that he surround himself by able men, that he avoid the delusions of ambition and the seductions of passion, that he aid in restoring the government to its original conceptions, and that he show moderation in the use of victory. He had always considered that it was one thing to win victories but quite another to use and improve them.[11]

Whatever may have been his distrust of the chieftain under whom they had fought, there is every evidence that Ritchie understood the importance of the victory achieved by the Democrats in 1828. They had broken through the line of safe precedent under the slogan "measures not men," inaugurating a new era similar to that inaugurated by the Democratic revolution of 1801. However, deluded he may have been about the importance of "measures" in this personal triumph of a military hero, sufficient measures and principles were at stake to render necessary political accord within the victorious party if that victory was to be improved.

[10] *Richmond Enquirer,* November 21, 1828.

[11] *Ibid.,* November 21, 25, 1828.

Accordingly he used every energy to steer clear of the rocks of internal discord. He considered it a time to bind up the ties of friendship and to soothe the lacerated feelings of those who had been injured by eight years of bitter party warfare, a time to restore the press to a due consideration of virtue and intelligence, a time to restore the purity of our institutions, and a time to develop the internal resources of our common country. In reply to the rumor that Van Buren and Calhoun already sought the presidency as the successors of Jackson in 1832, he entreated the politicians and the editors to "save Rome" from her enterprising and ambitious citizens and to give the people a rest from the madness, the folly, and the heart-sickening effects of political strife. Had his advice been followed, granting that he himself would have been willing to abide by it permanently, Ritchie might today be rated among the great statesmen as well as among the great editors.

As the cabinet was expected to perform the most important executive functions under the new order of things, and as the leading politicians of Virginia expected to occupy the most important places in that body, Ritchie approached all discussions regarding it with a degree of caution. He did not share the common distrust of Van Buren, nor was he keen for the promotion of those radical state rights men who were willing to play fast and loose with Clay for political advantages. It is not certain, however, that he had been admitted to those administration secrets which contemplated sending the leaders of the old school to oblivion. He, therefore, quietly acquiesced in the local movement to make Tazewell, the solon of the Virginia lowlands, the premier of the new administration. Nor did he express a doubt that Floyd, who had refused to stand for a re-election to Congress, would be called to aid in the patriotic work of recalling the government to original principles. Meanwhile, the *Enquirer* lost no opportunity to urge Jackson to an independent course in the selection of his advisers. Although conspicuous because of the absence of Virginians, he was therefore able to announce the names of the new cabinet with disappointment but not with regret. Had local conditions permitted, he doubtless would have had even less hesitancy in seeing the line of succession pass to the younger statesmen.

Mistaking his praise of the elder statesmen in Virginia for sympathy with their ambitions, it was not long, however, before the editorial world began to chide Ritchie about the "crop of sour grapes" there. It was noted, moreover, that despite the inclemency of the season, the crop was unusually large but of a variety that would never ripen. He endured this pleasantry until it reached a point beyond which forbearance ceased to be a virtue and until some of the smaller plums had been allotted to the lesser politicians, and then he notified the amused public that there were no sour grapes in Virginia and that Tazewell had never desired a place in the cabinet.[12] He could not say as much for Floyd and refrained from saying anything.[13]

The slight shown the elder statesmen in the formation of the cabinet did not concern Ritchie half so much as the other innovations introduced by Jackson. Inured to the methodical habits of the Virginia dynasty and to those tenets of conservatism which made the Old Dominion a power when she had giants in politics but later left her stranded high and dry in the march of progress, the practical application of the spoils system shocked him. But he had cast his lot with the new regime as a matter of patriotism and was determined to fight within the party rather than out of it. On April 14, 1829, he protested by letter to Van Buren, thus early recognizing him as the power behind the throne, against the consideration being shown the army of office seekers which thronged the federal capital. He feared that they would hasten the calculations of the politicians by sending Jackson to an untimely grave. He therefore advised that the President himself peremptorily refuse to converse with all

[12] *Richmond Enquirer*, March 10, 1829.

[13] *Floyd MSS.* Floyd to Col. John Williams, December 27, 1830.

applicants for office. Instead he urged that the whole matter be turned over to secretaries empowered with authority to investigate each and every application and to make recommendations. Under such conditions he predicted a quiet dispersal of the office seekers and the restoration of a sounder tone to the body politic. He was equally alarmed at the growing practice of appointing editors to office as a reward for political or other service. "It is with great reluctance," said he, "I speak upon this point. I am seriously impressed with the conviction that too many of these appointments have been made; and certainly of all the measures of the present adm. it is the only one which has produced a deep and serious impression among its friends in this part of the country. Is it not time to stop? The more you appoint, the more, I fear, will harass you for office."[14]

After an attempt, only partly successful, to conciliate the proud and ambitious Virginians and to lay the basis of a new Democracy with them by sending Tazewell to the English,[15] Randolph to the Russian, and Rives to the French court, by making other liberal uses of the spoils, and by reaffirming her political faith, interest was suddenly diverted from the administration, as such, by a movement for the annexation of Texas. Mexico was being threatened with a loss of her independence, and under the circumstances it was feared that her northeastern provinces would be disposed of in such a way as to make them a menace to the further growth and development of the United States. Our subjects were already pouring into Texas in an effort to extend our territory. As all such movements, this one received the endorsement of the folk at home, and the articles by "Americanus," believed to have been Thomas H. Benton, urging annexation, were republished in the press of the whole country and received with popular favor.[16]

[14] *Van Buren MSS.*

[15] Tazewell declined the appointment. *Van Buren MSS.* Tazewell to Jackson, March 30, 1829.

[16] *Richmond Enquirer*, September 8, 1829.

Notwithstanding the fact that the *National Intelligencer* saw in the proposed annexation the creation of a new West, which would depopulate Virginia by opening up new lands to her citizens and eventually dismember the Union by making the slaveholding power formidable, Ritchie wanted Texas and wanted it then. Ever since the South's unfortunate acquiescence in the Missouri Compromise, he had looked to Texas as a compensation for what it had then lost. Fully versed in the expansive powers of a slaveholding society he knew that elbow room was necessary to sustain the power and prestige of the South. Besides, there were other circumstances which now made Texas desirable. He believed Mexico ready to sell, and thought the purchase necessary to remove the dangers of British aggression.[17] Then, too, the purchase of Texas might be used as a master stroke by Jackson to allay party discords and to stifle opposition, as Jefferson had used the purchase of Louisiana to accomplish similar ends.[18]

Even Texas could not divert the attention of the South Carolinians and the disappointed Virginians from the tariff. It had not taken a year to convince them of their impotency at court and of the doubts surrounding the political triumph of 1828. Nevertheless they had strong ground of hopefulness for a redress of their material grievances in the supposed anti-tariff attitude of Jackson. This was doubtless the reason why they had said so little, except in their private correspondence, about his indifference toward their political pretensions and about the promotion of the "little Magician" to the premiership. The first annual message had tickled their fancy regarding the tariff, and the Exposition had not yet wrought its mission. Thus while some of the state legislatures, notably that of Pennsylvania, were nominating Jackson for re-election, they offered no serious opposition, planning and hoping all the time to control the policies of his

[17] *Richmond Enquirer*, September 8, 22, 1829.
[18] *Ibid.*

second administration. This is why Jackson's toast, "Our Federal Union; it must be preserved," given on April 13, 1830, at the celebration of Jefferson's birthday, surprised them. It meant simply that the Union would be preserved regardless of what became of the tariff or of what course the Nullifiers ultimately took.

As with Jackson so with Ritchie, there was much doubt about the ends to which his anti-tariff sentiments would lead. For once he had ventured to disagree with his teacher, Madison, in insisting that a protective tariff was unconstitutional and not merely inexpedient.[19] But at the same time he had tried to reconcile the Virginia planters to the existing conditions by inducing them to employ their slave labor in factories. Thus he hoped to make the South self-sufficing and a recipient of the protective policy.[20] Moreover, he had welcomed Van Buren, the supposed custodian of the northern interests, to Richmond in 1829; he had declared for Jackson's re-election almost three months before the Legislature of Pennsylvania; and he had complaisantly acquiesced in denying to Floyd and Tazewell a place of influence in the new administration.[21] When he could see no more in Jackson's toast than a 'mild warning to all parties," Calhoun, Tazewell, and Floyd needed no other proof that the *Enquirer* would be henceforth for Jackson and a united Democratic party regardless of the tariff or anything else.[22]

During the days immediately following Jackson's bold declaration for the Union, the Nullifiers became more aggressive. By a confusion of their own doctrines with those of '98 they hoped to drive Ritchie and other strict constructionists into an active alliance. But the wily editor of the *Enquirer* continued to condemn their schemes as inopportune and ill-advised. In able expositions of the Virginia doctrines based upon his political Bible. (Madison's Report),

[19] *Richmond Enquirer*, December 27, 1828; *Ibid.*, January 3, 1829.

[20] *Ibid.*, January 27, 1829.

[21] *Ibid.*, January 12, 30, 1829.

[22] *Ibid.*, April 20, 23, 1830; *Ibid.*, June 4, 1830.

he showed that they were unlike and preferable to Nullification. At the same time he made every effort to keep Jackson true to the strict construction theory of the federal constitution, hoping thereby to counteract the Nullification movement by a milder and more logical method of opposition to the tariff. To this end he urged, through Van Buren, a veto of the Maysville Bill on constitutional grounds as an achievement "more glorious than the Victory of New Orleans."[23]

Though he did not entirely approve the principles of Jackson's veto of the Maysville Bill, he accepted it as a vindication of the middle course between nullification and centralization, and assured the public that it would be harmless to the administration even in the West. His belief in its beneficient effects both as a means to restrain Nullification and vindicate the Virginia doctrines was clearly set forth in a letter to his brother Archibald, from which the annexed extract is taken:

> "I have this day had a long conversation with Stevenson, and a pretty long one with McDuffie. I infer from the remarks and tone of the latter that the storm in S. Carolina is blowing over that the proceedings of Congress for the last few days previous to adjournment will have the effect of tranquilizing her excited politicians and of putting aside the measure of *nullification*. I told him very plainly that in my opinion Virginia would not co-operate in such a measure. He said that the most the politicians of S. C. had thought of doing was to declare the Tariff null and void by a Convention, and then leaving it to her Juries to refuse giving judgments on the Revenue Bonds. He seemed to think that even this course would now be abandoned, though he said he had no idea that Congress, organized as it now was, would modify the Tariff so as to make it acceptable or tolerable to his state. I suggested to him that the measure might be got rid of by breaking in pieces the Combinations which had carried it through, but this was to be done by degrees and required time—that next winter we might reduce the duty on sugar and thus lessen the attachment of Louisiana for the Tariff—that in reducing the duty on iron & wool we might strike N. Jersey & N. York from the Tariff States, and thus we might get back to the old times. He, however, contented that a reduction on sugar would be lost by a majority of 30 votes, and that the various interests which were involved would stick together, and defeat any gradual or detached attack. I confess upon the whole his tone is much softened down, and that I have almost lost all fear of a *storm from the South.*
>
> "Our friends are, of course, in high spirits for Gen. Jackson's

[23] *Van Buren MSS.*

Message on the Maysville Bill. It does not exactly come up to our Virginia Doctrines; but it does a great deal, by arresting corrupting local appropriations, for the benefit of this and that sectional improvement, which were wasting the public funds and bribing the members of Congress out of their Constitutional principles. When I heard of the way in which the "Old Hero" was beset, by members from the West telling him if he rejected the Maysville Bill, he and they were gone there, that it would scatter dissatisfaction through most of their districts—when I recollect how many interests he was going against in taking his ground, I am more & more impressed with the great moral courage he has exhibited. I understand Eaton & Ingham were for his signing the bill, Van Buren & Branch against it. On Sunday morning, after sitting up all night, the President was very much nettled in their forcing the Light House & Harbor bill upon him, filled with God knows how many little appropriations for roads and canals & &, in order to force them all down his throat, or by his rejecting them, rousing up so many various interests *against* him. He exclaimed with some warmth, 'Let them come on—all—I am ready for them.' That bill you know he kept by him on Monday morning & refused to pass upon. Webster was very anxious to continue Congress together in order to force him to act, and thus get material against him for the Summer Campaign. The obligations we owe "Old Hickory" for stepping in at this crisis & saving the Constitution almost at its last gasp are great indeed."

Accordingly Ritchie turned his chief attention to the efforts being made to open the West India ports to American trade. "This is a matter," said he, in a letter to his brother Archibald, "deeply interesting to you farmers, at this time too, would have much effect on the coming harvest. I wish to God that I could have the pleasure of announcing the opening of the W. India ports. No news can be more agreeable to the public.[24]

Ritchie was never more mistaken in anything than in considering Nullification dead in 1830. The supposed remedial developments had only heightened the opposition of the Carolinians to the tariff. During the summer of 1830 they effected working organizations and made determined efforts to extend their propaganda. To this end the Nullification doctrines were again described as being identical with the Virginia doctrines, and Ritchie was attacked as a nationalist who, in conjunction with Van Buren, had parceled out the

[24] *Richmond Enquirer*, June 8, 1830.

empire.[25] The *Salisbury* (N. C.) *Carolinian* even affirmed that he had been a Nullifier in 1822,[26] when his cousin Spencer Roane had sought the presidency as the leader of the strict construction wing of the Democratic-Republican party.

In sympathy with their war upon the tariff, but desirous of controlling the enthusiasm of the Nullifiers, Ritchie was now ready to admit that there was a point of forbearance beyond which a free people could not go in the neglect of their rights. He was certain, however, that the South Carolinians had not reached that point, and he hesitated to draw the veil, under the existing conditions, on what would happen, were they to resort to force to prevent the collection of the customs duties. To his mind nullification and secession seemed synonymous, and the former was without sanction or precedent. In suport of these contentions he quoted at length from the writings of Jefferson and Madison, and called attention to the edition of the Resolutions and Debates of '98 which he had recently published, together with a preface by himself.[27] He furthermore denied the existence on his part of any understanding with Van Buren looking to the promotion of the latter to the presidency to the exclusion of Calhoun.

Supported as he was by most of the younger politicians of the state and by the General Assembly, the effect of Ritchie's stand in favor of the administration was readily seen in a tendency of the opposition forces of all varieties whatsoever to unite as they later did to form the Whig party. It is doubtless true that the followers of Jackson aided this tendency by their efforts to prevent the re-election of Floyd to the governorship and by their haughty exercise of power. They thus led Floyd, and probably Tazewell, to believe that Jackson's hostility to Calhoun had ante-dated the presiden-

[25] *Richmond Enquirer*, June 18, 1830; *Ibid.*, July 2, 13, 1830, and August 3, 13, 1830.

[26] *Ibid.*, August 3, 1830.

[27] *Ibid.*, July 2, 1830; *Ibid.*, August 3, 31, 1830; *Ibid.*, October 1, 1830.

tial election of 1828, and that the old guard had been treacherously betrayed into voting for a gang of spoilers. His Indian fighting blood was thus aroused, and he now sought sweet revenge to be "marked by the effects of the tomahawk." The following extract from a letter to Col. John Williams of Knoxville, Tennessee, shows plainly that he did not hesitate to join forces with Clay to attain such results:

"When I wrote to you that Mr. Clay and myself could not be reconciled it was for the reason that there was not in my opinion ground enough for us to occupy with the freedom of former friendship and not that I had the slightest enmity to him or remotest disposition to check his future hopes in this State or any where else—but perfectly willing my friends should deal with him as their judgment of the *present* and belief of the *future* shall dictate." [28]

The final breach between Calhoun and Jackson, which came when the latter discovered the attitude of the former toward his conduct in Florida in 1819, and the odium cast upon the administration by the presence of Mrs. Eaton in the official family, marked the parting of the ways between the politicians of the old school and those whom the natural course of events had made leaders in Virginia in 1829. In their short sightedness and lack of confidence in the power and influence of the new democratic revolution, Floyd, Tazewell, Tyler, Thomas W. Gilmer, and others thought that the time for sweet revenge had arrived, that the new order was rapidly disintegrating for want of experience and knowledge in the art of statecraft, and that they themselves would soon be vindicated by restoration to a commanding place in the councils of the republic. Even the friends of the administration admitted that Calhoun was the favorite of the Assembly for the presidency. Under the circumstances it seemed possible to win a large part of the followers of Clay. In the midst of such encouraging conditions the old guard became militant. With Floyd in the governor's chair and with Tazewell and Tyler in the federal Senate they anticipated little

[28] *Floyd MSS.* December 27, 1830.

difficulty in marshaling the state behind Calhoun's candidacy and thus checking the Nullification movement by making it unnecessary. To this end Ritchie was to be driven from his commanding position by Gilmer, who was to establish an anti-Jackson organ in Richmond, and that "wretch of a printer," Amos Kendall and those "miserable reptiles," William B. Lewis, John Eaton, and Martin Van Buren, were denounced as political dictators who had usurped the government by taking advantage of Jackson's credulity. Patriotism had thus called the old guard to the rescue. The lurking desires for revenge and the longings of ambition made it impossible to ignore the call.

The following extract from Floyd's Diary, commenced at this time to record what he believed to be the downfall of our experiment at government, tells the story as he and other Virginians saw it:

> "The President has disappointed friends and foes. All his enemies said of him before the election has been realized. The future historian will regret to record the error these states committed in raising a victorious general of their army to the first office in the States of a civil kind, merely because he had become popular in winning a great battle and closing a war with a splendid victory over the English army at New Orleans. * * * I thought Jackson had mind, which by practice in the affairs of government, would be qualified to manage the machine and in a short space of time he would be a statesman. That all the talents of the Union were at his command, I knew, and did believe in common with all others of his friends, that he would call around him the talented and distinguished gentlemen throughout the confederacy and make as strong and splendid an administration as Jefferson's. How sorrowfully all have been disappointed. We believe that Landon Cheves, Littleton Waller Tazewell, John McLean of Ohio, Thomas Benton, James Hamilton, Jr., of South Carolina, Hayne, a senator of that State, Hugh L. White of Tennessee, and so forth and so forth would have been called; and that Mr. Calhoun, the Vice-President, would have been consulted and allowed his due weight, he being considered a man of the first talents in the Union, the one on which we place the highest value. Instead of giving us such men, he has surrounded himself with men of narrow minds, some of them hardly gentlemen and none of them have much character and no principles, moral or political, except Ingham and Branch. Jackson has given himself up to the management of these wretches and has even had the folly to engage in the little petty quarrels of the women." [29]

[29] *Floyd Diary.*

To the honest conservatives, whatever may have been their political ambitions, their disappointments, and their estimates of the value and nature of their own public services, the exigencies of the times were indeed alarming. It is not strange that they turned to their hero, Calhoun, for deliverance and let pass no opportunity "to keep the long end of the lever in case of his (Jackson's) death." To this end Duff Green suggested that the General Assembly of Virginia place Calhoun in nomination with Jackson for re-election to the vice-presidency. Fearing and hoping that Jackson might die before the end of his first term, Floyd doubted the wisdom of the course suggested by Green, because Calhoun could not then ask for the presidency with the same grace that he could if his name had not been used in connection with the second place. Despite occasional tendencies toward conciliation and concerted action with the followers of Clay, the dissatisfied politicians of Virginia were willing to aid in the re-election of Jackson to defeat Clay and to be in a position to determine the succession in any event.[30]

Had not Clay been in the way the disaffected elements of the Democratic party in Virginia would have urged Calhoun's candidacy in 1831. With him and Jackson alone in the contest, Floyd was certain of their ability to carry the state. It mattered not that Duff Green, editor of the *United States Telegraph,* was being driven from his strategic position in conection with the press of the country to make a place for Blair and the *Globe,* and that the press of Virginia, under the leadership of Ritchie, was being brought into greater accord with the administration. Floyd's hope lay in getting Clay to see that the people would not satirize themselves by turning Jackson out and putting him in, and that he could attain the presidency only after Jackson's successor had served one or two terms. But unlike Judge Brooke, Clay's confidential adviser in eastern Virginia, the leaders of the western and the northern parts of the state, who favored

[30] *Floyd MSS.* Floyd to Calhoun, April 16, 1831.

federal appropriations to works of internal improvement and were not hostile to the protective tariff, were not willing that the author of the American System "should decline for a time" to be a candidate for the presidency.[31] Clay doubtless shared their opinion, and, though the inter-party feeling against Jackson raged, the time seemed inopportune for Calhoun.

Jackson's decision to have a political house cleaning, to be accomplished by forcing the resignation of his cabinet and by its complete reorganization, brought a revival of hopes for the anti-Jackson program. True, Floyd saw in the proposed house cleaning only "another of those manifestations of weak sagacity" by which Van Buren thought to save himself and Jackson and to suspend public judgment upon their conduct.[32] There was, however, a noticeable, falling off in Jackson's strength in Virginia about this time, and the advisability of launching Calhoun's candidacy was seriously considered by his friends. Despite the happiness over what was believed to mark a decline in Ritchie's power and influence, the chief difficulty lay now not with Clay but with Ritchie. To Floyd he had become a veritable thorn in the flesh. On June 24, 1831, he wrote to J. S. Barbour as follows:

"I am informed that Ritchie still adheres to Jackson, and to Van Buren; some think for the sake of the latter and 'for other purposes,' though he has but few, very few in his train. The Trabea is falling from his shoulders; every step he takes is digging his own pit; and every apology he attempts for the violation of the Constitution is lessening his influence, and for the outrages upon morals and private rights by the favorites of power, is preparing for himself future regrets. To talk about the benefits this administration has brought or will bring to State Rights, is an insult to the plain understanding of all and a satire upon the whole of Ritchie's former political opinions." [33]

There are few better examples anywhere of the inability of politicians to bring about things of consequence or to know what is of consequence and possible than that shown in 1831

[31] *Floyd MSS.* Floyd to Calhoun, April 16, 1831.

[32] *Floyd's Diary*, April 25, 1831.

[33] *Floyd MSS.*

by Calhoun's friends in Virginia. With a skill and adroitness equalled only by that of the Albany Regency, W. S. Archer, Geo. C. Dromgoole, and the Junto recently recruited by the addition of Ritchie's brother-in-law, Judge Richard E. Parker, Peter V. Daniel, and others of equal skill as politicians, understood both the temper and the desires of the voters and the limitations of their opponents both in and out of the Republican party. By smoothing over the attacks of the *Globe* upon "our Senators," Tazewell and Tyler, by offering the voters Jackson and reform in preference to Clay and the tariff or to Calhoun and Nullification, by a loyal devotion to the Union, and by throwing cold water upon the rumors which had brought Mrs. Eaton into the limelight and disrupted social and political circles in Washington, Ritchie made it almost impossible for such politicians as Floyd, Tazewell, and Tyler to bolt Jackson, while he at the same time prevented Calhoun from winning a popular following. Plainly nothing but victory was to crown such efforts and such sagacity. On April 4, 1831, Andrew Stevenson wrote Van Buren to have no alarm about the rumors of "mighty changes in the Old Dominion." He did not doubt that there would be "war to the knife" accompanied by the loss of some of his former friends, but he was determined to beat no retreat.[34]

Even the disruption of the cabinet did not alarm Ritchie and his associates. Indeed, they saw in it a political asset. They expected the resignation of the "little Magician' and the "magnanimous utterances" which accompanied it to put an end to "the discords and ambitions which have appeared in our party," and Ritchie expressed it as his opinion that Van Buren would not again accept office at the hands of the President.[35] A second thought, prompted doubtless by information from Washington and sustained by a desire for party unity, produced a change of mind, however, and he with the

[34] *Van Buren MSS.*

[35] *Van Buren MSS.* Ritchie to Van Buren, April 20, 1831. See also R. E. Parker to Van Buren, April 28, 1831.

approval of the Junto, concluded that it would be better for Van Buren to go to the Court of St. James rather than remain in this country and scramble with Calhoun for the vice-presidency. While the *New York Herald* was certain that Van Buren would not go to London, but would remain in this country and run for the vice-presidency, Ritchie was equally certain that he would go, and that he was not and would not become a candidate. Both publicly and privately, even to Van Buren himself, he opposed all attempts to run him against Calhoun.[36] The degree to which these declarations of a semi-friendship were reassuring to the friends of Calhoun would be difficult to determine.

Ritchie and the Junto had meanwhile developed a profound respect for Jackson as a man of integrity, character, culture, and principles. They thought it ridiculous and even unpatriotic for his own countrymen to denounce and villify, as a barbarian, a tyrant, a corrupter of the public morals, and a tool of magicians and juntoes, a man who would grace the society of any European court. It was, said they, the same type of justice as that given Jefferson in his life time. The *Winchester Republican,* controlled by Judge Parker, was certain that Jackson could carry Virginia against the combined forces of Clay and Calhoun.[37] It is interesting to note incidentally that such a combination was desired by some at this time as a means of depriving Ritchie of his power. If friends of Calhoun dared to assemble to make formal protest against the re-election of Jackson, their gatherings were written up as "Clay meetings," and those who took part were chided with the prediction that they would ultimately vote for the father of the American System for President.[38]

The friends of Calhoun knew as well as Ritchie himself that Jackson's strength in Virginia lay in the western and

[36] *Van Buren MSS.*, Ritchie to Van Buren, April 30, 1831; *Richmond Enquirer*, May 17, 24, 1831.

[37] *Ibid.*, July 22, 1831.

[38] *Richmond Enquirer,* September 9, 1831.

particularly in the Valley counties, each of which was at this particular time seething with discontent over the subject of internal improvements. While Baltimore had carried off the fruits of Hesperides, Ritchie had tried in vain to arouse the "sluggards and talkers" of his own state to the necessity of availing themselves, by the use of turnpikes, canals, and railroads, of the benefits which nature had lavished upon them. Since the incorporation of the Baltimore and Ohio Railroad Company and the Chesapeake and Ohio Canal Company he had repeatedly held out to them the advantages of connecting the East and the West by way of the James and the Kanawha rivers. From both the political and the economic view it is not surprising therefore that he now opposed the efforts of the South Carolinians to make Charleston the outlet of the Valley of Virginia by connecting the two by rail.[39]

Meanwhile Nullification had gained additional momentum. Although it had practically ruined his chances for the presidency in 1832, had Jackson not been in the running, Calhoun no longer concealed his paternal connection with that movement, and it was generally known that he had inspired some and written others of the elaborate arguments and expositions made in its defence in the summer and autumn of 1831. The talented and patriotic source of their origin commanded for the Nullification doctrines, therefore, a more respectful hearing then had hitherto been accorded them, and necessitated a more exact and thorough exposition of Ritchie's views regarding them.

He readily admitted Calhoun's courage and patriotism in opposing the tariff, but he could not subscribe to his method, Nullification of a federal law. That was to place a state in the impossible position of being both *in* and *out* of the Union at the same time. He admitted the right of a state to interpose by peaceful and constitutional means to arrest a deliberate, palpable, and dangerous encroachment of the federal government upon the rights of the states, such an interposi-

[39] *Richmond Enquirer*, June 17, 1831.

tion as Virginia had made in 1798, but he insisted that no state could veto a federal law until its constitutionality had been passed upon by the several states. Any other course might prove fatal to the Union, because three-fourths of the states might not act in accord with the nullifying state. He evidently considered that Calhoun, in his efforts to preserve the Union and to control the sentiment of his state, had either mistaken or ignored the logical conclusion of the Virginia doctrines which conceded the right of a state to secede or to revolt after due notice to her sister states and after all means to secure a redress of intolerable grievances had failed, but did not even imply that a single state or any number less than three-fourths of all had a right to nullify a law.[40] Although Ritchie later admitted that Jefferson was the father of Nullification, in that he had used that term in the Kentucky Resolutions, he would not admit that Jefferson's doctrine of Nullification was applicable to the tariff, because it was not plain that the protective tariff acts were abuses of delegated or an assumption of undelegated powers. Nor did he admit that Jefferson's ideas of Nullification were identical with the system worked out by Calhoun.[41]

However formidable Calhoun's doctrines might appear, Ritchie did not now consider the dangers from the tariff menacing. He saw clearly the near approach of the time when the public debt would be extinguished and when the public lands would be a source of sufficient income. Such conditions he hoped would make a tariff unnecessary and impossible. Accordingly he opposed the interposition of the individual states, except by resolutions on federal relations, and requested the co-operation of all aggrieved parties in an antitariff convention to be held at Philadelphia on September 30, 1831.[42] This he now considered a peaceful, constitutional, and adequate means for stating their grievances and for obtaining redress. In the same editorials which de-

[40] *Richmond Enquirer*, August 16, 1831; *Ibid.*, August 19, 1831.

[41] *Ibid.*, March 13, 1832.

[42] *Richmond Enquirer*, July 27, 1831.

nounced Nullification as opposed to the Virginia doctrines, he praised the Union party in South Carolina and urged the counties in Virginia to select delegates to the proposed anti-tariff convention. When the convention met Virginia had fifty-one delegates, thanks to his vigilance, a number greater than that from any other state. Among the number were some of Ritchie's most intimate friends: P. P. Barbour, John Brockenbrough, Geo. C. Dromgoole, Randolph Harrison, W. H. Roane, and others.[43] Ritchie was confident that the effects of their deliberatons would be remedial, but suggested that, in case they were not, the southern states call a convention to revise the constitution. In case this resort failed to bring redress he would then have sanctioned a convention of the southern states to devise the best means of appealing to the sister states. Secession or revolution were to be used only as the last resort—Nullification never. It is thus plain that he desired anything but Calhoun's plan.[44]

With such a conciliatory and compromising attitude, Ritchie might have endorsed Clay's proposal of 1832 for modifying the tariff by a downward revision. Other Virginians accepted it as better than the Tariff of Abominations, but his antipathy to Clay's political ambitions had now become chronic. In every move of that gentleman he saw an attempt to reach the presidency. Clay had become to him a modern Themistocles who could not sleep for thinking of the triumphs of Miltiades. Accordingly he pronounced his proposal for modifying the tariff only a "new bill of abominations" and gave warning that the South would not end the matter there. She demanded remedial legislation not as a favor but as a right.[45] Then, too, he and Blair of the *Globe* stood in constant fear lest a compromise of the differences on the tariff would lead to a coalition between Clay and Calhoun

[43] *Richmond Enquirer*, October 11, 1831.

[44] *Ibid.*, November 1, 1831.

[45] *Ibid.*, January 24, 1832.

to defeat Jackson. The tariff issue had thus become a political asset.[46]

Meanwhile Duff Green, out of the bounty of his sordid though fertile brain, sought to expose Ritchie. First he affirmed on the authority of "an intelligent gentleman from western Virginia," that Ritchie and John Randolph had gone into the service of Van Buren, and that they were organizing the state so as to give him its vote for the vice-presidency, regardless of the wishes of Floyd, the governor, and Tyler and Tazewell, the Senators in Congress. Then came the report that W. C. Rives was to supplant Floyd for governor, that Peter V. Daniel was to succeed Tazewell, that Ritchie was to succeed Van Buren at the Court of St. James, and that the tariff, as an issue, was to be surrendered.[47] Finally it was reported and freely reiterated by the *New York Journal* and the *National Intelligencer* that a move was on in New York, Pennsylvania, and Virginia to make Van Buren President by securing his election with Jackson, who had promised to resign to permit his promotion.[48]

Ritchie at once assigned Green to a place in the Ananias Club. He also challenged him to produce any proof that he had ever sought office from Jackson for himself or for others. His very nature revolted against the spoilsmen and their methods, and he now laid bare the "vigilant inquisitor to the teeth." "We defy both him and his spies," said he, "who go prowling into the public offices, and hold conversation with the heads of departments, which are afterwards garbled, and retailed to the public by the Editor of the *Telegraph*. We defy all such men. We ask no favor of any of them—and may as truly add none of Mr. Van Buren himself—nor of Gen. Jackson."[49] Furthermore, Ritchie declared that he then had in his possession a letter from Van Buren, in which

[46] *Van Buren MSS.* F. P. Blair to Van Buren, January 28, 1832; *Ibid.*, R. E. Parker to Van Buren, February 3, 1832.

[47] *Richmond Enquirer,* December 22, 28, 1831.

[48] *Ibid.*, December 30, 1831.

[49] *Ibid.*, December 28, 1831.

he had declined to run for the vice-presidency, that there was not a man in the General Assembly of Virginia, who pressed his claims, and that he had never heard a single member express the slightest desire to vote for him.[50]

The refusal of the Senate to confirm Van Buren's appointment, after he had actually repaired to the Court of St. James, acted as a bomb in the various political camps throughout the Union. Immediately plans and policies so shaped themselves in Virginia as to give an appearance of truth to Duff Green's falsehoods and conjectures, but the correspondence of those concerned more than refute his charges. Although he considered Van Buren wholly unfit for the presidency,[51] John Randolph, who now desired to be minister to England himself, felt that the part which "the thrice double ass," Calhoun, had played in bringing about his recall had made it "as easy for Benedict Arnold to get the vote of Virginia as for him" (Calhoun).[52] To Ritchie it was a memorable event in our annals,[53] and he urged Van Buren's reappointment at once. The *Winchester Republican* nominated him for the vice-presidency, and Richard E. Parker boldly predicted that he would succeed Jackson.[54] After a conference with Jackson, Andrew Stevenson informed Ritchie that he must take the field "in the spirit of victory" and that his "former scruples as to Mr. Van Buren being nominated for the vice-presidency must give away."[55] Furthermore he advised that delegates to the proposed Baltimore Convention be selected at once and that they be instructed to vote for Van Buren. In the following lines Floyd committed to the pages of his diary what the obstinacy of the old guard had wrought in Virginia: "Ritchie, that profligate son of a Scotch Tory, and the Richmond Junto are at work trying to procure a

[50] *Richmond Enquirer*, December 30, 1831; *Ibid.*, January 3, 1832.

[51] *Jackson MSS.* Randolph to Jackson, March 18, 1832.

[52] *Ibid.*, March 26, 1832.

[53] *Richmond Enquirer*, January 31, 1832.

[54] *Van Buren MSS.* Stevenson to Ritchie, February 4, 1832.

[55] *Ibid.*, *Van Buren MSS.* Stevenson to Ritchie, February 4, 1832.

party to nominate in this state Van Buren for the vice-presidency.'"[56] Clearer vision would have enabled him to see that they already had a party both able to nominate and elect Van Buren.

In his opposition to the plans to force Van Buren's proposed candidacy, Ritchie was true to his conservative tendencies and displayed superior political sagacity. Despite the vigilance of dame rumor the idea was a new one, and Virginians then as now moved slowly. Time was needed to pave the way in the popular mind for an explanation of Van Buren's former attitude toward the tariff, his relation with the peace party of 1814, and his attitude toward the Missouri Compromise. Then, too, Virginia had a natural feeling of distrust for political spoilsmen and magicians, of whom he was the reputed prince.[57] Furthermore, he feared the consequences of such a course upon the national campaign. In hope of carrying Virginia and North Carolina, and of throwing the election of the vice-president into the Senate, where Van Buren had about as much chance of election as he had to be minister to England, the friends of Calhoun had launched P. P. Barbour's candidacy for the second place. Already there was talk of withdrawing Sergeant, Clay's running mate, from the race in the border states for any man who could carry them against Van Buren. Under the circumstances Ritchie thought it wise to sound the public before taking an irretrievable step.

Notwitstanding Ritchie's attitude, leading members of the Junto made a determined effort to commit Virginia to Van Buren's candidacy. The first trial of strength came in the Democratic State Convention which met in February, 1832. The contest was hotly waged, and the friends of Van Buren, led by W. H. Roane, now a member of the Junto, forced a *sine die* adjournment, when it was found that they could not win and after Jackson had been re-endorsed.[58]

[56] *Van Buren MSS.*, February 5, 1832.

[57] *Richmond Enquirer*, February 4, 1832; *Ibid.*, March 17, 20, 1832.

[58] *Richmond Enquirer*, March 17, 20, 1832.

After an interval of two weeks the matter was again taken up in a caucus of the Democratic members of the Assembly, which, after a heated discussion, decided to refer the whole matter, together with the selection of delegates to the Baltimore Convention, to the people.[59] As a result, the spring election of 1832 was largely a contest between rival candidates for the vice-presidency.

The decision to refer the contest to the people was a tactful move, and was largely the work of Ritchie. He rarely made a move of any kind without previously making a diligent effort to ascertain the sentiment of Virginia. Then he generally moved in the direction it indicated. As a result of the plebiscite Barbour received the support of Virginia, voting under the unit rule, in the Baltimore Convention,[60] but the result of the contest for that support had made it evident that Van Buren was almost equally strong, and that his candidacy would, in due time and as the result of his being the regular nominee, develop a strength greater than that of any combination which could be made against him. Accordingly Ritchie dismissed his former scruples and reluctantly espoused the candidacy of the New Yorker. Henceforth the battle cry was Jackson and Van Buren, the choice of the people, against the triumvirate, Clay, Calhoun, and Webster.[61]

Many of Calhoun's friends in Virginia did not concur in the nomination of Van Buren and continued to support Barbour. Those of them who attended the Baltimore Convention had refused to make its action unanimous.[62] Accordingly a Jackson-Barbour ticket was placed in the field, and there was talk during the summer of a coalition with the opposition to support it. But the disaffected reckoned without their host. Although a strict constructionist of the most approved type, Barbour now had an eye on the supreme bench, and was not willing to antagonize the only man who could gratify his

[59] *Richmond Enquirer*, March 20, 23, 1832.

[60] *Ibid.*, May 25, 1832. The vote was: Van Buren 39, Barbour 45.

[61] *Ibid.*, May 29, 1832.

[62] *Ibid.*, June 5, 1832.

ambitions. Those who desired to use him as a tool to accomplish the defeat of Van Buren were disgusted at his non-committal attitude regarding the vice-presidency and his reverence for party unity. But the cause of their chagrin was the capital which Ritchie and his associates used to effect Barbour's complete withdrawal from the race.[63]

Ritchie's reluctance in supporting Van Buren for the vice-presidency, even after he had secured the nomination and after his candidacy had become popular in Virginia, was due to a careful consideration of the best interests of the party locally, and not to any feeling of hostility or distrust. His record on the tariff had not been satisfactory, and it was feared that unnecessary enthusiasm would fan the opposition of the Nullifiers and anti-tariff men. Since 1828, when Ritchie had suggested that greater honors were in store for him than the governorship of New York, and when Van Buren had desired to make Ritchie the national spokesman of the Jacksonian party, they had been friends and confidants. Besides, there is every evidence that the Junto now had greater confidence in Van Buren than in Jackson, and that they desired the presence of the former at court as a sort of balance wheel. New York's iniative in undertaking and carrying to a successful completion her works of internal improvement and the flush condition of the federal treasury had simplified the national issues upon which he had been found wanting, and it was now thought that he was the only man who could steer the ship of state safely through the storm which continued to blacken the southern skies. In a letter written so that it would reach him immediately upon his arrival in this country from England, Ritchie requested that he "hasten without delay to the city of Washington to do all you can to assist in settling the tariff on just principles." "Take your stand," said he, "boldly like a patriot. Come out fearless of all consequences—and trusting to your country

[63] *Richmond Enquirer*, June 1, 12, 1832; *Ibid.*, July 3, 1832; *Ibid.*, October 20, 1832; *Floyd's Diary*, October 26, 1832.

and your God." [64] One week later he begged him to open his mind to the President and to beseech him not to sign the bill then pending for appropriations to certain works of internal improvement. About the same time Daniel expressed a belief in Van Buren's influence for good at Washington. John Randolph's invitation for him to partake of Virginia's hospitality followed, as did Parker's assurance that the vote of that state would be for him for the vice-presidency.[65]

Jackson's veto of the Bank Bill gave a new and more important issue to the campaign and permitted Van Buren to retire from the limelight. Henceforth Clay and his policies became the chief objects of attack, permitting Ritchie to revive the story of the corrupt bargain of 1825, to ridicule "Nick" Biddle, and to ferret out and publish all evidences of and tendencies toward a coalition between Clay, Calhoun, and Webster to defeat the choice of the people. In some quarters it was feared that the predilection of the inhabitants of the western counties for the American System and their dissatisfaction with the results of the Constitutional Convention of 1829-'30 would combine with the disaffected elements in the east to give Clay the electoral vote of the state, but Van Buren's popularity with the German elements of the Valley, Jackson's complete impersonation of the West, of which western Virginia was really a part, and Ritchie's previous services in the cause of reform more than offset these tendencies. The success of Jackson was accordingly hailed by Ritchie as a triumph for the people, a rebuke for the federal Senate in rejecting Van Buren's appointment to be minister to England, and the death knell of both Clay and Calhoun.

Meanwhile the Tariff Bill of 1832 had become a law, and the Nullifiers, failing to obtain redress by it, were pressing South Carolina to radical measures. While the bill was pending Ritchie had predicted that McDuffie, Calhoun, Hayne,

[64] *Van Buren MSS.* Ritchie to Van Buren, June 25, 1832.

[65] *Ibid.* From June to September, 1832.

and Hamilton would be naughty, if Congress failed to grant remedial legislation. "The Union party," said he, "are too weak to resist them. There is no knowing where the dissatisfaction may stop. The whole South is indignant at the opposition and obduracy of the Tariffites. Virginia is now cool, but very excitable and determined not to send a man or musket to put down S. Carolina. Events may hurry us further. I fear, Sir, many of our most sagacious patriots are now beginning to tremble for the Union. It is on all hands admitted to be the most alarming state of things which has existed since the Revolution."[66]

Now that these prophetic utterances were about to become true, Ritchie's chief concern was to keep Jackson "cool" and "firm." His panacea for all crises of state was "conciliation and compromise," to which haven he now fled. While the Nullifiers were preparing to resist the collection of the customs duties by making them illegal within the limits of South Carolina, and while Jackson was preparing to collect them by the use of federal troops, Ritchie suggested that the annual message to Congress recommend a gradual reduction in all duties until they should be only twenty per cent. of what they then were. This was the principle of the compromise later agreed upon, but it now went unheeded. Even after the adoption of the famous nullification ordinance by South Carolina, Ritchie thought Jackson should take the initiative in moving for compromise. It was a glorious opportunity to make a masterly use of his great popular victory at the polls. He could now kill Calhoun by magnanimity, whereas he had led the people in their execution of Clay. The moderate tone of the annual message pleased Ritchie greatly and led him to the false conclusion that the "Old Hero" was not going to hang Calhoun, or what was more important to Ritchie, disrupt the Democratic party by precipitate action. The *Enquirer* praised its moderation and again

[66] *Van Buren MSS.* Ritchie to Van Buren, June 25, 1832.

congratulated the people upon their wise choice in electing Jackson to the presidency.[67]

Every precaution to keep the Old General cool was for naught. It mattered not that he had been lenient in dealing with Georgia in her conflicts with the Union about the Indians. Now the Union had been assailed by an enemy, Calhoun, and as Jackson was at its head, the assault was taken as personal. He had no intention of passing it by unnoticed. While Ritchie was praising his moderation in dealing with the Nullifiers, his Secretary of State, Livingston, was at work upon the famous Proclamation to the people of South Carolina, which made its appearance on December the 10th, six days after the regular message. Its masterly and defiant refutation of the Nullification arguments was popularly received, and thus in little more than a month after he had vanquished Clay, Jackson again found himself a national hero in the battle with Calhoun.

The Proclamation, as it came to be called, swept aside the bad logic and the impracticable theories of the ordinance of nullification and proclaimed the doctrines of the supremacy of the Union, which at that particular time meant the supremacy of Jackson. The following is possibly the most important passage in it: "I consider the power to annul a law of the United States, incompatible with the existence of the Union, contradicted expressly by the letter of the constitution, unauthorized by its spirit, inconsistent with every principle on which it is founded, and destructive of the great object for which it was formed." Jackson insisted, also, that it mattered not how the tariff had been enacted or how unequally it operated upon any section or sections, it was the law of the land and had to be obeyed. Moreover he attacked the compact theory of our government, thereby questioning the right of a state to secede or to be an arbiter in the adjustment of grievances.

The effect of this state paper, the ablest of the Jacksonian

[67] *Richmond Enquirer*, December 4, 6, 1832.

era, was to arouse the Carolinians almost to the point of defiance and to strike terror to the hearts of Virginians. Few of the latter sympathized with nullification, except as a means of harrassing Jackson, but they did believe in the compact theory of our government and in the ultimate right of a state to secede. Immediately a friendly Assembly which had elected W. C. Rives, an ardent follower of Jackson, to the federal Senate without opposition, was converted into an unfriendly body which elected Tyler, his enemy, to fill the vacancy caused by the resignation of Tazewell; W. S. Archer wrote C. C. Cambreleng of New York that it would simply be out of the question to think of having Virginia endorse the Proclamation; and Floyd rejoiced to see "the poor unworthy dogs, Ritchie, Van Buren, Jackson and Co." completely deserted. So phenomenal was the transformation that Jackson suspected the Virginians of a secret alliance of long standing with the Nullifiers. "You see," said he, in a letter to Van Buren, "the course of the Nullifiers in the Virginia Assembly. I was aware of the combination between them and Calhoun and Company."[68]

The Proclamation placed Ritchie in a most embarrassing position. He endorsed every word of its argument against Nullification, but could not agree with its "doctrinal points" regarding the right of a state to secede. But there was also the practical side. Jackson had carried Virginia by 25,000 majority in 1832, and the Assembly was overwhelmingly Democratic. Now all these advantages seemed to be lost as in the twinkle of an eye. The main issue, however, was Nullification and not secession. On this subject Ritchie was in accord with the Proclamtion and the voters in the western counties who, after all, made up the rank and file of the Democratic party in Virginia. Accordingly he accepted the general principles of the Proclamation in the hope that it would appeal to the good sense and patriotism of the South Carolinians in such a way as to be effective. By an occa-

[68] *Van Buren MSS.* Jackson to Van Buren, December 23, 1832.

sional airing of his opposition to its doctrinal points he was also able to lead the disaffected elements of the lowlands.

The time seemed opportune, however, to destroy Ritchie's influence. His attitude was not wholly pleasing to Jackson; Nullifiers called him a Federalist; nationalists called him a Nullifier; Floyd's wife was certain that he took his cue from the Albany Regency; and Floyd himself spoke of him and others of the Junto as "wretches" who had "deserted their principles and the liberties of the people" for the smiles of a tyrant."[69] After discovering that only a few Virginians were in active alliance with the Carolinians, Jackson's assurances that all was well in the Old Dominion, "regardless of the mad theories of a few demagogues & politicians," gave credence to the report that Ritchie was his chief informant and that he secretly approved the Proclamation and the contemplated use of force in dealing with South Carolina.

The charges against him were too numerous to answer, and many of them were too trivial to deny. Accordingly Ritchie persisted in his devotion to the Union and in his fight for compromise. The same issue of the *Enquirer* which contained his chief comments on the Proclamation contained, also, a letter from Lewis Cass, written probably at Jackson's request, suggesting that Virginia, by a committee of her Assembly, entreat South Carolina to retrace her steps and to petition Congress for a reduction of the tariff. Three days later, December 18, 1832, the *Enquirer* announced that Clay and Webster had surrendered and that the tariff would in all probability be gradually reduced to what it had been in 1816. His devotion to the Union finally righted him with the administration and greatly increased his favor with the westerners who now poured out an avalanche of resolutions endorsing the Proclamation and condemning Nullification. Meanwhile his insistence upon the compact theory of government and his personal antipathy for Calhoun kept him

[69] *Richmond Enquirer,* December 22, 1832; *Floyd's Diary,* December 15, 1832; *Ibid.,* January 1, 1833.

straight in the course between nationalism and Calhoun's variety of particularism. Of the many aspirants to direct the ship of state he was one of the few who kept an eye upon "the Rights of the States" and "the Union of the States," the light-houses established by the fathers. Amidst the storm then raging he had the satisfaction of seeing his pet policies, mediation in dealing with South Carolina and compromise in disposing of the tariff, carried into effect in such a manner as to restore peace and harmony to the country. His heart certainly beat with pride when he recorded the events which had saved the Union, restored tranquillity, opened to the South a prospect of justice, and revived the spirit of those friends of liberty who had sighed because of the threatened shipwreck to the only great republic in the world.

CHAPTER VI.

JACKSON AND THE WHIGS.

Had not the nullification movement ended when it did and as it did, the followers of Clay and Calhoun would have united into a formidable opposition at the very beginning of Jackson's second administration. The alliance of the state rights men of eastern and the nationalists of western Virginia, the incongruous elements of which its local and national Whig party was later composed, had been practically completed in the winter of 1833. It remained only for the party as a whole to find a common platform which was soon forthcoming in the belated and questionable efforts of each faction to save the country from executive usurpation, ignorance, and general inefficiency.

Ritchie always insisted that the opposition factions had, in some instances, combined to prevent Jackson's re-election, and he was confident that the Compromise Tariff was the offspring of their intercourse. The fact that Tyler, Floyd, and John Hampden Pleasants now spoke of their old friend of 1825, Henry Clay, as "our great ally of the West" and as the deliverer and preserver of the Union, the value of which they had so recently calculated, and the fact that these believers in the Virginia doctrines were now willing to make concessions regarding both a national bank and the tariff, following Clay's magnanimous sacrifice upon the altar of his country, all strengthened Ritchie's conjectures.[1]. The following extract of a letter from Tyler to Floyd, written at this time, would have confirmed them:

> "In one word I go for the Union, not in word but in feeling and sentiment. Would northern men believe it that the manufacturers are safer in the hands of those wicked S. Carolina nullifiers than of the *non descript*, and yet it is true."[2]

[1] *Richmond Enquirer*, April 12, 16, 1833; *Ibid.*, May 17, 1833.
[2] *Floyd MSS.* January 10, 1833.

Union of the opposition and disaffected elements was not, however, yet possible. Intensity of interest and disinterestedness of purpose had not wrought them into a coherent working party. Because of his "magnanimous sacrifice" on the tariff Clay sought and expected to win the South and to become the logical and acceptable candidate of the whole country for the presidency in 1836. On the other hand, Calhoun already regarded himself as the spokesman and leader of the South and hoped, by adding the West to his following, to reach the presidency as the leader of a powerful section.[3] In November, 1833, Duff Green despaired of any concerted action on the part of the opposition factions, being, as he was, unwilling to give up Calhoun's pretensions and program. Meanwhile he lost no opportunity to sow discord in the ranks of the administration. To this end Colonel R. M. Johnson was to be made Speaker of the House of Representatives that he might become an independent candidate against Jackson's choice for the presidency and that the ranks of the administration might be thus broken.[4] At the same time Floyd, also a follower of Calhoun, thought it possible to detach Clay from the "Northern harpies" and to induce him to play a second fiddle to his favorite. This was to have been attempted in the effort to unite the South and the West, and to establish another line of succession which would have given the presidency first to Calhoun and then to Clay.[5] These conflicting interests and ambitions only delayed concerted action.

This delay operated to extend the Junto's hold upon the political power of Virginia. In the face of a hostile Assembly, which had condemned the Proclamation and the Force Bill and re-elected Tyler to the federal Senate only two months after it had elected W. C. Rives, a devoted follower

[3] *Floyd MSS.*, April 16, 30, 1833.

[4] *Ibid.*, Duff Green to Floyd, November 10, 1833.

[5] *Ibid.*, Floyd to W. C. Preston, November 23, 1833; *Floyd's Diary*, November 24, 1833.

of Jackson, Ritchie appealed to Virginia to endorse the administration. The response from the mountain and hill counties, where the people disapproved of Clay's Compromise and his coquetting with Calhoun and where the Old Hero was still an idol, was immediate and overwhelming. The new Assembly contained National Republicans or Clay men, Democrats or administration men, and seceders and nullifiers or ultra state rights men, and the members of Congress elected at the same time were similarily divided.[6] But the administration stood vindicated with a majority in both houses of the Asembly, and Ritchie was able to thwart all efforts to remove him from the office of public printer,[7] which he had held by successive re-elections for almost twenty years.

In these days of loose party ties political victories were as useless as they were meaningless. Although he had won the elections, the temper of the people of Virginia was not such as to sustain Jackson in a further war upon the bank such as that which a removal of the federal deposits would necessitate. As has been shown Calhoun's friends in Virginia were not always hostile to a national bank. Now that war upon that institution seemed to strengthen Andrew Jackson politically and to spread panic throughout the land, they hesitated more than ever. Accordingly Ritchie became an unwilling spectator while the fruits of his recent political victories slipped from his very grasp, and the regular opposition and the disaffected elements formed themselves into a majority party in the Assembly, henceforth to be known as the Whig party, a name given the new organization by James Watson Webb of the New York *Courier and Enquirer*. Following the course of the federal Senate in condemning the President for the removal of the deposits the Assembly of Virginia took a similar course, forced the resignation of W. C. Rives from the federal Senate and elected Benj. W. Leigh, a friend of the national bank, to the vacancy,

[6] *Richmond Enquirer*, April 23, 26, 1833.

[7] *Ibid.*, December 3, 10, 1833.

elected Tazewell, a Whig, over the administration aspirants to the governorship, and the majority party therein agreed upon a program for preserving harmony within its own ranks.[8] The course followed in 1832 after Nullification and the Proclamation had thus been repeated, but it had also led to the formation of a great political party.

In its eagerness to win political victories and to serve the material needs of its members, the Whigs now scrupulously avoided any references to the constitutionality of the federal bank and to its alleged political activities. But Ritchie claimed that these were the all important issues before the people and threw all the strength of the *Enquirer* into a determined effort to keep them alive. The public prints give a very inadequate account, however, of the depression which had fallen upon the administration party in Virginia and of the actual conditions which existed there. This is revealed only in the private correspondence of the leaders. Ritchie himself wrote Rives that "The times are out of joint in politics,"[9] and Gooch, his former partner, compared the party violence and proscription to that of the days of the Black Cockade and observed that the merchants and farmers were being made to feel the fangs of the dying monster;[10] respect for its venerable editor was all that saved the *Enquirer* from mob violence; John Rutherford wrote that none thought of the constitution but only of self-interest; and Peter V. Daniel was threatened with the destruction of his business but continued to decry the "contemptible slaves of the bank"; and the merchants of Richmond refused to buy from those countrymen who supported Andrew Jackson.[11] Such were the conditions under which the party of the "wise and the just," which was to rule that city for ten years first saw the light in Richmond.

[8] *Richmond Enquirer* January 18, 21, 23, 1834; *Ibid.*, February 27, 1834.

[9] *Rives MSS.* Ritchie to Rives, January 6, 1834.

[10] *Van Buren MSS.* Gooch to Van Buren, March 24, 1834.

[11] *Stevenson MSS.* Rutherford to Van Buren, March 19, 1834; *Ibid.*, Daniel to Stevenson, March 29, 1834.

Never before had Ritchie entered a campaign under more threatening auspices. He owed the banks of Richmond large sums and his defence of them and denunciations of the national bank were constantly construed as due to subserviency to the former. Then, too, General Jackson, despite the attitude of the General Assembly, was preparing to protest against the federal Senate's resolutions of censure. The effects of the Proclamation were not yet dead and Ritchie dreaded the appearance of such a state paper and entreated Stevenson to do all in his power to suppress it. "If such a paper is sent," said he, "it must do great mischief. It may turn the tide completely in Virginia. I pray heaven that this message may not ruin us. You can not act too promptly and decisively. Show this, if you please, to the President."[12]

On the day before Ritchie's letter to Stevenson, urging Jackson to use moderation, was written the famous "Protest" was sent to the Senate. Had they reached Washington in time a dozen letters like that from Ritchie and others as prominent in the councils of the party as he, would have availed nothing. The Old Hero was furious at the presumption of Clay and Calhoun in daring to censure him, and, as usual on such occasions, it was impossible to restrain him. Conscious that "The eyes of the world are upon us," a favorite expression, Ritchie returned to his efforts to save the Assembly of Virginia from the control of the hated "piebald" party. He was determined that his children should never reproach him for sitting idly in his domicile "while the measures were being prepared for a loss of our liberty."[13] The monster was to be decapitated that it might be rooted out of Virginia and Clay be sent to a deserved oblivion.

The campaign resulted in a complete victory for the Whigs, and Ritchie was forced to endure his first great political defeat. The re-election of Leigh to the federal Senate was assured, and all the Democratic accomplish-

[12] *Stevenson MSS.*, Ritchie to Stevenson, April 18, 1834.

[13] *Ibid.*, Ritchie to Stevenson, April 10, 1834.

ments stood in danger of being reversed. In a characteristic manner. Ritchie forgot himself in his sympathy for his friends who had been overtaken by defeat. The following extract from a letter to his friend Stevenson tells the whole story:

"Roane's defeat stung me worse than any other electors? I have ever known. Even J. Q's was not so bitter to me. But I tried to keep up my spirits hoping for better things elsewhere.

"Blair would not believe me last August—& you would scarcely listen to me in November, when I predicted to you the mischievous consequences of removing the deposits. I fear we shall rue the precipitate step in sackcloth & ashes. But what is now to be done? It requires wiser heads and firmer hearts than mine to say. I am not in a mood to speculate upon these events. But unless we are wiser than we have been, our enemies will crow over us & our party will present nothing but a splendid ruin. The terrors of the Bank are now carefully kept out of view by a desperate opposition, and the cry is that the President, in his usurpation, has seized upon the public purse, &. &. &.

"Have you, my dear Sir, consulted with him about the proposition I suggested of coming before Congress, recommending a wise system of state banks stript of executive control and abuse, &. &.

"God knows when I am to write you good news.

"Pray burn this and the other letter. I unbosom to you in the utmost confidence of my friendship, think, consult the strongest heads of our party, and coolly and firmly, or else we are lost. For myself and those who are dearer to me than my life (he expected to lose the public printing), I would eschew politics forever & live upon bread and water. * * * I have one consolation in the utmost frankness against these unfortunate measures, but in vain. I have destroyed all our confidential scraps for fear of accident. So do with my two last."[14]

Political sagacity kept Ritchie's heartburnings from the public. Before the smoke of the battle had cleared he came forward in a "prediction," which shows clear political insight and that its author had lost none of his ability or determination as a fighter. "A strange and unnatural combination," said he, "has gained a temporary ascendency which it must lose as soon as its object is accomplished. When it comes to act upon any subject of policy or principle, not connected with hatred to Jackson, it must fall to pieces, and commence a war *inter se*. It contains all the elements of dis-

[14] *Stevenson MSS.* Ritchie to Stevenson. (No date.)

solution, and is destined to share the fate of other monstrous alliances.

"Never was there a party in which the seeds of its own dissolution were more deeply sown. Principle may divide them—policy may sever them, but the presidential election is being organized at this very moment; and it must break them to pieces. True, Mr. Clay said the other day in the Senate in reply to Mr. Grundy: 'For one, I can assure the Senator from Tennessee that I am no candidate—that I do not desire to be a candidate—and, that, if it depends upon me alone, I never shall be a candidate for any office whatsoever!' But, Mr. Clay has not yet acquired the very first principle of the ancient Metaphysicians: *'He knows not himself.'* He who has been three times a candidate for the highest honor in the world will not suffer it to escape him, if he thinks he is able to clutch it. He will not suffer all his late labors in the Senate to pass for naught. If hope whispers him of success, he will attempt to reap the harvest. Even if his own modesty would withdraw him from the contest, the zeal of his friends will hurry him into the arena.

"But even ambition does not burn so intensely in his bosom, as it does in the heart of another leader of the Senate (Mr. Calhoun). If recent signs do not deceive us, this extraordinary man (extraordinary every way for the vigor of his mind, the variety of his principles, and the intensity of his ambition) will soon take the field, with feeble hope of winning the voices of the South, as well as the support of the Bank. Then shall we see under which king the *various* members of the opposition will range themselves."

Following the triumphant victory of the Whigs, politics in Virginia were in a hurly-burly. The indications were that the new party had come to stay, and the usual professions of faith and reaffiliations on such occasions of those willing to do the bidding of the people and to keep in pace with the progress of the times were in order. When submitted to the scathing ridicule of Ritchie and Daniel, the parting respects of W. S. Archer and other former Democrats who now climbed into the Whig band-wagon attracted state-wide interest. In the enthusiasm of their success the Whigs began to suggest some of their more prominent partisans, such as Tyler and Leigh for the presidency or the vice-presidency, but Ritchie refused to follow the decoy and repeatedly warned the people that the "monster" proposed to make Clay and Calhoun in turn President.

Adversity frequently points the road to success, and so it now proved with the Democrats of Virginia. Recovery from the shock of their defeat was rapid, and they now began to prepare for the future. Hitherto the *Enquirer* had coped almost single-handed with a numerous and ably conducted opposition press, at the head of which stood John Hampden Pleasants, a foeman worthy of the steel of any "knight of the quill" of his day. A movement was now set on foot to establish administration presses throughout the length and breadth of the state to aid Ritchie in his work of reclamation. After their characteristic methods for finding out things and executing policies, the politicians had awakened to the fact that Jacksonian Democracy carried with it an obligation to educate the people, and they very reluctantly complied with that demand to secure their own self-interest. Accordingly Democratic presses were established in most of the leading towns, whence the seeds of discord were sowed among the ranks of the opposition.[15] To this end the ambitions of Clay and Calhoun were made to run counter at every possible turn.

Finally it was decided to prevent the re-election of Leigh to the federal Senate. Relying upon the anti-bank sentiment which prevailed in Virginia, a large majority of the Assembly being unwilling to endorse that institution, his known friendship for the national bank, and his unpopularity in the western counties, which did not like his course in the Constitutional Convention of 1829-'30, a bold attempt was to be made to force the Whig party to repudiate one of its ablest leaders or incur odium in refusing to do so. To this end numerous post-election polls, frequently determined by

[15] *Richmond Enquirer*, July 25, 1834.

house to house canvasses, were made in those counties of which the Whig assemblymen were willing to vote for Leigh regardless of his opinion upon the constitutionality and necessity of a national bank. Ritchie took an active part in these canvasses, urging the sacredness of the time honored right of instruction. When the Assembly met in December, 1834, he was confident that the backbone of the Whig party had been broken, because the electors in both the eastern and western counties had responded in no uncertain terms to the campaign against Leigh.[16]

With Virginia ripe, as Ritchie thought, for another change his greatest solicitude was regarding Jackson. At one time the ill-fated Proclamation had robbed the Democrats of Virginia of the fruits of their political victories and sent Tyler to the federal Senate, and at another the removal of the deposits and the famous Protest had driven Rives from that body and sent Leigh to fill the vacancy. On each occasion Ritchie had opposed the action of the administration as suicidal to the party. Now it was rumored that war upon the bank was to work a forfeiture of its charter and that Jackson was on the point of granting Letters of Marque and Reprisal upon the commerce of France to force that proud nation to a quickened sense of its financial obligations to us. A conservative by nature, Ritchie thought he saw in such ill-advised steps the complete annihilation of the Democratic party in Virginia. Certainly, Leigh could not be defeated, if they were persisted in. Accordingly he pled with Van Buren and Stevenson against the use of any "bold and questionable proposition" regarding the bank that would furnish a new "handle to his (Jackson's) and our enemies," and he expressed surprise that any one at Washington had thought of Letters of Marque and Reprisal. "The measure is too hasty in any event," said he. "It is not called for by the present state of the question. I have not seen a single

[16] *Van Buren MSS.* W. C. Rives to Van Buren, October 14, 1834; *Richmond Enquirer*, August 29, 1834; *Ibid.*, October 3, 1834; *Ibid.*, December 4, 1834.

person who is in favor of the measure. Rely upon it that the people will be decidedly against it. * * * I should be under the necessity of raising my humble voice as strongly as I could against it."[17] Instead he would have let the bank alone and referred the subject of our international relations to Congress.

None of Ritchie's precautions could save him and his party in Virginia from the penalties of their defeat. Amid one of the most exciting contests ever witnessed at the state capital, Leigh secured a re-election to the Senate, and Ritchie himself later became "a martyr" to the political proscriptions which were now revived for the first time in more than thirty years. The public printing was given to Samuel Shepherd; Linn Banks had a close call for re-election to the Speakership of the House of Delegates; and P. V. Daniel lost his place in the Governor's council.[18] It was more than "Old Nous Verrons" could endure gracefully, and he now began to fight like a stag at bay. Long editorial articles appeared in the *Enquirer* on the right of instruction and the duty of obedience, on the unprecented use of political proscription in Virginia, on the dangers with which a probable restoration of the monster would surround the state banks, and on the consuming ambition of Clay and Calhoun to reach the presidency. Under the slogan "heads up" he rallied the unterrified for the election of 1835, confident that the people would resent the ruthless manner in which their instructions had been disregarded by the "piebald Whigs" in the re-election of Leigh. All the available letters and resolutions of protest against Leigh's election were now published at length, and appeal after appeal was made to the sovereign people to redress their wrongs.[19]

Meanwhile the abolition had swallowed up the anti-slavery movement and in so doing had pressed negro slavery to the front as a political and economic question. Until

[17] *Stevenson MSS.* Ritchie to Stevenson. (No date.)

[18] *Richmond Enquirer*, December 9, 1834; *Ibid.*, January 29, 1835.

[19] *Ibid.*, February 28, 1835.

1830 Virginia had maintained a studied silence on this all important subject, because silence had meant security at home and political friends abroad. But, when a band of deluded negroes had rushed like a pack of hungry wolves upon helpless women and children in the dead of night, assaulting and murdering them in what was called "Nat" Turner's Insurrection, and when the political skies were growing ominously dark, it became impossible "to keep things quiet south of the Potomac." Accordingly, Ritchie, as the faithful spokesman of the people, warned his fellow countrymen of the folly of shutting their eyes and averting their faces from "the black and gnawing evil, "which stood at their doors. In no equivocal terms he urged the gradual abolition of negro slavery and the removal of the free people of color from the Commonwealth. In support of this bold stand he showed that every census made the black cloud larger and more appalling; that the laws of the sister states to the southward against the domestic slave-trade would cut off the market for surplus negroes; and that thousands of Virginia's non-slaveholders were pouring into the West and the Southwest to escape the evils of an institution which had already impoverished them and was now threatening to debase them. He also urged immediate action, insisting that it was not a time to sit quietly down in the consolation that their grand children would eliminate "the black curse," but that it was a crisis requiring the immediate attention of statesmen and patriots.[20]

Like a spark to the parched prairie Ritchie's bold stand soon attracted attention throughout the entire Union and aroused all the latent indifference of the Old Dominion. For days the Assembly had hesitated to break the profound silence; but now that it had been broken by the fearless leader of all reforms, the people of the western counties responded in petitions and resolutions urging the gradual abolition of negro slavery, and the slaveholding aristocracy stood aghast, hesitating between the dictates of conscience and

[20] *Richmond Enquirer*, January 7, 1832.

their material well being. Some sided with Ritchie, who was himself a slaveholder, but others planned his destruction, as his enemies had done in 1829-'30. The following letter indicates the attitude toward him in parts of the "south side":

> "Messers Editors:—Owing to the late publication in your paper advising the gradual emancipation of our slaves, you will discontinue sending the *Enquirer* to my post-office & consider me no longer a subscriber to a paper so reckless in its course and so regardless of the safety and property of others.
>
> Yours, etc.
>
> Nath. Alexander."

But Mr. Alexander was not willing to stop here. In an address to the people of Halifax and Mecklenberg, two of the largest slaveholding counties in the state, he attacked the practicability of emancipation, pointing out especially the dangers of agitation, and urged the slave-holders to discontinue the *Enquirer,* which, he maintained, was trimming its sails to the "winds which seemed to be blowing westwardly."[21]

To both friends and assailants Ritchie's replies were firm and sane. He discontinued Mr. Alexander's paper with pleasure; reiterated his former remarks upon the subject of negro slavery; and assured the slave-holders that he would have adhered to his customary silence in dealing with that subject, had not "the still small voice of conscience" made such a course impossible. At the same time he pled for the freedom of the press, quoted from Jefferson and others of the fathers to justify his position, and disclaimed any sinister design upon the west.[22] Despite the opposition which he encountered, Ritchie's editorials were doubtless potent in committing the House of Delegates, by a vote of 60 ayes to 67 noes, as favoring some measures for the gradual abolition of slavery.[23]

Ritchie's subsequent silence upon the subject of abolition, continuing, as it did, nearly uninterrupted for almost

[21] *Richmond Enquirer,* January 12, 1832.

[22] *Ibid.*

[23] Journal, House of Delegates, 1831-'32, p. 110.

two years, was doubtless due to his desire for accord within the Democratic party and not to the intimidating threats of his assailants. It was plain to his mind that much of the agitation in both the North and the South and in Congress, that the proceedings of American Anti-Slavery Society, and the demands for the abolition of slavery in the District of Columbia had no other object than that of keeping Van Buren from the presidency. If they had other purposes, then he saw in such movements a menace to the Union and refused to give them publicity. Already he suspected Calhoun and Duff Green of a design "to pick a quarrel with the North about the negro" in an effort to unite the South, that Calhoun might reach the presidency as the leader of a powerful section. When he did speak upon the subject of negro slavery it was only to condemn the abolitionists as disunionists and to expose the political designs of Calhoun. By the use of elaborate extracts from the northern prints he attempted to show, what was doubtless true, that the inhabitants of the North were for the most part friendly to the South and to her institutions and that Calhoun and his followers had greatly exaggerated the nature and scope of the abolition movement.[24] It is not surprising therefore that the *United States Telegraph,* edited by Duff Green, placed the editor of the *Enquirer* in a class with the abolitionists and denounced his subserviency to the North.

Though eager to win in the local elections, disposed to discount the importance of the abolition movement, and practically committed to Van Buren, Ritchie hesitated to espouse his candidacy openly. He still placed a high value upon the alliance between the northern and southern Democrats, but the persistency of the abolitionists, together with the teachings of Thomas R. Dew, had wrought a complete change in his mind regarding negro slavery. By 1835 he, in common with many other Southerners who had formerly favored abolition, saw that any possible solution of the

[24] *Richmond Enquirer,* April 16, 20, 1833; *Ibid.,* June 28, 1833; *Ibid.,* July 26, 1833.

slavery problem would leave behind it a greater, the negro problem. Without admitting Calhoun or any of his friends to his council and after the Democrats of the Assembly had endorsed Van Buren's candidacy in secret caucus, Ritchie tactfully sought to ascertain by letter his opinions upon the right of Congress to interfere, constitutionally, with slavery in the states and upon the expediency of abolishing the slave-trade in the District of Columbia.[25] In due time a favorable reply was received through Silas Wright, and the *Enquirer* began forthwith to demand justice and gratitude for the man whose only magic was his good sense and good humor.[26]

Having decided upon a national standard bearer, Ritchie buckled on his armor to retrieve the defeat of 1834. Meanwhile new conditions had arisen which promised to perpetuate the Whig rule. The referendum on the senatorship had exposed Leigh's unpopularity and had put an end to the premature efforts to strengthen the Whig party locally by rallying the voters to him for the presidency. Accordingly the Whigs now endorsed Judge White, whose candidacy had been launched in the hope of defeating Van Buren and of disrupting the Democratic party. Locally the Whigs were not so much concerned with White's candidacy for the presidency as they were with electing "White men" to the Assembly, who would be willing to join with the regular Whigs against the administration and thus control the patronage. From the very first Ritchie saw through their designs and expressed the hope that the "old man" (White) would soon understand the efforts being made to use him as a stalking-horse for others, and that he would return to the Democratic fold.[27]

The campaign which followed for members of the Assembly and for representatives in Congress was one of the most hotly contested ever waged in Virginia. Ritchie and others

[25] *Van Buren MSS.* Ritchie to Van Buren, March 2, 1835.

[26] *Richmond Enquirer*, March 20, 31, 1835.

[27] *Van Buren MSS.* Daniel to Van Buren, February 22, 1835; *Richmond Enquirer*, March 3, 1835.

of the Junto fought for their political lives with odds greatly in their favor but with a majority to overcome. The good crops and high prices of 1834 had dissipated the panic scare; the re-election of Leigh had proved suicidal; and the Whigs of the western counties preferred Van Buren to White, if Clay was to be abandoned. Both parties fought for the presidency. Had the Whigs secured a majority in the Assembly, they might have been able to unite upon Judge White for the presidency with a hope of carrying the state for him. Though Van Buren was favored by Jackson and the North, such a contingency would have been a powerful factor toward eliminating him from the contest in favor of some man who could carry the South. The story of "a corrupt bargain" between Ritchie and Van Buren looking to the promotion of the latter to the presidency and supposed to have been made about 1829 was launched but to no avail. The administration leaders were steadfast and achieved a victory which for completeness surpassed their most sanguine expectations. The importance of the result was evident. Judge Parker assured Van Buren that all was well in the Old Dominion,[28] and Ritchie wrote that all opposition to his candidacy in the South would now quickly disappear.[29]

This triumphant victory of the Democrats in Virginia did more than place the candidacy, if not the election, of Van Buren beyond the question of a doubt. It inspired Ritchie and the Junto with an ambition to name his successor in the presidency. The political alliance between New York and Virginia, which they had so zealously maintained, had relegated the politicians of the old school in Virginia, Floyd, Giles, and Tazewell, to oblivion, made Stevenson Speaker of the House of Representatives, placed Virginians in the most important foreign missions, determined the personnel of the Supreme Court, and made Ritchie political arbiter of his own and the neighboring

[28] *Van Buren MSS.* May 8, 1835.

[29] *Rives MSS.* Ritchie to Rives, May 19, 1835.

states. That same alliance was now to be used to elevate W. C. Rives first to the vice-presidency and later to the presidency. The few days intervening between the election of 1835 and the meeting of the Baltimore Convention were given up almost entirely to furthering this plan. The following extract from a letter by Ritchie to Rives himself throws light upon the situation:

"You know I have carefully foreborne touching upon the Vice-Presidency. Not a word, line, or syllable has been exchanged between us on the subject. But I think it high time to tell you (P. P. Barbour being out of the question who in my opinion has superior claims to any one in the Union, on account of his long service) that my heart is now set upon your elevation from the Floor to the Chair of the Senate. I had hoped that the thing was fixed; and I had given myself less concern than I ought to about it, but I am informed since Friday night that some of our strongest friends at Washington think that Richd. M. Johnson ought to have the nomination, great as they admit your claims to be. What is the desire of Mr. V. B. on the subject I am unable to say; though it seems to me that he would prefer yourself. I will not inform you of all that has passed since Saturday morning. But I have not hesitated with all the respect I feel for Col. Johnson, to press your name in every way that appeared proper to me. I have this evening written two letters to two of the delegates of the Convention, one from Virginia and the other from the West, and I have also addressed myself to a gentleman at Washington, who can, if he thinks fit, exercise a sort of 'potential voice' upon the proceedings of an important part of his Delegation. I am assured by every man that I have seen that you are the favorite candidate of this state. I think from what two of the N. C. Delegation told me you will receive their support. Col. Watkins (ever zealous and efficient) & Col. Morgan, who took the steam boat on Sunday, will go by way of the Potomac & Washington. Peter V. Daniel has been induced by the emergency of the case to go to Baltimore, and will take Washington in his way. What the result may be it is utterly impossible to guess. I shall be most deeply disappointed if we do not prevail. I have freely told & written my friends that with your name associated on the ticket, I think Virginia and the South will be safe, with Col. Johnson less than safe.

"I beg you for the present to say and write as little upon the question as possible. I have no authority now to tell you why. But be content if you receive the nomination, to accept it in a way which you so well know how to express, and if the Cup be unfortunately passed to another lip, to bear your disappointment as becomes you." [30]

When the Democratic convention met in Baltimore on May 20th, one day after Ritchie wrote the letter to Rives

[30] *Rives MSS.*

from which the above extract was taken and almost eighteen months before the election, the Virginians semed omnipotent. In a speech overflowing with optimism, its president, Andrew Stevenson, himself a member of the Junto, defended the convention system, then in use for the second time by the Democrats, and pointed the way to Van Buren's nomination by such interrogations as "Who will best preserve the unity of the Democratic party? Who best understands the principles and motives of our government?" and "Who will carry out the principles of the Jeffersonian era and General Jackson's administration?" After some debate the two-thirds rule was readopted, and amid the smiles of its obedient members the convention ratified General Jackson's choice for the succession.

This apparent unanimity was destroyed in the vote for the vice-presidential nomination. With the aid of New York, Johnson defeated Rives, receiving barely the necessary two-thirds majority. The only attempted explanation of New York's vote was the necessity of crippling Clay or Harrison, each prospective nominees of the opposition for the presidency, by running a western man on the Democratic ticket for the vice-presidency. Politically it was sound, but the Virginians were not always willing to play politics, even with their New York allies and teachers, when they themselves could not be the beneficiaries. As Silas Wright now expressed it they were "wild" and "too astute as to their principles and too little practical in their political course."[31] In view of this betrayal they did not hesitate to lay violent hands upon the ark of the covenant and announce on the floor of the convention their intention to oppose the election of Johnson whose principles and character they could not respect.

Thus was struck the first effective blow at the coalition between New York and Virginia, which had placed Jackson in the presidency, was about to name his successor, and has been a potent, though not always a wholesome factor, in

[31] *Van Buren MSS.* Silas Wright to Van Buren.

American politics from that day to this. The blow had been struck by personal ambition which has always been the greatest menace to political coalitions. Separated by powerful rival commonwealths at sufficient distance to remove local friction nothing remained in a material way, except possibly the tariff, which neither has ever taken seriously, to mar their industrial and commercial relations, and, as political principles and issues frequently find their basis in self-interest, it has always been easy for New York and Virginia to co-operate in political movements. Thus the Grand Old Commonwealth has been kept subservient to Tammany Hall, while its citizens praised their leaders as patriots and statesmen and strangers looked on with contempt and frequently with jeers in imitation of Calhoun's attitude in the thirties and the forties. In view of the fact that Calhoun is today regarded as one of the South's greatest statesmen, the question naturally arises what will the South and Virginia, fifty years hence, think of those who have recently tried to break the political dependence of the South upon New York?

The healing of this schism, which always left a scar, called for skill and diplomacy. Silas Wright and Van Buren each sent personal letters to Rives, Ritchie, Parker, and Daniel; Van Buren himself visited Rives in his home at Castle Hill;[32] and the northern prints were profuse in their praise of the Virginians, tactics familiar and effective even in this day. After some delay Van Buren was received into full fellowship, a favor never extended to Johnson, and the flag of Democracy was again unfurled with the slogan "heads up" and to the contest. Van Buren's letter to Dr. William McK. Gwin of Mississippi in further explanation of his attitude toward negro slavery, together with B. F. Butler's Exposition,[33] were taken as further evidences of their candidate's southern principles, and his election was now urged as

[32] *Van Buren MSS.*

[33] *Richmond Enquirer,* July 28, 1835.

necessary for the preservation of the Union and the national Democracy.[34]

But others, notably the leaders of the lower South, were not so sanguine over Van Buren's candidacy. They doubted his southern principles, suspected the intimate relations existing between Richmond and Albany of being fraught with evil, and began to plan for a southern convention that they might more effectively protect the rights and interests of their section. Naturally Ritchie oposed the proposed convention and tried to soothe his fellow southerners into a feeling of security, but the annexed extract from the *Atlanta* (Ga.) *Chronicle* makes it plain that he was dealing with conditions and forces which he did not understand:

> "Mr. Ritchie and Old Virginia will not meet with a Southern Convention, because Virginia must be a border state in the event of a dissolution and because Mr. Ritchie would lose the rewards he has been earning from Mr. Van Buren and the Albany Regency. Be it so. Let Virginia occupy neutral ground then, or take sides with the North as she may prefer. We shall lose some great and good men (who might go farther South and be saved). Yet, when we get rid of Ritchie, Stevenson and others of that kidney, we need not count the cost, and *we shall be greatly benefitted by having Virginia a slave state between us and the North without being compelled to contribute to her defence.*"[35]

At this time Ritchie was doubtless more interested in the success of the Democratic party in Virginia than in the rights and interests of the whole South. Consumed by a desire to preserve the ascendancy of the Mother of Commonwealths in a great nation and never over suspicious of the ulterior motives of men, he had little sympathy with Calhoun's program for a united South, if, indeed, he understood that movement. His patriotism was circumscribed by no sectional lines and was as broad as the legitimate interests and commendable ambitions of every American citizen. He advised the united action of the South against the abolitionists and other disunionists only as a means of preserv-

[34] *Richmond Enquirer*, July 21, 1835; *Ibid.*, August 4, 1835; *Ibid.*, September 18, 1835.

[35] *Ibid.*, October 6, 1835.

ing the Union and of maintaining the rights and interests of all. He would doubtless have been willing to conciliate and compromise. Virginia had scarcely been rescued from the clutches of the Whigs, and Jackson's time for throwing fire-brands, the regular meeting of Congress, was near at hand. He desired no repetition of the experiences which had followed the Proclamation and the Protest. In a letter to Van Buren he, therefore, advised that the annual message be written in "the language of dignified moderation."[36] Especially was war with France to be avoided, because war would arrest the spirit of internal improvement then abroad in the land, restore the protective system and the bank, and entrench the Whig party in power both locally and nationally.

Contrary to expectations Jackson showed moderation in dealing with France. It is not probable, however, that the local conditions in Virginia or the desires of her politicians to win elections there influenced him in the least. But as much can not be said of Ritchie's influence, exercised as it was through Van Buren, upon the larger and more important policies of the administration as set forth in the message in dealing with France. However that may be, Ritchie accepted the message as a vindication, and, had the press known his part in shaping it, his unqualified praise of that state paper would doubtless have been accepted as another evidence of his alleged monumental conceit and consuming vanity. The message was spoken of as the most "conciliatory, dignified, enlightened, and noble paper which has ever been given to the country."[37]

Triumph in national affairs was also attended by a vindication at home. The Assembly, by a vote of 95 ayes to 68 noes, restored Ritchie to the office of public printer and by a vote almost equally large reinstated Daniel in the Executive Council. Though aware of a desire to keep him from all places of influence, Ritchie had furthermore the satisfaction

[36] *Van Buren MSS.* Ritchie to Van Buren, November 28, 1835.

[37] *Richmond Enquirer,* December 12, 17, 1835.

of hearing those who had voted against his re-election disclaim any personal feeling in their efforts to secure a "practical printer." He now said not a word about political proscription, but characterized the leading Whigs as the "oily orator" from Petersburg, the "rampant lawyer" from Richmond, the "Beliol delegate" from Albemarle, the "rumbling thunderer" from Northampton, the "county court lawyer" from James City, and the "bewitching spoiler" from Pittsylvania and defied the whole "mongrel pack," Tray, Branch, Sweetheart, and all.[38] A declaration of war upon Leigh and Tyler, members of the "aristocratic" Senate followed, and was accompanied by a hearty approval of Benton's efforts to expunge from the records of the Senate the resolutions of censure against Jackson for the removal of the deposits.[39] Thus Ritchie found himself indirectly approving the very measures he had formerly disapproved and even willing to drive opposition senators from office that Jackson might be vindicated.

Although he deplored its injection into both local and national politics abolition would not down. Even Virginia played with the fire with all the eagerness of childish curiosity. In his annual message of December, 1835, to the Assembly, Governor Tazewell endorsed the proposed plan for concerted action among the slave-holding states against abolition and requested that he be authorized to communicate with the non-slave holding states upon the subject. Following up his message the Whigs tried to place the Assembly on record as opposed to the right of Congress to interfere with negro slavery in the District of Columbia, as reaffirming the right of a state to regulate and determine its own domestic institutions, and as demanding the suppression of all abolition societies by a resort to punishment for those who persisted in belonging to them.[40]

These new issues were annoying at their best, but under

[38] *Richmond Enquirer*, December 12, 1835.
[39] *Ibid.*, December 17, 1835.
[40] *Ibid.*, January 7, 12, 14, 1836.

the conditions prevalent in 1835 and 1836 they became positively embarrassing. Ritchie recognized in it all an attempt to injure Van Buren's candidacy and not a patriotic effort to serve the southern weal. But there were Democrats ever ready to listen to the Whig press and the Whig politicians in their studied attempts to make it appear that the Democratic party was in alliance with the abolitionists and not in full sympathy with the best interests of the South. It took real skill and masterly statesmanship to tide the feeble members of his party over such ordeals as those imposed by the Whigs in these attempts. Ritchie's slogan for all such exigencies was "The federal Union, it must be preserved." He now insisted that Tazewell was not and never had been a friend of the Union and that he should not therefore be entrusted with the care of an explosive which might destroy it.[41] Like many other loyal patriots to be found in the South at this time and twenty years later he did not think the election of a northern man to the presidency a sufficient cause for the united action of the slave-holding states to prevent such a contingency. Accordingly he lent his best energies to the support of a less radical course on the part of the Assembly than that desired by the Whigs. The right of a state to regulate its domestic institutions was reaffirmed, the non-slave holding states were simply requested to restrain the activity of the abolitionists, a protest was made against the proposed abolition of slavery in the District of Columbia, and confidence in the desires of the North to deal justly with the South was expressed.[42] True, Whigs and even Democrats cried "subserviency to New York," but they could not deny that Ritchie's subserviency contained a large proportion of patriotism and that they themselves in their attacks upon the abolitionists were resorting to the stock argument of all minority parties in the South.

Another subject used most effectively against the administration party in Virginia and to the great annoyance of

[41] *Richmond Enquirer*, December 17, 1835; *Ibid.*, December 29, 31, 1835.

[42] *Ibid.*, January 21 1836.

Ritchie was that connected with banks and banking. The vast enterprises being launched in the western counties and the general quickening of industrial activity created a demand for such credit as only banks could extend. This came at a time when the death throes of the Bank of the United States, the efforts to reform the national currency, and the uncertainties of the panic made it almost impossible for the state banks to live. Having abandoned the national bank, as a local party, the Whigs now suddenly developed a remarkable affection for the state banks, demanding an increase in their number and in their capital stock. In addition to the general conditions arguing in their behalf they defended their course as necessary to encourage internal improvements and to prevent the threatened depopulation of Virginia and attacked the banking monopoly of "King Ritchie and his prime minister, Dr. Brockenbrough." Despite Ritchie's great popularity, as a friend of the people and the spokesman of the Jacksonian Democracy, these were taking arguments in the western counties.[43]

As in dealing with the subject of abolition, Ritchie discussed banks and banking frankly but diplomatically, and there is every evidence that his arguments in defence of the existing system were based upon a sounder foundation than his financial obligations to the banks of Richmond. In defence of his opposition to an increase of the number of the independent banks he reviewed the early experiences of Kentucky, insisted that those Virginians who were leaving their lands for the far West where banks were unknown were not in search of bank credit, and predicted a restoration of the national bank in case the states did not act conservatively in their banking operations. To offset the political advantages which the Whigs contemplated from their change of attitude toward the local banks, he held before the rural inhabitants, naturally inclined to favor the exclusive use of hard money, the evils of excessive banking and of a consequent restoration of the monster. In view of the fact that

[43] *Richmond Enquirer*, December 10, 1835; *Ibid.*, February 23, 1836; *Richmond Whig*, April 22, 1836.

Pennsylvania had rechartered the Bank of the United States and that several states were expected to charter branches thereto, he saw and made others see how Biddle could evolve another monopoly and bring the "whole confederacy . . . under bank government." If free banking was permitted or even an undue increase in the number of local banks allowed, he was confident that these calamities would be immediate. The common horror which the inhabitants of the western counties felt toward the national bank and the traditional conservatism of the east coupled with the fact that a large part of the state's internal improvement and literary funds were invested in bank stock enabled Ritchie to defeat the Whigs at every turn, to retain his own political influence amid trying and perplexing conditions, and to maintain Virginia's record for conservative banking.

The time, energy, and skill necessary to keep the state right on abolition and banking did not restrain Ritchie from prosecuting his declaration of war upon Leigh and Tyler. With a majority of the Assembly at his command he now planned to drive them from the Senate, as the Whigs had driven Rives, by instructing them to vote for a proposition which they could not endorse, knowing that sufficient pressure could be brought upon them to compel obedience. Except in 1811, when Wm. B. Giles had protested against it, the time honored right of instruction had never been questioned in the "sovereign state of Virginia." Finally amid stirring scenes equaled only by those which had attended the actual expunging of the Senate's record or the re-election of Leigh by the Virginia Assembly, he and Tyler were instructed to vote for Benton's resolutions. As Governor Tazewell refused to communicate the resolutions of instruction, talk of impeachment proceedings followed. But Tyler's subsequent resignation and Leigh's refusal to follow his course simplified conditions in two ways; it gave the Democrats an opportunity to re-elect Rives and a winning issue with which to go before the people in the contest which was then at hand for members of Assembly.[44]

[44] *Richmond Enquirer*, March 5, 1836.

Thus the Virginians entered the preliminary skirmish for the presidency, that contest for members of the Assembly which came in the spring of the presidential year, and was as carefully watched as are the political vanes, Vermont and Maine, to-day, with many new and perplexing issues. But abolition, banking, expunging, and the right of instruction were not allowed to eclipse the main issue, the contest for the presidency. Already White and Tyler had been placed in nomination by a caucus of the Whig members of the Assembly for the presidency and the vice-presidency respectively, but the western Whigs desired General Harrison for the first place and preferred Webster or Calhoun to so recent an apostate as White.[45] This lack of accord within their party led to a Whig state convention which nominated Harrison for the presidency and Tyler for the vice-presidency but accepted the electors committed to the support of Judge White, with the understanding that they should vote for that one of the two candidates who received the largest popular vote. By such a combination the Whigs hoped to carry Virginia and to make it possible for no one to sacrifice his principles in supporting the "piebald" ticket. All were urged to vote against the abolitionist, Van Buren, who, it was now claimed, desired social and political equality for all races.

At first the Whig plan of campaign seemed formidable, but as the contest advanced the "double-headed" ticket commanded a constantly diminishing support. Following the example of Virginia Ritchie expected the opposition at large to run Webster in New England, Harrison in the Middle and Western states, and White in the South, in an effort to throw the presidential election into the House and to effect the possible elimination of Van Buren entirely by making the three candidates to whom the constitution restricted the choice on such occasions all Whigs. It was all the more important therefore to defeat the Whig party in Virginia in

[45] *Richmond Enquirer*, January 2, 1836; *Ibid.*, February 13, 1836; *Richmond Whig*, January 1, 1836.

its efforts to control the Assembly and to win a popular majority of the votes in the local election. Thus no opportunity was lost to unite all factions in support of Van Buren's candidacy which had already been endorsed by the Democrats of Virginia but was now re-endorsed by a state convention in which Wm. C. Rives spoke of him as "the first choice over all others in the Union."[46] In spite of the fact that the Democrats refused to place Johnson's name upon their ticket for the vice-presidency, the most possible was made of the lack of accord within the opposition party. To this end Harrison was attacked in the eastern counties as an abolitionist and a friend of the American System, while White was attacked in the western counties as a Nullifier and a seceder.

Ritchie's generalship, General Jackson's popularity, and the disorganized condition of the Whigs saved the day to the Democrats, who now carried the state by a popular majority aggregating 5,000 and retained control of the Assembly.[47] An end was thus put to the fear of possible Whig combinations, and Van Buren's election seemed assured. Again members of the Junto assured him that all was well in the Old Dominion, and the Whig press now spoke of the *Richmond Enquirer* as the *"Albany Enquirer."*

Now that the presidential contest seemed won in Virginia, Ritchie and the Junto attempted to divert interest from those local and national issues which were perplexing them and to keep Van Buren awake to his obligations to the South by launching a movement for the annexation of Texas, never dreaming that their efforts if successful would complicate the abolition question and give rise to a score of other questions equally perplexing. In 1819, 1829, and again in 1835 Ritchie had cast longing eyes to the southwest, a small part of which he now possessed in fee simple. Now his dreams had come true, and Texas was making a noble fight for her independence of Mexico and was thought to be

[46] *Richmond Enquirer*, January 16, 1836.

[47] *Ibid.*, May 17, 1836.

friendly to annexation to the United States. Accordingly when Santa Anna talked of arming the slaves of Louisiana, of planting his banners on the Capitol at Washington, and of plucking the laurels from the brow of General Jackson, if the Americans did not desist from their attempts to dismember his country by aiding the Texans, Ritchie urged that we acknowledge their independence. The daily reminders from the opposition press that his enthusiasm for Texas was not wholly disinterested went unheeded.[48] He had long regarded Van Buren as friendly to annexation, but he did not know to what extent he would carry his friendship when placed in a position of responsibility and faced by a growing abolitionist sentiment. Accordingly, Ritchie now informed him of their previous understandings, though thinking it impossible that he could have changed his mind and assuring him that the South counted upon him "to carry the measure against the prejudices of the Northern oppositoin." He was not certain how the measure was to be brought about, "whether by waiting the overtures of Texas or Mexico—or, by initiating the proposition—whether by recognizing the independence first, or smoothing the way to the affiliation in the first instance—whether now or at the next session—whether by admitting Texas in the chrysalis from a territory or immediately as one of the sovereign states of the Union—whether as one state, or as one *subject to the qualification of making her into several,* as they obtain the necessary population." He was willing to leave these and "various other questions" to Mr. Van Buren's "long head," but he ventured the suggestion that no more than three states be made out of Texas, lest the North prevent its annexation.[49]

Fearing that agitation of this subject would not enhance his chances to reach the presidency Van Buren followed the advice of Jackson and of Ritchie's close friend, Judge Parker, and carefully refrained from any expressions regard-

[48] *Richmond Enquirer,* October 30, 1835; *Ibid.,* May 13, 24, 1836.
[49] *Van Buren MSS.* Ritchie to Van Buren, June 9, 1836.

ing Texas. There is no evidence that he answered either directly or indirectly Ritchie's letter and suggestions. Had he now taken a stand, his course eight years hence might have been greatly simplified and the possibility of an abrupt breach between himself and his friends in Virginia might have been obviated.

Meanwhile the federal treasury had become embarrassed by the almost unprecedented experience of having more money than it could spend. The proceeds from the public land sales, which were enormous at this period of expansion, and the revenue from customs had extinguished the public debt and was piling up a vast surplus. If the Compromise Tariff was to be maintained and if settlers were to be given access to the public domain at any reasonable price, the causes which were producing these conditions could not be disturbed. Nevertheless, some would have lowered the tariff regardless of the Compromise, and others would have lowered the price of the public lands or have given them to the states in which they were located. But the desire to keep faith between the sections regarding the tariff and to conserve the nation's resources by restricting the public land sales and appropriating the benefits of the common territory to all prevailed, and on June 23, 1836, Congress passed an act distributing the surplus proceeds of the land sales among the several states in proportion to their representation in that body. The pill needed a little coating before Jackson could swallow it, and the distributions were therefore made in the form of loans, but with the understanding that they were never to be returned.

Dr. Brockenbrough's interest in retaining the federal deposits in his bank at Richmond was not the only nor indeed the chief reason for Ritchie's opposition to the distribution act. He saw in that measure a tariff bill in disguise and the final destruction of the sovereignty and respectability of the states in a mad scramble for the flesh pots of Egypt. Instead he would have used the surplus already existing to provide an adequate defence, to exterminate the Indian titles to the public domain, and to secure the annexation of Texas. He would have prevented the further accumulation of surpluses by reducing the tariff. Piqued at Jackson's refusal to veto the bill and elated with Van Buren's bold declaration against it, he now proclaimed the latter the real and not the nominal leader of the Democracy.[50]

The flurry over Texas and the agitation over the surplus diverted attention only temporarily from the contest for the presidency. In Virginia the rival parties continued to vie with each other in picturing the abolition records of the opposing chieftains. The rapid strides made by Harrison's candidacy in the western counties created alarm in the Democratic camp, but Ritchie never let pass an opportunity for picturing the calamities which might result from an election by the House. The danger narrowly averted in 1801 and the experiences of 1825 were drawn upon constantly. It was not known how many Whigs would stick to the declining fortunes of Judge White, and, therefore, the "double-headed Janus-faced mongrel ticket" worried Ritchie no little. On September 20th Judge Parker wrote to Van Buren that "nothing could draw him (Ritchie) away from his press at this critical juncture."[51] Nevertheless, he was never more resourceful. From picturing Van Buren as a strict constructionist he turned to praising the "Tenth Legion"[52] and deploring the election of a Nullifier and a seceder like White. From a denunciation of Harrison's abolition record he turned to a defence of Van Buren's free negro vote and his part in the Missouri Compromise.[53]

Though now prominently mentioned in connection with the governorship, Ritchie announced the results of the Democratic victory in Virginia, which had greatly enhanced his own prestige, with characteristic modesty. The chief recipient of its benefits was not, however, unmindful of the

[50] *Richmond Enquirer*, June 21, 28, 1836; *Ibid.*, August 23, 1836.

[51] *Van Buren MSS.*

[52] The Tenth Legion was the name applied to the Democratic stronghold of the Valley.

[53] *Richmond Whig*, August 12, 1836; *Richmond Enquirer*, November 4, 1836.

one who had done most to make it possible, as the annexed extract of a letter from Van Buren to Ritchie indicates: "There is, I assure you with great sincerity, no man in the country in whose patriotism, political intelligence and personal integrity I have more confidence. I know I have not a better friend in the world and be assured that your suggestions will always be duly considered."[54] As he reviewed Jackson's administration by which he proposed to to shape his own, it was plain that questions might arise upon which he and the Virginia editor could not agree, but he was certain that their general objects would always be the same.

Virginia readily acquiesced in the election of Van Buren, but the prospective election of Johnson to the vice-presidency by the federal Senate was a bitter pill which was not swallowed readily. Rather than submit some were willing to apply the knife as the only remedy for the disease with which the spoilsmen and the abolitionists had infected the body politic. Their opposition went further than their friendship for Rives; it was founded in enmity for the American System and the rumors about the dusky origin of Johnson's wife. The Whig press contained many rhymes on "Johnson's Wife of Old Kentucky," and a laurel crown was given by "the Chaste Southern Dames" to the author of one of these doggerels.[55] Virginia's electors had been selected to vote for Wm. Smith of Alabama for the vice-presidency, but it was now proposed that they cast their vote for Tyler, the Whig candidtae, to keep the election from the Senate and to accomplish the defeat of Johnson.[56]

Although he did not attempt to defend his record or his character, Ritchie regarded the assaults upon Johnson as attacks upon the Union and as so many unnecessary and useless attempts to inflame the anti-abolition sentiment at the South. He classed the "madmen" who made them with those

[54] *Richmond Whig*, November 4, 1836; *Van Buren MSS.*

[55] *Richmond Whig*, December 2, 1836.

[56] *Ibid.*, November 25, 1836.

pessimists who predicted the downfall of our glorious experiment in government, but assured them that "There is an attachment to the Union among the people of this country so strong that it will baffle all the parricidal attempts of such infuriated incendiaries." This attitude was wholly sincere and sprang from a love for the Union of the fathers and not from a desire to preserve accord within the Democratic party. It is almost needless to say that the electors of Virginia kept faith by casting their vote for Wm. Smith for the vice-presidency.

The election of Van Buren, following as it did two brilliant victories for members of the Assembly, marked the period of Ritchie's greatest power. With his incessant war for principles he was not, however, a practical politician. Thus he did not always make the best use of his political victories or aid others in using them to the best advantage. In a sort of ultimatum he now advised the Assembly regarding the use of the federal surplus, regarding appropriations for internal improvements, and the state banks.[57] By aid of the party caucus he was re-elected public printer, his friend, David Campbell, was made Governor, and his brother-in-law, Judge Richard E. Parker, took Leigh's place in the federal Senate to be succeeded in a few weeks, after he had found a place better suited to his tastes and abilities, by Ritchie's cousin, Wm. H. Roane.[58] He did not hesitate to advise Van Buren in the formation of his cabinet, or Jackson regarding the proper way in which to close his brilliant administration.[59] It is thus not strange that he was called an autocrat and that the *Richmond Whig* spoke of him as a self-constituted politician who bestowed offices of honor and dignity as a reward for relatives and partisans.[60] But the *Whig* did not consider that Ritchie had played a prominent part in bringing about the tariff compromise, the destruction

[57] *Richmond Enquirer*, December 24, 1836.

[58] *Ibid.*, December 13, 15, 17, 1836; *Ibid.*, January 6, 1837.

[59] *Van Buren MSS.* Parker to Van Buren, February 7, 1837; *Rives MSS.*, Ritchie to Rives, February 25, 1837.

[60] *Richmond Whig*, December 6, 1836.

of the national bank, the suppression of the nullifiers, and the election of Van Buren, and that he could stand in the federal Capitol to see the new President take the oath of office and shake hands with the potentates who took part on that occasion with some feeling of personal triumph and that he could dictate to the local Assembly and even to the powers higher up with some claim to authority, if not to the finer qualities of a politician and a statesman.

CHAPTER VII.

VAN BUREN AND THE INDEPENDENT TREASURY.

Through the calm which surrounded Van Buren's inaugural ceremonies the evidences of political discord were apparent even to the casual observer. The clashing ambitions of W. C. Rives and N. P. Tallmadge on one side, and Thomas H. Benton, whom Jackson had placed second in the line of succession, on the other, were making for an irreparable schism in the Democratic party. The former leaders sought to win by merit the popular favor which Benton hoped to inherit. By overwhelming majorities they had already succeeded in committing Congress against Jackson's famous specie circular requiring all payments for public lands to be made in specie, and they had also induced Congress to claim its alleged constitutional right to be the custodian of all federal moneys. Encouraged by these successes, they were furthermore resolved to make Van Buren abandon the specie circular which Jackson had continued in operation by a bold use of the pocket veto. As the author of that state paper, the leader of a large party opposed to banks of whatsoever description, and as the friend of Jackson and the spokesman of Van Buren, Benton, now called "Old Bullion," was a formidable barrier to their ambitions. As early as January, 1837, the Whig press had gleefully noted the personal character of the contest.[1]

The conditions at the beginning of Van Buren's administration were well portrayed by Ritchie in one of his "strictly confidential" letters written this time to Benj. F. Butler, Attorney General, under the new administration. To inquiring parties desiring to invest capital in America, Andrew Stevenson, Minister to the Court of St. James, had expressed

[1] *Richmond Enquirer*, January 6, 10, 17, 1837.

the belief that the national bank, upon which Jackson had made a war to be continued by his successor, would not be put down. His indiscretion became known in America and was interpreted by the *Globe,* in a caustic editorial, as evidence of a disposition to repudiate Van Buren and Jackson, and of a possible alliance with those opposed to Benton and friendly to Rives and Tallmadge. Ritchie's letter was a defence of Stevenson, and because of its thorough and able presentation of the whole situation is here given in full as follows:

"TUESDAY, MORNING.

"*My Dear Sir:*

"I have been prostrated two days on the bed of sickness, and though I am rapidly recovering, I am compelled to pillow up my head, for the purpose of addressing you on a subject which deeply interests me. Perhaps I am going too far. Perhaps, I may be taking a liberty which our short acquaintance may not seem to justify. Perhaps, I am too boldly breaking through that state and dignity, that hedge in men of affairs. But, when I recollect the simplicity of character which best adorns a man,—when I recall to mind the cordial terms you used towards me, at the last night I had the pleasure of seeing you, I feel irresistibly impelled to address you upon a subject, which interests me as a friend and as a patriot.

"Without further circumlocution, then, I call your attention to the editorial article which appeared in the *Globe*, containing some severe criticism on the conduct of Andrew Stevenson. It is scarcely necessary to tell you how much pain it has given many of his and the President's friends. May I frankly inquire of you, whether it is to be regarded as a true exponent of the President's feelings and sentiments? I well know the solicitude which this article will occasion in the breast of Mr. Stevenson, not only on account of the character of these strictures, but from the *source* from which they emanate, *the official organ of the government*. You will readily imagine, Sir, how very unpleasant must be his situation, until he shall be apprised of the President's feeling on this subject. You can well conceive, too, that if he shall ascertain the article in question to have received the President's sanction, he might feel himself constrained to resign his commission and return home. I feel solicitous that Mr. Stevenson and his friends should be put at ease on this subject, if, indeed, I am right in the conjecture that Mr. Blair, without consulting his official friends, has only given expressions to his own views, stimulated as they no doubt have been by the conduct of the agents of the Bank, as well as the insidious comments of the Press on Mr. Stevenson's London letter.

"May I call your attention to the few remarks I made in the last *Enquirer*, on the article in the *Globe?* They were written, Sir, I am free to confess to you, under some little embarrassment. While I thought on one hand, that Mr. S, did not deserve the severe strictures he had received, even admitting that he may not have sufficiently weighed the phraseology of his letter,—I could not on the other hand, lose sight of the importance of pressing the harmony of our party, and of maintaining an unbroken front towards our opponents, who are ready to make the most of every division in our ranks, and indeed of every thing which may avail in the opposition which they seem determined to wage against the Administraton. I feel constrained too, by those personal sentiments I entertain towards Mr. Blair, by the recollection of that cordial and confiding kindness, which he had so freely poured out to me, on my last visit to Washington. Of all the the articles I had ever seen in a newspaper, I confess to you, the article in the *Globe* had given me the most poignant concern. I liked Mr. Blair, sincerely, ardently. You can then very readily conceive under what feelings I penned my brief comments on this severe stricture. But, Sir, I think myself bound to tell you, that the Republicans in this quarter of Virginia will not sustain the course which the *Globe* has sustained towards Mr. Stevenson. His sentiments in regard to the Bank, the persecution he has received from the opposition, and his feelings towards Mr. Van Buren, both politically and personally, and let me add, Sir (because it is a fact which fell within my own knowledge), the memorable efforts which he made to sustain Mr. Van Buren in the days of *his* trial or persecution, and while others were shrinking from the storm, *his* coming forward, and being one of the most active and determined men to press the rejected minister for the Pesidency,—these and other circumstances are too well known, to permit his friends in Virginia to view with indifference any attempt to strike him down! I will not cavil with you, Sir, about the amount of Mr. S.'s indiscretion. I will not deny, if you please, that he might have written rather a more prudent letter; because we now see that the one he has written is susceptible of some misconstruction. I will not say, whether taking even the worst view of the matter, Mr. S. ought or ought not to have spoken a syllable about the Bank, and whether if asked at all in the frankest spirit by any gentleman who was preparing to withdraw his funds from America, he ought not to have said, that he did think the Bank would not be put down, an opinion which seems to be countenanced by the report of the Republican Committee of Pennsylvania.

"Admit, then, that the private letter from London is correct; which I am prepared to deny in all its extent,—admit that Mr. Stevenson has been guilty of some indiscretion, yet does it therefore follow that he was at once to be put under the ban—that there was no other mode of correcting the error?

"I have no question that his own letter, which is the only authentic testimony we have before us, *has been* misconstrued. It is perfectly obvious, at least to me, that Mr. S. was not aware at the time he wrote it of the construction that would be placed upon it, both as regards Mr. Rush, for whom I know he entertains the kindest feelings; or the sentiments expressed in Mr. Van Buren's letter to Mr. Williams, which no man more cordially approved. I attribute the whole style and phraseology of the letter, to the indignation he felt at the article in the *Commercial Advertiser*, and not as the *Globe* supposes, to any disposition to repudiate either Mr. Van Buren's or Mr. Rush's opinions in relation to the Bank.

"On this subject you have no doubt formed your own opinion. And you will pardon me, I trust, for the liberty I take in advising you at all upon the subject. My own course on this occasion proceeds not only from my regard for Mr. Stevenson, but from the great interest of my party. My feelings for him are certainly very warm, both as a public and private man, and I feel the strongest desire that he should not suffer in the public estimation. But I am equally solicitous for the union and harmony of the Republican Press, and for whatever course may be most likely to promote the success and prosperity of the administration. I am but poorly read in the signs of the Heavens, if a lowering storm is not coming on, which may require all our strength and discretion. Our Currency is in a most distracted condition. The spirit of speculation has involved the community in danger and embarrassment. Thousands will fall victims to circumstances, of which they had no presentiment, and over which they could exercise no control. The picture of the distress in this City is already most appalling. The strongest houses, as they were supposed, are bowing beneath the tempest. The Hermans of N. Orleans, the Josephs of New York, the Philips of Philadelphia, and the Warwicks of London have prostrated several of our capitalists, and our new Bank Bills, admirable as they are in many respects, by abolishing the small notes and requiring 3/5 of their Capital to be preserved in gold and silver, are yet calculated to add to the distress of our existing banks. The Treasury Circular has disturbed the equilibrium of circulation, and by unnecessarily accumulating the specie in the Western States, will prevent us from eking out the capital of the new Banks except by heavy drafts on the old. Instead then of extending accommodation, the Banks will be compelled to curtail their Customers. In such a state of the elements the clamor is always directed to the government. The opposition, of course, have seized upon the Treasury Circular. Some of the friends of the Administration who believe it to have been a wholesome measure, originally, have changed their view. They contend a change of circumstances demands a change of policy, that, as Mr. Burke said 'circumstances are infinite—and infinitely combined, are variable and transient; that he who does not take them into consideration, is not erroneous, but stark mad, he is, metaphysically mad; that a statesman *never losing sight of his principles,* is to be guided by circumstances and judging contrary to the exigencies of the moment, he may ruin his country forever.' Some of his friends also maintain that whatever respect might at first have been due to the Circular of General Jackson, yet a decided voice of both houses had condemned its continuation, and that it is the duty of Mr. Van Buren to consider not so much what had been done by his predecessor, as what would promote the good of the country.

"In a word, Sir, it cannot be concealed that the time is not far distant, when from the confusion and turbidness of the elements, we will require all our sincere friends to support us against the common enemy. Union and not discord must become our watchword. If within three weeks from the commencement of the Administration, we have the signs of two important dissensions in our ranks;—if in addition of the *contre temps* of Mr. Forsyth, we are to have such men as Stevenson struck down and sacrificed, men who like him have hazarded everything for our cause, who have suffered so severely from our opponents, and whose interests and feelings are so naturally and deeply enlisted in the success of the present Republican Administration—what I frankly ask you, are we next to expect? The President's path may be strewn with roses, but it will also have thorns enough.

"My intercourse with Mr. Van Buren has been so cordial and confiding for ten years past,—my confidence in his good sense and magnanimity, so strong, that I am sure he will excuse me for asking you unreservedly to submit this hasty letter to his inspection. I beg you to consider it in every other respect as *strictly confidential.*

You will best judge what ought to be done. I do not not ask for anything to appear in the *Globe* on this subject. Far from it. I do not even ask the privilege of putting a line in the *Enquirer*. My respect for Mr. Blair forbids that course. All I wish is, to put myself at ease about the matter, and the immediate friends of Mr. Stevenson; and to put him also at ease. But I will consult your own wishes rather than mine. In a word then, let me assure you, that whatever information you may give me shall be considered *strictly confidential*, and that no use will be made of your reply, except so far as may be *expressly allowed* by yourself. Fear not, Sir, that I will trouble you in this way again. I am too well aware of the drafts made upon your precious time, as well as too sensible of the reserve which it becomes me to observe towards yourself to think of repeating this transgression, but on the most urgent occasion.

"If I could be vain enough to hope that Mrs. B. retains any recollection of the eccentric Virginian whom she met for the first time in the East Room on the 4th of March, I would add my best wishes for her, as well as those for yourself, from,[2]

"Yours truly,

Thomas Ritchie."

It is evident that Ritchie contemplated more in this letter than a mere vindication of his friend Stevenson. At the point of a threat he was fighting for the state banks and for a continuation of the credit system, each of which was endangered by the specie circular and the new banks which had sprung up in the West. In a few well regulated state banks, such as the Bank of Virginia, of which his cousin, Dr. Brockenbrough, had been president for twenty-five years, he saw the only possible means of continuing the credit system by the use of bank notes and the only alternative to a national bank. Besides, Virginia was wedded to the old order of things, having invested her literary and internal improvement funds in state bank stock and agreed to accept bank notes in payment of taxes.[3] In opposing the proposed return to an exclusive use of metallic money, Ritchie stood by Virginia, but in so doing he was forced into the conservative following which was now rapidly crystalizing about W. C. Rives in Virginia and N. P. Tallmadge in New York.

On the other hand Benton and his policies were popular in Virginia. Disgusted because of the monopoly enjoyed by

[2] *Van Buren MSS.*

[3] *Ibid.*, P. V. Daniel to Van Buren, October 20, 1838.

the Richmond bankers and accustomed to the use of hard money only, the rural population accepted what "Old Bullion" said as gospel. They were ably led by James McDowell of Rockbridge and Thomas Jefferson Randolph of Albemarle county. McDowell's connection with Benton, being his brother-in-law, and Randolph's commendable efforts to prevent Rives from appropriating to himself the political legacies of Madison and Jefferson, gave prestige to their leadership.

Van Buren had scarcely entered the White House before the contest, already noticeable in national affairs, was on in Virginia. All realized that it involved the presidential succession, and the hope of having Rives displace Benton in the popular favor aroused local pride and added spice to the contest. Many were now willing to accept Rives at his own estimate as the logical successor of Jefferson and Madison, and as the one man who could restore the prestige of Virginia. The ambitions and interests of each faction were plainly evident in the elections of April, 1837, for members of the General Assembly and of Congress.[4]

Standing aloof and eager to profit by the results of faction was a vigilant and, since the election of Van Buren and the financial panic which followed, growing opposition. This opposition was ably directed by John Hampden Pleasants of the *Richmond Whig,* who lost no opportunity to sow seeds of discord in the ranks of the administration. By constantly referring to Benton as "the Great Expunger" and to Rives as the "Little Expunger" and by creating anxiety as to which of the two the "Little Magician" would ultimately favor, he wounded the pride of the latter and drove deeper the wedge of discord.[5] When Jackson had used the pocket veto for the resolutions suspending the specie circular order of 1836, Pleasants had cried conspiracy and tried to give the impression that Rives would never be permitted to aspire to

[4] *Richmond Whig.,* April 21, 1837; *Richmond Enquirer*, April 11, 1837.

[5] *Richmond Whig,* February 23, 1837; *Ibid.,* March 3, 1837.

the presidency. But when it seemed that the breach in the Democratic party was irreparable, he suddenly ceased to find fault with the "Little Expunger" and actually vied with him in professions of friendship for the state banks and in condemnation of the panic producing qualities of the specie circular.[6]

The financial alarm and distress which enveloped the country during the months of April and May, 1837, were seized upon by Ritchie as forceful means of inducing Van Buren to rescind the specie circular. To this end Rives was given a conspicuous place as the spokesman of the people in his congressional fight against that measure.[7] Meanwhile Dr. Brockenbrough, president of the Bank of Virginia, made flying trips to Washington;[8] Ritchie pictured the dire calamities which would befall the country in case the credit system were abandoned; and Rives reminded the President through the correspondence which they maintained and the agency of friends, that he could not defy the people by adhering to the specie circular.[9] It was all to no purpose; Van Buren remained non-committal and doubtless determined.

Unlike Rives, Ritchie was unwilling to force Van Buren's action in regard to the specie circular. Next to his love and ambition for Virginia was his love for the Democratic party, which was now in danger. Then, too, he did not, like others opposed to the specie circular, attribute all the financial ills of 1837 to it. Wiser councils had prevailed, and from his friend, Dr. Brockenbrough, he had learned that "the panic" was due mainly to over banking, wild speculation, and unwise uses of the federal moneys.[10] His confidence in the state banks had also been shaken by their suspension of specie payment and their apparent unwillingness to resume it. Such institutions were plainly unsuited for federal depositories

[6] *Richmond Whig*, March 7, 1837; *Ibid.*, April 4, 21, 1837.

[7] *Ibid.*, March 28, 1837.

[8] *Stevenson MSS.* Ritchie to Stevenson, April 20, 1837.

[9] *Van Buren MSS.*

[10] *Richmond Enquirer*, April 21, 1837; *Ibid.*, May 16, 1837.

and unsound bases for the state's credit at a time when credit was most needed for the construction of works of internal improvement. Precipitate action might also result in a political triumph for the Whigs and the consequent restoration of "the monster." Besides, Congress had been summoned to meet in extra session to deal with the situation, and he was willing to thrust responsibility upon it.

To the eternal credit of Virginia and even to the Junto, a solution for the crisis was forthcoming. Going back to a recommendation, first made by John Randolph to Albert Gallatin, when the latter was Secretary of the Treasury, and again renewed, in 1834, by Wm. F. Gordon, Dr. Brockenbrough now suggested to Van Buren a complete separation of the federal finances from all banks whatsoever. To this end he proposed a system of federal depositories, two or more for each state, under the charge and management of federal commissioners. In such an expedient Brockenbrough saw security, both to the state banks and to the federal government. In the first place it would make a national bank unnecessary, and familiarity with local conditions would make it possible for the federal government to accept the notes of specie paying banks in payment for lands. Thus the credit system could be maintained which he considered necessary "in a rising and enterprising country like ours," where "a mere metallic currency is too silly for any man of sense to dwell upon." In the second place, the proposed system provided a suitable financial agency which could be freed from the embarrassments of an occasional suspension of specie payment.[11]

As a way out of his dilemma, Van Buren readily accepted Brockenbrough's suggestion and hastened to enlist Rives and others in support of it. Without mentioning the specie circular he laid before them three methods for caring for the federal moneys, viz: a national bank, the continued use of the state banks under certain regulations and restric-

[11] *John P. Branch Historical Papers*, Vol. III., No. 3, p. 253.

tions, and the proposed independent treasury system. The first of these propositions he himself was unwilling even to consider, but he expressed no preference as between the remaining two. In keeping with the purpose of the politicians for maintaining accord within the party, he suggested to Rives that he write to Benton, Wright, Buchanan, and Tallmadge upon the importance of coming together in a conciliatory spirit for the consideration of these propositions.[12]

At once Rives saw in the proposed independent treasury a scheme to give the whole country "an exclusively metallic currency" or to give the government "one money and the people another," both of which its author had clearly endeavored to avoid. From the standpoint of the constitution and of expediency he considered a national bank unthinkable, even going beyond Van Buren in his opposition to it. Accordingly he informed the President that he, "with Jackson and Taney," believed "selected state banks under proper regulations adequate to the wants of the federal government" and helpful auxiliaries in "the improvement of the currency of the country." Though it may have been unable to meet the exigencies of the panic, he was also unwilling to discard a system which had worked well for three years for "a new and very doubtful experiment."[13] Thus it became plain that there was to be no compromise with Rives.

Other Virginians, notably Judge Parker and Judge Daniel, to whom Van Buren had submitted Brockenbrough's proposal, saw in it a scheme to continue the specie circular and even to put the whole country upon a hard money basis, but they did not hesitate on that account to approve it. They were willing to go further than Brockenbrough and to accept the whole of Benton's program. They each thought that the government had come to a choice between an independent depository and the use of specie and a national bank and the continued use of discredited paper. Their opinions were doubtless potent with the President in determining his sub-

[12] *Van Buren MSS.*

[13] *Ibid.,* June 3, 1837.

sequent actions. "The bankers of Wall Street," said Parker, may have to say 'Othello's occupation is gone,'" but he was confident that the "people will rejoice and bless the day which emancipates them from the iron yoke of the moneyed aristocracy." He therefore advised Van Buren, if for nothing else than politics, to take a stand against the credit system and the discredited banks and "to trust all to the people."[14]

To Ritchie there remained one of the three possible courses. He could have gone to one or the other extreme—followed Benton or Rives—or taken the middle course as outlined by his cousin, Dr. Brockenbrough. Political consistency and expediency, not always virtues, and his friendship for and confidence in Rives as the hope of Virginia, left him little choice. To Butler he had already committed himself to the credit system, and to the public at large he had committed himself against the independent treasury, when proposed as a Whig measure in 1834. Accordingly he now sided with Rives, and to remove the objections to the state banks as federal depositories and as agencies for preserving a sound currency he began to urge an early resumption of specie payment and their more rigid regulation and control, insisting meanwhile that the panic would soon be ended and that the country would return to its former prosperity. During its special session of twelve days, in June, 1837, the General Assembly was completely under his influence and did nothing hostile to the interests of the state banks.

But the panic continued; business demoralization increased; and the public became daily more hostile to the state banks. Something in the line of immediate resumption had to be done, or the days of the banks were numbered. Thanks to Rives, Ritchie, and Brockenbrough, they had escaped the wrath of the Assembly in Virginia, but angered solons elsewhere now planned to force resumption or a forfeiture of the banks' charters. Then, too, rumor had it that Van Buren had cast his lot with the hard money party and

[14] *Van Buren MSS.*, May 27, 1837.

that he proposed to recommend an independent treasury. After a conference with Dr. Brockenbrough[15] Ritchie threw himself into the breach with "A Proposition" for a convention of bankers to meet in Baltimore on September 18th, two weeks after the date set for the meeting of Congress. The object of the proposed meeting was to devise "means for bringing about a resumption of specie payment," but it also contemplated greater security for the state banks and a formidable stand of the conservative elements of the Democratic party.

The Proposition met with small encouragement in the states, and it soon became definitely known that Van Buren would adhere to the specie circular, and furthermore that he would recommend the proposed independent treasury. Thus Rives had lost his fight one month before Congress met, when he had expected to carry everything before him. At once he set about to rally his followers under the conservative banner. Tallmadge in New York and other conservative leaders elsewhere took a similar course. Their organ, the *Madisonian*, now first saw the light in Washington, and Rives began to be openly mentioned for the presidency. In vain did Dr. Brockenbrough plead for harmony in the party and endorse the independent treasury. In his letters of "Camillus," which now appeared in the *Charlottesville Republican* and later in the press of the whole country, Rives declared his platform and proclaimed relentless war upon those who were overthrowing the Jacksonian Democracy.[16]

Ritchie was now in a dilemma. On one side stood the administration and a number of his personal friends, among them Judge Daniel, Dr. Brockenbrough, and his brother-in-law, Judge Parker. On the other side were Rives and, as Ritchie believed, "a majority of the Democratic party" in Virginia. The results of the proposed campaign of education in behalf of the administration remained unknown, but

[15] *Van Buren MSS.* Brockenbrough to Rives, August 5, 1837.

[16] *Ibid.; Richmond Enquirer*, August 18, 1837.

he proposed to remain loyal to the Conservatives without breaking with the administration. To Rives he expressed a preference for the independent treasury over a national bank, but he advised him, "as a wise and prudent man" not to "brave the executive power." "It is," said he, "fearful odds why."[17] To Van Buren, who had taken Ritchie into his full confidence explaining why he favored the independent treasury and adhered to the specie circular, he expressed alarm because of the increased power which would be given the executive by the proposed changes, but he took particular pains to make his position on them clear to the administration, as the following extract from a letter to Van Buren shows:

"When I first expressed them (his opinions on the independent treasury) I was aware that they differed with two of my most intimate, most trustworthy friends, Judge Parker and Dr. Brockenbrough. I was told you were going also for the Sub-Treasury system, and no man can be ignorant of the fearful odds to be encountered in the Executive power. I expected to meet with the opposition of every Press friendly to the Administration, and I scarcely knew one man in the Republican party who had made up his mind against the supposed Executive project. I was not certain of the course which Mr. Rives would take. But I made up my opinion on the reasons, which both the *Enquirer* and the *Globe* took in 1834. If you have the *Enquirer* for Oct. 3, 1834, you will find the strong grounds, which my friend Blair took against the Sub-Treasury system at that time, and which, I have no doubt, he has forgotten. My plan was to bring back the State Banks to specie payment. For that purpose partly, I was in favor of a Bank Convention. . . . In a word, to pursue in some degree, the course which was pursued in the parallel period of 1815-'16. I did not believe that the State Bank Deposits had been fairly tried. I did not think with Mr. Adams that they were as bad or worse than counterfeiters, nor with Gen. Jackson that they had been instigated by their subserviency to Messrs. Biddle & the Barrings to suspend payment, nor that they were suspending to speculate in their paper or to sell their specie. But I did believe that they might be induced to resume payment at some early period, and that with proper precautions, they might serve as useful agents of the public Revenue. . . . It is impossible for me to say positively what the public sentiment is in Virgina. I can only speak of the very few persons who are around me. This short letter is written to you in confidence, and I may, therefore, say, that Judge Parker & Dr. Brockenbrough are yet, I believe, for the Treasury Scheme—the former, however, is for the Bank Convention, the latter is decidedly so, and now thinks the new system cannot be carried out unless the resumption has taken place. Judge Daniel goes strongly for the Sub-Treasury System. On the other hand, Mr. Rives, James Garland, Nicholas, Rawlins, the

[17] *Rives MSS.* Ritchie to Rives, August 10, 1837.

President of the Farmers Bank, are decidedly against it. Fontaine of Hanover (a senator of our State Senate) is on the same side. I do not really know how my friend Roane (the U. S. Senator) stands affected. But judging from other indications and especially from the general tone of my domestic correspondence (for the *Enquirer*) I am disposed to think it probable that the majority of the Democratic party *in Virginia* will be opposed to the Sub-Treasury System as compared with the State Banks."[18]

When Congress assembled in September, Ritchie remained loyal to Rives. Facing the praise of a united press the *Enquirer* and the *Charlottesville Republican* condemned the President's message. When the *Richmond Whig* saw Calhoun returning to the Democratic fold, it daily expected "Father Ritchie" to take a "flip-flop" to the administration which seemed to be reuniting as of old, despite the talk of disintegration. But the flip-flop did not come, and it turned to chiding the editor of the *Enquirer* because of his alliance with the "nullifier," but he remained aloof and even defiant. He felt that the new policies would wreck the party, and he mistrusted Calhoun's motives and loathed his ambitions. In a leading editorial he assured the public that "Mr. Calhoun has not gained our confidence by his recent moves on the chess-board, however, much he may have won on the hearts of our brethren, "He is," said he, "too much of a metaphysician for us. His late speech has been cried up by his friends to the skies—but we will thank them to tell us how it comes to want the non-committalism genius of Mr. Van Buren's Message. How so many persons have been puzzled yet to see from its zig-zag statements and balancing expressions whether Mr. Calhoun is now or not a friend of the Bank of the United States.[19]

From his retreat at the Hermitage the "Old Hero" tried to prevent Rives from pursuing further the road which Judge White had followed to oblivion and to arrest the schism in his beloved party. Through his influence pressure was brought to bear upon Ritchie, but consistency, loyalty to friends and devotion to principle made it impossible for him

[18] *Van Buren MSS.*, August 20, 1837.

[19] *Richmond Enquirer*, October 3, 1837.

to face about abruptly. He was always ready, however, to compromise and conciliate. Accordingly he came forward with a second "Proposition," this time the Special Deposit System, a sort of halfway measure between the use of the pet banks and the proposed independent treasury. Under this system the federal moneys were to be deposited with approved state banks which would permit federal inspection and regulation and refrain from the use of the federal moneys in their banking operations.[20] Ritchie urged its adoption as a means of restoring business tranquillity, perpetuating the state banks, making a national bank impossible, and preserving the unity of the party. As the following extract from a letter to Rives shows he hoped to enlist him in its support:

> "We must not divide and break down the party. I should think that you might all agree upon some plan. It seems to me that Calhoun is easing off and even Benton a little.
>
> "What think you of the plan of the Special Deposites? See the *Enquirer* of Friday. Even Dr. Brockenbrough says, if there be supposed insuperable objections to the S. Treasury System, the Special Deposite System will work well." [21]

Congress and even Rives paid little attention to Ritchie's proposed compromise, and adjournment came without an agreement upon a suitable depository for the federal moneys. The time was, therefore, thought opportune for launching the Conservative party in Virginia. J. M. Mason, James Garland, Geo. W. Hopkins, and W. S. Morgan, representatives in Congress were ready to join it, and the reports of a successfully contested election, in which the united action of the Whigs and Conservatives had made W. H. Seward Governor of New York, inspired confidence.[22] The home-coming of Rives was attend by demonstrations of popular approval of his course in Congress; Ritchie praised "our worthy Senator" and endorsed his determined stand; and Governor Campbell's message to the General Assembly, endorsing the insurgent movement and commending its objects was re-

[20] *Richmond Enquirer*, October 20, 1837; *Van Buren MSS.*

[21] *Rives MSS.*, September 20, 1837.

[22] *Van Buren MSS.*, R. E. Parker to Van Buren, November 27, 1837.

ceived with enthusiasm. So alarming did the situation become that Judge Parker began to conjecture about the future of the Democratic party, if it were to be deprived of the masterly direction of the *Enquirer*.[23]

In the face of such developments and confident of the outcome the administration leaders resolved upon drastic measures to hold their disintegrating party together. A movement was started for an independent press in Richmond with Hugh A. Garland as editor;[24] the "Calhoun Whigs" entering the Democratic party were everywhere treated with the kindest consideration, and open bids were made to John Tyler, Abel P. Upshur, Henry A. Wise, Thomas W. Gilmer, and others to follow their example; the *Globe* was admonished to deal gently with Rives; and Van Buren was advised to say as little as possible upon the subject of the independent treasury in his regular message to Congress. Finally it was arranged that Judge Parker, a politician of the "gum shoe" variety, should be on hand for the meeting of the General Assembly with a letter from Van Buren which could be shown to a "few and in circumstances which would satisfy them."[25]

This bold stand effectively checked Ritchie who did not contemplate a breach with his party, but it only spurred Rives to renewed efforts. The regular session of Congress for 1837-'38 had carried him too far adrift to permit a return to the fold, and he, an "expunger" and a "remover of the deposits," was royally hated by the Whigs. Thus there was nothing left for him but to persist in the third party movement. He could not join the Whigs as the Conservatives in New York were doing, because the Whigs did not desire his help and had within their party such men as Tyler and Leigh whose ambitions ran counter to his own. Besides the Conservative strength had never been tested before the people, and the contest for members of the General Assembly was at hand.

[23] *Van Buren MSS.*, January 18, 1838.

[24] *Ibid.*, Daniel to Van Buren, January 23, 1838.

[25] *Ibid.*, Parker to Van Buren, November 14, 27, 1837.

As the time for the spring elections drew near and it became daily more evident that Congress would adjourn without agreeing upon a suitable depository for the federal revenues, the cause of the administration in Virginia became alarming. The "campaign of education" by which the leaders had hoped eventually to win had thus far been unsuccessful, but like the Conservatives, they too were anxious for the verdict of the people and apparently willing to abide by it. Silas Wright, a special emissary from Van Buren, came to Richmond to confer with Ritchie, who was now greatly concerned about the movement to destroy his press. As a result of this and other conferences, it was agreed that the whole weight of the *Enquirer* would be thrown to the administration in the fight then to be waged before the people in Virginia and elsewhere, provided, however, that the war on Ritchie was to cease and that he was to be left to follow his independent course in case the administration failed in its campaign of education. Accordingly Ritchie switched the issue from Rives and the independent treasury to Van Buren and the national bank. In the very beginning of the conservative movement it will be remembered he had left a loop-hole for such an exit by informing Rives that he would go for the independent treasury to defeat a recharter of the national bank. Protesting against the design of the "piebald" Whigs to restore the monster, he now entered the list of those fighting for the regular Democracy, and Parker's letters to Van Buren became more encouraging.[26]

Despite Ritchie's good faith in carrying out his part the election in Virginia resulted in defeat for the Democrats, who found consolation only in their continued control of the state Senate and their ability thus to prevent the Whigs from instructing Roane out of the federal Senate and endorsing the national bank. The Conservatives won twenty-three Delegates and four Senators, which gave them the balance of power in the House and on all measures requiring a joint vote, such as the election of a federal Senator.

[26] *Van Buren MSS.*

Ritchie attributed the defeat to apathy, discord, and panic,[27] but others, among them some of his uninitiated friends, attributed it to Rives and Ritchie. Van Buren was informed that the "vacillating and wavering course" of the latter had done "more harm than all other things beside,"[28] and prints outside of the state maintained that he had desired and planned the defeat hoping to force upon Congress his plan for the special deposit banks.

Not perturbed by the charges against him but fearful lest the results of the elections elsewhere would duplicate those in Virginia, Ritchie appealed at once to Van Buren on behalf of his proposed compromise. On July 2, 1838, he wrote as follows:

"I am about to write you a very free letter. I have no time to study the graces of composition. I must tell my tale right straight on. The mail closes within a short time, and it was only within a few minutes past, that upon a long conversation with Dr. Brockenbrough, I have determined to take this mode of addressing you, instead of taking the cars in the morning for Washington. He thought it would be best for me to go on political grounds, but advised me on personal considerations to decline the visit. He said that I would be watched, hampered, & belittled. But these considerations should not have prevented me, if I had not supposed that the special friends of Calhoun in the H. of R. might suspect the object of my visit, and then set themselves to defeat it.

"Sir, you ought to know me. From the first moment of my acquaintance with you, I have been your personal & political friend. How warmly I have been so, let my actions speak more than my professions. No man more sincerely rejoiced in your election—no one could have more highly regretted that the first measure of your administration should have called forth my opposition. But I have ever been most anxious to conciliate and to compromise this vexatious question. I have spared no pains to bring our friends together. Were any one at Washington, who had the ear of both, with an address and weight of character to enforce his recommendations, I think the matter would have been settled before this. But each side complains that the other will not compromise, and nothing is done.

"I wrote Mr. Balch last Thursday that if I could do any good at Washington I would cheerfully go on. He gave me no sort of encouragement. I had almost abandoned the whole matter in despair, until I received the three letters marked A. B. & C. I trust them to your most sacred honor.

"I beg you to read most carefully the letters of Messrs. Rives and Hopkins in particular. Call around you, my dear Sir, your closest

[27] *Richmond Enquirer*, May 1, 11, 1838.

[28] See *Van Buren MSS.*, for April and May.

friends, if it be not too late. You know the means of bringing about such results far better than I can undertake to advise. Cannot Mr. Poinset approach Mr. Lagare, and thus make a *point d' appui* between the two wings?

"If Congress could be induced to postpone their adjournment for a few days, everything might be settled. I beg you in the most emphatic terms to close up this vexatious question now. Read the letter of my friend Rutherford (the Lieut. Governor, and a Sub-Treasury man) and of Fontaine our amiable, pure & sensible Senator.

"I pray you not to listen to the infuriated counsels of those bitter Hotspurs, who advise you to appeal to the Polls. Before the Fall Elections the schism in our party may produce the direst results. We shall all be distracted whether Mr. Wright's bill passes or is rejected. We shall probably be beaten, and then a National Bank may be fastened upon us.

"Mr. Calhoun is for agitation, agitation. But you know him sufficiently to know how far he is to be trusted for motives or measures. John P. King has drawn this politician to the life.

"I am interrupted. I have no time to pour out the thousand reflections that run in my brain. Your own sagacity renders it, however, unnecessary.

"I entreat you to act and to save our Party, as I took the liberty of telling you, through my letter of last year to Mrs. B. in the spirit of a liberal compromise.

"Believe me to be, your friend,

THOMAS RITCHIE."

"(Please return my letters.) Dr. Brockenbrough fully agrees with me in all my calculations & he is the only person who knows of this letter."[29]

With characteristic tenacity Van Buren refused to be moved even by this ardent appeal from his old friend. He yet had confidence in his proposed campaign of education, and, as soon as Congress adjourned, set out to reason with the Virginians on their native heath at the White Sulphur. On his way thither he made it convenient to eat "bacon and beans" with Rives at Castle Hill and to break bread with T. J. Randolph, Rives' rival and neighbor. While Daniel and Parker criticised this condescension as "calculated to inflate the vanity and self-importance of one (Rives) who ridiculously imagines himself to be holding the destiny of the administration and of the Republican party in his hands,"[30] Ritchie accepted the visit in a gracious spirit and

[29] *Van Buren MSS.*

[30] *Ibid.*, Daniel to Van Buren, August 8, 1838.

was loud in his praise of the Commonwealth's distinguished guest.[31]

Ritchie evidently misunderstood the object of Van Buren's visit. It was not, as he supposed, to pave the way to a compromise but to prevent a further widening of the schism within the party. In the last days of the regular session of Congress Rives had expressed a willingness to accept the Special Deposit System with important modifications, and there was thus ground for Ritchie's false conjectures. On the verge of what he considered a triumph for his proposition he now pled more earnestly than ever for conciliation and compromise, as the only condition under which the Democrats could win in 1840. In the efforts of the *Globe* to make the President's sojourn both pleasant and profitable he saw also a supposed disposition to abandon the independent treasury.[32] Had Ritchie's advice been followed, the Democrats would doubtless have fared better in 1840, but Van Buren's administration would have stood for naught instead of a brilliant period in the executive history of our country.

Both Rives and Ritchie made their greatest mistake in under-estimating the effect of the "campaign of education" being conducted by the administration and in over-estimating the popularity of the credit system as maintained by the state banks. They also placed too much emphasis upon the conditions in and vote of Virginia. If Van Buren accepted any compromise with them in 1838, it was certainly only by taking the lion's share. Ere he reached the springs the tone of the *Charlottesville Republican* made it plain that he had offered Rives nothing in the line of conciliation, except the honor of his presence for a two day's visit in his own home. The work of winning Virginia had already been entrusted to T. J. Randolph, James McDowell, Judge Parker, P. V. Daniel, Geo. C. Dromgoole, and Dr. Brockenbrough, and the President had simply offered Rives a last

[31] *Richmond Enquirer*, July 31, 1838.

[32] *Stevenson MSS.*, Ritchie to Stevenson, August 4 and 5, 1838.

opportunity to right himself with the party which had honored him and from which ambition had driven him astray. Contrary to expectations the autumnal elections in the other states were generally favorable to the administration, and the independent treasury stood justified in the sight of the people. True to his promise made to Silas Wright, Ritchie accepted this last chance to get into the band-wagon, and, in the words of J. M. Mason, who also had seen the light, was now ready to "sink or swim" with Van Buren. Some suggested Calhoun as a compromise leader, but Ritchie was unwilling to be rocked in the same "truckle-bed" with the man who had defeated Crawford and fathered Nullification.[33]

Such changes of attitude as this have subjected Ritchie to the severest criticisms, among which were disloyalty and ingratitude. When considered in connection with his promise to Silas Wright, the best explanation for this change is found in a letter from Daniel to Van Buren. "Mr. Rives," said he, "ought to have known Ritchie better. Should have known that altho' he is glad to acquire favor throughout the nation, that his special horizon is limited to the State of Virginia; that he never will go beyond what with assiduous industry he strives to ascertain is the sentiment of this state. To that he will adhere no matter who stands or who falls. He believed, I have no doubt, from the unfortunate connection of the state with her banks, thru' her literary fund and fund for internal improvement vested in their stocks, and from her unwise pledge to receive their notes in payment for taxes, that she would be constrained to sustain these banks to any and every extent, and therefore, he sided with them: he now believes the state will not countenance an outbreak with an administration which sustains her familiar and great constitutional doctrines; therefore, to keep with the majority in the state, he will abandon Mr. Rives, if necessary and save himself from falling to the earth. I sus-

33 *Richmond Enquirer,* September 28, 1838; *Stevenson MSS.,* Ritchie to Stevenson, March 4, 1838; *Ibid.,* Rutherford to Stevenson, July 28, 1839.

pect, too, that Ritchie's own involvements with the banks have had their influence."[34]

The signs of the times carried no warnings for Rives who adhered to the third party, defying the advice of friends and the Whig coquetry. In the defeat of the Whigs at the polls in the autumnal elections of 1838 and in the successes of the Conservatives in Virginia he saw a possibility of making the latter the real opposition party and of placing himself in Clay's shoes.[35] His "Principles and Policies of the Conservatives," declaring for an "armed neutrality," was a revised statement of his political platform, first set forth in the letters of "Camillus."[36] Brockenbrough now questioned his Democracy, alleging that it had been shattered by his failure to reach the vice-presidency in 1836; Parker and Daniel ridiculed the armed neutrality and the presumption of its chief exponent;[37] and Ritchie, now fearing a union between the Whigs and the Conservatives, warned him not to throw himself into the hands of the Volsci.[38]

Forced to abandon his friend and doubtless wounded in pride, Ritchie now sought consolation in the quiet of Brandon, on the James, whither he was accustomed to go in times of adversity. The *Enquirer* could not retreat, however, and turned temporarily to a discussion of non-partisan subjects. Its attacks upon the abolitionists were renewed and intensified; greater aggressiveness in the work of internal improvements was urged; and agriculture and manufacturing came in for a share of attention. It was just as unwilling to permit Calhoun to tap Western Virginia and divert its traffic thence to Charleston as to see it made tributary to Baltimore and Philadelphia. Without endorsing protection the *Enquirer* tried also to show how prejudice against the tariff had prevented the rise of a belt of manu-

[34] *Van Buren MSS.*, October 20, 1838.

[35] *Richmond Enquirer,* April 11, 1839.

[36] *Ibid.*, January 11, 1839.

[37] *Van Buren MSS. and Stevenson MSS.*

[38] *Richmond Enquirer,* December 20, 1838.

factures in Virginia along the granite belt separating the Tidewater from the Piedmont. It also contained able letters and editorials setting forth the advantages and profits to be derived from scientific farming and from silk culture.[39]

Although in a mood for reforms his dependence upon the state banks now blinded Ritchie to an opportunity for real service. He saw little merit in the system of "free banking," which was then so successfully divorcing the banks of New York from politics by admitting competition into the banking business. Such practices were in keeping with his principles of political economy and with his former suggestions, but the proposition now came as another "northern fad" and was therefore under the ban from the beginning. Besides, if Biddle's "hydra-headed monster" was to be kept down, Ritchie thought it now necessary that the Democrats should retain control of the banking business. He knew that Biddle's genius was equal to the task of organizing a second monopoly, if it were given free range in a field open to competition.[40]

The intense interest in the impending senatorial contest in Virginia made it impossible for Ritchie to abandon politics even temporarily. As has been shown the Conservatives held the balance of power in the General Assembly. They were now determined to force the re-election of their leader. A majority of both the Democrats and the Whigs were willing to combine with them to effect this object. The Democrats asked only that Rives cease to oppose the administration, but the Whigs made no conditions as to the price of their help and thus rendered their coalition with the Conservatives possible. Nevertheless an election was rendered impossible, because there were "impracticables" in each of the old parties, notably the thirteen Whigs, who would not countenance such an alliance and who thus constituted themselves a second and third balance-of-power party. Not even so tempt-

[39] See *Richmond Enquirer*, September to December, 1838.

[40] *Ibid.*, November 30, 1838; *Ibid.*, December 18, 1838; *Ibid.*, January 12, 1839.

ing a plum as the vice-presidency, though believed to have been tendered by Clay, could induce the "thirteen impracticables" to vote for Rives.[41] Consequently Virginia was cut off from her equal representation in the federal Senate.

Though never willing to admit the possibility of a reelection for Rives, Ritchie grew nervous when the vote in the Assembly fell only two or three short of that goal. In such an event he saw the possibility of a permanent union between the Conservatives and the Whigs, which would wrest the electoral vote of Virginia from the Democrats in 1840. Accordingly he urged Rives to retire to private life rather than turn Federalist and desert the principles of Jefferson and Madison.[42] As a solution of the question of the senatorship he urged a referendum. "They (the people) are," said he, "the foundation of power, and in all doubtful cases their servants are bound to consult them."[43] It is extremely doubtful, however, whether he would have endorsed a referendum for a proposition to increase the number of independent state banks or to confirm the banking monopoly of Richmond, questions indirectly involved in this issue.

Rives chose to lead the Conservatives into their second contest before the people, that of April, 1839, as an independent party, fighting under the banner of the armed neutrality. He yet hoped for greater defections from the Democrats, and it is not certain that he now contemplated a permanent alliance with the Whigs. To this end the Conservatives of the Assembly issued an address to the people, and Rives himself published a letter defending their course and reasserting their claims to be the original Democrats. In proof thereof it was pointed out that only one Democrat had voted for the Sub-Treasury Bill when first proposed in 1834 and that a large majority in each house of Congress had opposed the specie circular in 1837. Rumors of a

[41] *Richmond Enquirer*, January 24, 1839; *Ibid.*, February 2, 7, 14, 1839.

[42] *Ibid.*, January 24, 29, 1839; *Ibid.*, February 14, 1839.

[43] *Ibid.*, February 21, 1839.

tentative understanding between the Whigs and the Conservatives looking to the presidential election of 1840 were also denied. There were, nevertheless, visible traces of a Conservative leaning to the Whigs. Their alliance with them in the attempt to re-elect Rives was now defended, and Rives himself now assured the public that all Whigs were not lepers and that he would never be deterred from duty by any "Brutum fulmen."[44]

The fifth rib thrusts which Rives now gave Ritchie on every occasion led to a suspension of friendly intercourse between them and spurred the venerable editor to renewed efforts to control the General Assembly. There was much at stake: a senatorship in Congress and the electoral vote for 1840. Besides Ritchie had to redeem himself, if possible, and to rehabilitate his friends. Stevenson would not have refused a place on the ticket with Van Buren in 1840,[45] and James McDowell, whom Ritchie liked scarcely more than Benton, was now the acknowledged leader of the Democracy in Virginia, thanks to the confusion wrought in the Junto by Van Buren's policies. It was indeed one of those times that "try mens' souls," and as usual Ritchie was equal to the test. The press of the whole country spoke of it as "one of the battles of his life."[46] With a skill and adroitness equal to that of Tweed at a later day, he now extended the olive branch to Impracticables and to Conservatives alike; resurrected the ghosts of the dead monsters, the national bank and the tariff; and decried Clay in his finessing to reach the presidency. The annexed extract from the *Enquirer* was a typical rallying cry:

> "People of Virginia . . . are you prepared to put down 'the Northern President with Southern principles?' Are you prepared to disgust the whole Northern Democracy, the best friends, as a party, which we have there, by discarding our staunchest friends in all the North? Are you prepared to paralyze such a man, to spread abolition over the free states, and to shake the pillars of the Union itself.[47]

[44] *Richmond Enquirer*, March 20, 1839.

[45] *Stevenson MSS.*, John Rutherford to Stevenson, April 10, 1839.

[46] *Richmond Enquirer*, April 13, 30, 1839.

[47] *Richmond Enquirer*, April 13, 1839.

The independent stand taken by the Conservatives made success for the Democrats impossible. In counties where they had no candidate of their own members of the former party either absented themselves from the polls, following the example of their leader, Rives, or supported the Whig candidates, thus dividing the nominal Democratic vote. As a result the new Assembly had practically the same political alignments as its predecessor. Ritchie found consolation only in the fact that the total popular vote of the administration candidates for the House of Delegates was greater than the combined totals of the Conservative and Whig candidates.[48] This, to his mind, was sufficient assurance that Virginia would vote right in 1840. Regardless of the fact that the Democratic majorities came from the western counties, where James McDowell's influence was greatest and the hard money sentiment strongest, the press of New York gave Ritchie chief credit for the showing of the administration party.

Regardless of Ritchie's contentions the results of the election of 1839 indicated doubt about the vote of Virginia in the presidential election of 1840. Accordingly each of the national parties during the months immediately following made every effort to heal its schisms and to attract strength. To this end it was proposed that the Whigs and the Conservatives unite to make Rives Governor and to elect a Whig to the federal Senate. In convention assembled at Staunton the Whigs also nominated Tallmadge for the vice-presidency on a ticket with Clay, and their prints and orators throughout the state sowed dissension among the Democrats by keeping Benton before the public for the presidential succession and McDowell, his kinsman and the terror of all slave-holders, for the governorship.[49] It was even asserted and with some evidences of truth, that McDowell and Benton were getting control of the press in the western

[48] *Stevenson MSS.*, Ritchie to Steveson, May 15, 1839; *Ibid.*, July 28, 1839; *Richmond Enquirer*, June 14, 1839.

[49] *Richmond Enquirer*, September 10, 13, 1839; *Ibid.*, October 1, 4, 1839.

counties, preparatory to establishing their ascendency in Virginia and to putting the Junto out of control. On the other hand, the "sink or swim party," a name now applied to the followers of Van Buren, in ridicule of Ritchie, were equally active. Stevenson was suggested for the vice-presidency; McDowell was to take Rives' place in the Senate, provided Brockenbrough or some other eastern man was made Governor; public dinners were attended without distinction as to faction; and Ritchie persisted in the contention that one hundred state rights Whigs, now called "Ritchie Whigs," were ready to take the place of each Conservative who deserted, a contention confirmed by the absence of the Impracticables from the Whig State Convention.[50]

The month of December, 1839, was fruitful of events of consequence to the people of the whole country, but particularly those of Virginia. On March 4th the Whigs in what Ritchie termed the "Thaddeus Stevens Convention" surprised the country by renominating General Harrison for the presidency and John Tyler for the vice-presidency. It is true Tyler's nomination was generally expected, but as the running mate of Clay. A few days later the Whigs and Conservatives placed a young Virginian, R. M. T. Hunter, in the speaker's chair of the House of Representatives, where he, as leader of the Calhoun party in Virginia, was able to serve the interests of that faction most effectively. These events were followed in the last days of the month by a rconciliation between Van Buren and Calhoun and by Ritchie's unequivocal declaration for the independent treasury. Thus more than a *modus operandi* for the coming presidential campaign had been effected. The way had been paved for the Calhoun faction which had hitherto fought in vain for a footing in Virginia to fasten itself upon that Commonwealth. When abolition and the extension of negro slavery became the sole issues, as they soon did, this faction clinched the hold secured first in 1840.

50 John Letcher became editor of the *Valley Star* in 1839. See *Richmond Enquirer* March 19, 1840.

Under the changed conditions the contest over the vacant senatorship from Virginia lost none of its interest. A new situation had developed to prevent the election of Rives. Some of his Conservative followers had become impracticables to the extent that they would not vote with the Whigs who were now ready to give Rives their undivided support, provided the Conservatives would do likewise. Early in the session of 1839-'40 John T. Anderson, himself a Conservative member of the Assembly, had made clear their reasons for refusing to unite with the Whigs in a letter to Mr. O'Callaghan of New York. Had General W. S. Scott been the Whig nominee for the presidency instead of General Harrison, there would have been no barrier to such a union and to the election of Rives, since Tyler had been nominated for the vice-presidency. Under the circumstances Rives could not openly ally with the Whigs, because some of the Conservatives would then have supported John Y. Mason, Democrat, who was popular with all parties. The result was another deadlock, and Virginia continued to be represented by only one Senator.[51]

When it became apparent that the vacancy in the federal Senate would not be filled Rives put a timely end to the life of the third party in Virginia by declaring for Harrison for the presidency. This new change of attitude came when Clay and other leading Whigs were gathering at Richmond to launch the campaign of 1840 for members of the General Assembly and was doubtless made in preparation for that event. Henceforth it was to be a straight out fight between Whigs and Democrats. The letter anouncing Rives' affiliation with the Whigs was dated February 15, but was not published until ten days later. It disclaimed against executive usurpation, the abuse of federal patronage, and Benton's "Graduation Bill" for the sale of public lands and was especially vehement in its denunciation of the independent treasury, which it claimed was capable of becoming a greater menace than the national bank had ever been. It set forth

[51] *Richmond Enquirer*, January 22, 1840; *Ibid.*, February 1, 4, 1840.

a good negative program and thus entitled its author to full membership in the Whig fraternity.

The political caldron never boiled hotter than in Virginia during the period between the adjournment of the Assembly and the April elections of 1840. The last skirmish before the great fight for the presidency was in progress. The Conservatives seem to have divided almost evenly between the two old parties, but many state rights Whigs, such as Wm. O. Goode and Wm. P. Taylor followed Calhoun into the Democratic party. Abolition entered into the contest as at no previous time. It was now recalled that General Harrison, as a young man, had belonged to a society for the abolition of negro slavery; that both Ritchie and McDowell had been abolitionist in 1832; that Van Buren, as a member of the constitutional convention of 1821 in New York, had voted to enfranchise free negroes; and that R. M. Johnson, the Democratic vice-president and candidate for re-election, was an abolitionist who had married a wench. Each side was able to furnish "positive proof" for its statements and equally able to refute all attacks upon its own candidates. In this game of crimination and recrimination little progress was made on either side, but, at a psychological moment in the contest, some one sprang Poinsett's Report on the proposed reorganization of the army and turned the tide completely to the Whigs. Under the proposed changes of the Secretary of War, which were known to have the President's approval, the state militia was to be used as a part of the national army, which the Whigs now claimed would pave the way for a contemplated executive usurpation.[52] Virginia's pride was at once wounded, and before the smoke of battle could clear Ritchie was forced to admit defeat and to concede the re-election of W. C. Rives to the federal Senate as a Whig.

The end of this contest did not produce even a truce in the bigger one of which it was a part. Without the slightest disposition to "give up" Ritchie continued to attack Harrison's anti-slavery record and his federalistic leanings and to

[52] *Stevenson MSS.*, Rutherford to Stevenson, May 19, 1840.

herald his incompetence and obscurity. He was present everywhere on the firing line, exhorting his followers to organize and to rally. He even refused an invitation from the President to come to Washington, giving as an excuse his unwillingness to leave Virginia before she had been redeemed.[53] By a personal letter to Poinsett he tried to determine the facts about his recommendations regarding the organization of the army and to exonerate Van Buren from any blame for them.[54] Expressing a desire to use the remaining days of his life in a defence of those principles for which his life had been spent he was determined that the Whigs should raise no "new issue" and that the war for vindication should be carried "boldly into the heart of Africa." Calhoun was welcomed to Richmond as a spellbinder, and a new paper, *The Crisis,* was put into the field by Ritchie to aid the *Enquirer* in its campaign of education.[55]

The Whigs were equally active. They were confident of success provided the old issues which had divided Federalists and Republicans could be kept out of the campaign. Van Buren's supposed anti-southern leanings were brought into vivid review, and he was pictured as a spendthrift who had used the federal moneys to purchase French bedsteads and gold knives and forks for the White House. Their chief asset, however, was Poinsett's Report, which they begged in vain to have published in the *Enquirer*. The least possible was said about the tariff, the bank, and internal improvements. Despite their alleged monopoly upon the wisdom and decency of the Old Dominion the Whigs now conducted a campaign of advertising. Log cabins decorated the public squares of all the leading towns and cities, and the clans rallied nightly at their Tippacanoe clubs. Whig orators visited every nook and corner of the state, Clay, Webster,

[53] *Van Buren MSS.*, Ritchie to Van Buren, June 1, 1840.

[54] *Richmond Enquirer,* June 12, 1840.

[55] *Richmond Whig,* July 28, 1840; *Ibid.*, August 11, 1840; *Ibid.*, September 29, 1840.

and Rives appearing upon the hustings. Webster's visit to Richmond was made the occasion for a grand demonstration, when log cabins surmounted by living raccoons and canoes, filled with white boys dressed as Indians, were transported through the leading streets in ox-carts and when the children of the "wise and good" dangled strings of buckeyes about their necks in all the glee of a savage revel. It could not be denied that Harrison had, as a young man belonged to an abolitionist society in Richmond, but it was urged that he had since seen the light, and in extenuation for his former opinions reference was made to the anti-slavery tendencies of the Father of his Country, the Sage of Monticello and the Orator of Roanoke.

Ritchie anounced the results of the contest as follows: "The Goths have taken Rome," but he was proud that "the Citadel," Virginia, had been saved. "There is an asp among their (the Whig's) roses," said he. "The proud and noble Commonwealth of Virginia is against them. 'Yet all this availeth me nothing, so long as I see Mordecai, the Jew, sitting at the King's gate.' Like Fabricius she despised the seductive pageant, and their intimidating threats. . . . Seduce Virginia by their log cabins, and hard cider, and their Belial orators! Intimidate her by threats of revolution! Humbug her by their arts and devices! How little did they know the character of this people."[56] Van Buren's satisfactory answer to the letter addressed to him on the traiff, negro salvery, etc., Calhoun's active support of his candidacy, and Ritchie's repeated expressions of confidence in the Tenth Legion, and the western counties in general, had saved Virginia to the administration but not the presidency.[57]

The first returns from the contest had indicated that the result in the country at large would be very close and that it would in all probability depend upon the vote of Virginia.

[56] *Richmond Enquirer*, November, 1840.

[57] *Ibid.*, August 7, 1840; *Ibid.*, October 15, 1840; *Richmond Whig*, December 4, 1840.

Confident of success the leading Whigs of that state were exultant, but, as usual, the returns from the Valley counties dampened their ardor and created grave fear as to the final outcome. At once the *Richmond Whig* began to revile and ridicule the ignorance and stupidity of the "Suabian Dutch" and to declare its unwillingness to see the results of a national election turn upon "300 spurious Dutch votes" in Shenandoah and Rockingham counties. A vigilance committee was organized resolved to carry war to the knife rather than submit.[58] As later evidence showed a coup d' etat was planned by which Van Buren was to have been seized on the eve of his second inaugural and carried to the mountains of North Carolina. Thence a revolution was to have been declared in the name of justice and in defence of our representative institutions. Although Pleasants later denied the existence of any such revolutionary plan, explaining it all as hoax upon Father Ritchie, it can not be denied that the Whigs regarded their predicament as serious and that they contemplated a resort to force.

Though rarely forced to fight on the defensive, Ritchie was a militant leader of an opposition. Despite their strength in the South, he firmly expected the Whigs, when once in power, to return to the tenets of the Federalists. Accordingly he now thought that Virginia, aided by "chivalrous South Carolina," which, of course meant Calhoun, was specially called upon to become the "flag bearer" of the South and of the Union in an effort to restore the government to the doctrines of '98. He urged the necessity of organization and of refraining from all discussions of the relative merits of Van Buren, Benton, Calhoun, and Buchanan for the presidency. He reprinted the Resolutions of '98 and announced that they would be the beacon flag by which Virginia would judge the incoming administration.[60] Mean-

[58] *Richmond Enquirer*, November 6, 10, 13, 1840; *Richmond Enquirer*, December 8, 1840.

[59] *Richmond Enquirer*, November 13, 1840.

[60] *Ibid.*, November 20, 1840.

while he never lost sight of "our northern allies."[61] He was evidently playing the role of a conciliator and compromiser in an effort to hold together the anti-slavery and protectionist North and the pro-slavery and free trade South in preparation for another fight for the presidency.

[61] *Richmond Enquirer*, November 27, 1840.

CHAPTER VIII.

TYLER AND TEXAS.

While Governor of Virginia, David Campbell made public some astounding revelations regarding the status of learning in that state. After a careful investigation he showed that one-fourth of the white population could not read or write. The effect of this revelation and of Governor Campbell's frequent references to it were humiliating and gave birth to one of those spasmodic but fruitless reform movements which characterized the South during the ante-bellum period.

As in other movements for the social betterment so in this, the people of the western counties took the lead but found an able and sincere lieutenant in Ritchie. Already under the influence of the "Yankee school teacher" and impatient with a system of education which provided a university training at public expense for the sons of the "eastern nabobs" and reserved its lesser benefits for the indigent poor," the middle classes, the small farmers, now demanded public free schools, even if they necessitated the destruction of their far-famed University. Educational conventions, attended by leading educators from all parts of the Union, were held in the western counties and sent mammoth petitions to the General Assembly setting forth the objects of their meetings and asking aid from the state to accomplish them.

Ritchie lent his best energies to a presentation of the requests and to furthering the general educational movement. The "buncombe," "coon-skin fooleries," and "hard cider jests" of 1840 had temporarily shaken his confidence in the wisdom of the people, and he now pled for the public free school as the salvation of the republic. He would now have restated Montesquieu's celebrated maxim, "Virtue is the basis of a republic," so as to make it read, "Virtue and information constitute the basis of a republican government." That the Assembly might know what was being done for the cause of public education in other states, he caused his own duplicate of the library then in use by some of the public schools of New York to be placed in the Capitol where it could be seen daily.[1] Aided by James M. Garnett his pioneer efforts were of immediate service and planted those germs which later ripened into an abundant fruitage in the free school systems of both Virginia and West Virginia.

Among Ritchie's many services to the cause of primary education his address before the Educational Convention, held in Richmond, in November, 1842, deserves special mention. In one of the few public addresses ever delivered by him he there emphasized the wholesome influences of education as a means of lessening crime and of strengthening and maintaining our democratic institutions. He was appalled at the ignorance in the southern as compared with the northern states and attributed the cause in Virginia to a system of public education which pauperized its recipients and made no provision for a regular, systematic, and proper superintendence. He pointed to Prussia as the best example of the results to be derived from considering primary education as a common benefit to be borne as a common burden.[2] But the slave-holding aristocracy was then no more disposed to bear common burdens than is the moneyed aristocracy of to-day, and Ritchie was thus prevented from joining hands with Horace Mann in doing for the South what the latter was doing for the North, and what he was fitted to do both by education and training.

Ritchie's enthusiasm for free schools and his responsibility as the father of a large family of girls led him to espouse the cause of education for women. Even to-day the following from one of his editorials on that subject would be a sweet morsel for advocates of greater equality between

[1] *Richmond Enquirer*, December 4, 1840.

[2] *Ibid., November* 22, 1842.

the sexes: "We go for anything which promises to advance the improvement of women. Man, 'the tyranny man,' has too long degraded them into beasts of burden or into toys to entertain his dallying hours. We have cut them off from our political privileges. Their very name is sunk in ours—and we educate them in the most light and superficial manner, as if they had very inferior minds to improve and as if they had not the most important duties to discharge in the relations of wife, mother, helpmate, and companion. But several of them begin to assert their rights, to display their intellect, and to command our respect. We are now for enlarging the sphere of their information and influence; and hence we approve of any plan which is calculated to put them on more solid and useful studies."[3]

Scientific agriculture was another subject of great concern to Ritchie. His cousin, Edmund Ruffin, the prince of agriculturists of the South, was about to give up the editorship of the *Farmer's Register* just at a time when his services were most needed to redeem the farm lands of Virginia. Nevertheless, he did not despair. He endorsed the suggestion made by W. C. Rives for establishing a chair of agriculture in the State University, and he himself thought that the farmers should be educated in the rudiments of agricultural chemistry and of scientific agriculture. To promote these objects he advocated the formation of local agricultural societies centering in a state organization, the distribution of prizes and premiums for model farms and rare products and the founding and operating at state expense of agricultural stations.[4] His enthusiasm upon these subjects and the advantages from having their particular brands of flour mentioned in a journal of so great authority as the *Enquirer* induced manufacturers to send Ritchie sample barrels of flour and choice boxes of tobacco. Such receipts were always acknowledged in the most gracious manner. From the hospitable board of the venerable editor the

[3] *Richmond Enquirer*, November 9, 1841.

[4] *Ibid*, November 11, 1842.

flour went direct to the consumers, and the tobacco was distributed among his friends, as he did not use the weed himself.

But the subject of negro slavery would not down and, now that the abolitionists had taken it in hand, diverted attention from all local reform movements. At the best their activity was alarming and annoying; since the South had resolved to have Texas, it became positively unbearable. Together with other southerners, relying on that security which came when the White House was occupied by a "northern man of southern principles," and together with those Whigs who, like Wise, Gilmer, and Upshur were losing confidence in the power of the Whig party to preserve the Union with its diverse sectional interests, Ritchie had become more and more of a pro-slavery advocate and was now determined to have Texas that the institution of slavery and the expanding energy of the South might have a West of its own into which to retreat and fortify itself. Shortly after her declaration of independence he urged the representative of Texas in London to maintain terms of friendship with Stevenson, our representative at the Court of St. James, to whom Ritchie now made repeated suggestions about the possibility of annexing the "Lone Star Republic" to the United States.[5]

The new program threatened at once the political relations of New York and Virginia. The defection of the Conservatives had placed the former state in the power of the Whigs with William H. Seward as Governor, who had refused to extradite fugitive slaves. In return Virginia had refused to give up escaped criminals, and subsequently her Legislature enacted an inspection law for all vessels bound to and from New York. The differences between these "sovereign states" became menacing, and at times Ritchie seemed willing to part company with his former political ally. In a half-hearted tone he commended the retaliatory acts of the General Assembly, but he endorsed most heartily Upshur's article in the first number of Ruffin's *Southern Magazine*

[5] *Stevenson MSS.*, Ritchie to Stevenson, September 9, 1839.

and Monthly Review, calling upon Virginia to take her ground as a sovereign state in opposition to the abolitionists, "boldly and decidedly" and "at once."[6] A second thought, fathered doubtlessly by his political instincts, revived Ritchie's genius for an appeal to the constitution and brought forth the happy suggestion that all could live in peace and accord by adhering to its compromises.

The accession of the Whigs to power under the leadership of General Harrison did more than break the hold of the Albany Regency and the Richmond Junto upon the administrative machinery of the government. It struck a death blow to the schemes of the latter and its southern lieutenants for the annexation of Texas. The determination of the Whigs to proceed at once to put their program into operation would, if successful, have revived the political contests over the tariff, the bank, and internal improvements and blinded all interests to the golden opportunity for expanding to the westward. Accordingly Ritchie did not pause long in commending the military services, the patriotism, and the social qualities of the deceased chief executive, but proceeded at once to take advantage of "the act of God" which had given the South a doubtful opportunity in the elevation of Tyler to the presidency. If the opportunity were used, the political achievements of the past might be preserved and the opportunity for a greater nationality might not be lost. To this end the proposed extra session of Congress was condemned, and no opportunity was lost to widen the growing breach in the long-established friendship between Clay and Tyler. The former was pictured as a "designing politician" bent upon being President in all but name, and a "glorious immortality" was held out to Tyler, "should he be found faithful to the constitution." His closest friends, Wise, Gilmer, and Upshur, now known as the "corporal's guard," were hailed as members of the republican wing of the Whig party, and democracy and republicanism were made synony-

[6] *Richmond Enquirer,* March 6, 1841.

mous with strict construction and the Virginia doctrines for which the guard professed to stand.[7]

Tyler's message to the extra session of Congress made it as plain to Ritchie as to others that the days of Whig rule were numbered and that the object of his recent editorial efforts had been attained. The President's determination to adhere to the Compromise Tariff of 1833 and his advocacy of a "fiscal agency" as a depository for the federal moneys, could never be reconciled with Clay's schemes for a protective tariff and a revival of the national bank. But Ritchie sought no compromise or alliance with either faction. When the indignant Whigs of Richmond, Norfolk, and other points in Virginia rose in mass to condemn Tyler's vetoes of Clay's measures and to honor their idol by a legislative act perpetuating his name in that of a county of the Old Dominion, Ritchie exulted. He was witnessing the death throes of the hated Whig party, and, to make the work of the executioner in Virginia more complete by alienating completely the strict constructionists, he continued to praise Tyler's vetoes and to assure him of the support of the Democratic party and of the undying gratitude of Virginia.[8] His private correspondence shows, however, that he already regarded Tyler as "driftwood upon the stormy sea of Whig politics" and as the destined leader of a forlorn and hopeless third party.[9]

The first regular session of Congress under the Whig regime only widened the breach which the special session had made in their party, but the reaction to Clay and his nationalistic policies was so pronounced as to alarm "old state rights" men. Blinded to the advantages of a "union of Whigs for the sake of the Union" and, despite their protests to the contrary, eager for the spoils of office, the Whigs, now in control of the General Assembly of Virginia, refused to pass resolutions condemning the national bank and a pro-

[7] *Richmond Enquirer*, May 14, 1841; *Ibid.*, August 24, 1841.

[8] *Ibid.*, July 20, 1841; *Ibid.*, August 17, 24, 1841: *Ibid.*, September 24, 1841.

[9] *John P. Branch Historical Papers*, III., 247.

tective tariff, or to take any stand upon the subject of federal relations.[10] Fearing the eternal disgrace which he thought must follow, should Virginia go on record as favoring these things, Ritchie pled for the Virginia doctrines as never before and at once placed himself in greater harmony with the record and policies of his own party. Although adhering to the state banks as suitable depositories for the federal moneys, he was now willing to divorce them from politics and to give the country a metallic currency in so far as that desired end could be effected by substituting coins for paper notes of small denominations.

The end of his first regular session of Congress, also, found Tyler and his guard without a party. Although Clay was about to retire to private life, he was everywhere regarded as the real leader of the Whig party, and his retirement was looked upon as a grooming for the presidency. The circumstances presented an opportunity, however, to rally a party around the President. To this end an effort was made in administrative circles to classify all voters as adhering either to the administration or to the opposition, and the *Madisonian,* the organ of the defunct Conservative party, was accepted as the mouth-piece of the administration. Numerous mass meetings were also held, particularly in Virginia, at which letters were read from Tyler, Wise, Upshur, and Gilmer. But all efforts to adjust party alignments by executive dictum were futile, and resulted only in placing the President at the head of the expected "forlorn and forsaken" third party which Ritchie now pronounced as impossible as the "third estate in the Empire."[11]

With the Whigs rent asunder both locally and nationally, Ritchie considered the time opportune for the Democrats to reclaim Virginia. "Sentinel must answer sentinel," said he, "until the contest is over."[12] On the eve of the state election Tyler had sent a special message to Congress recom-

[10] *Richmond Enquirer,* January 13, 22, 1842.

[11] *Ibid.,* February 26, 1842.

[12] *Ritchie MSS.,* Ritchie to Charles Campbell, April 6, 1842.

mending a repeal of the federal law providing for a distribution of the proceeds of the public land sales. This came as a blow to the Whigs of western Virginia, who had expected to use their part of this fund for internal improvements and free schools.[13] Their consequent defection and the inability of Wise, Upshur, and Tyler to hold their following in the eastern part of the state paved the way for a brilliant and decisive victory for the Democrats. The growing pro-southern sentiment, that sentiment which was later to ripen into a passion for Texas, contributed materially to the Democratic success. Counties in the Tidewater, hitherto Whig and Federalist, now gave Democratic majorities for the first time in their history. It marked the beginning of that movement which at important crises was to make Virginia a united pro-slavery state under the leadership of the Democratic party. As Ritchie said, "The fiery cross has indeed passed over the state and the Republican clans have rushed to the rescue."[14]

In recognition of his services in this and other campaigns Ritchie's name was perpetuated in that of a new county in the trans-Alleghany;[15] his name was frequently used in connection with the vice-presidency;[16] and friends far and near supported the *Enquirer* more liberally than ever before in a gracious effort to relieve the financial embarrassments of its editor.[17]

Under the disintegrating influences of the Whig party and the reviving hopes of the Democrats, the presidential succession began to be of concern to the latter. Though formidable Clay was not feared, and Van Buren was discredited by his defeat in 1840. Regardless of Jackson's desire to have the succession pass to Benton after Van Buren had done with it, the followers of Calhoun in Virginia, in-

[13] *Richmond Enquirer*, March 29, 1842.

[14] *Ibid.*, May 10, 1842.

[15] *Ibid.*, March 2, 1843.

[16] *Ibid.*, March 2, 1843; *Van Buren MSS.*

[17] *Ibid.*, November 18, 1842; *Ibid.*, December 2, 1842.

spired by the Texas fever which was becoming chronic with them, began to groom their favorite for the race. He was put forward as the one candidate upon whom the "Tyler Whigs," now in ridicule sometimes called "Ritchie Whigs," and the Democrats of eastern Virginia could unite. His pro-southern program was attractive to them, and his followers realized that there was now a chance of removing the long standing objection of Virginia to his ambitions. Little fear was entertained regarding the course of the voters in the western counties. They had ever been willing to swallow diluted doses of strict construction, and they now lived under the illusion that the preservation of the Union which they loved depended upon the preservation of negro slavery. Besides they had always been ardent expansionists, and, with Texas as an issue, they were willing to follow the standard of any man who favored its annexation. Accordingly copies of a "Life of Calhoun," written by himself but fathered by R. M. T. Hunter, were distributed freely; newspapers in the south side placed Calhoun and Silas Wright in nomination for the presidency and vice-presidency respectively; and Calhoun himself addressed an enthusiastic following at Petersburg.[18]

But the friends of Van Buren in both the eastern and the western counties were not willing to be brushed aside thus ruthlessly. The fact that both Jackson and Benton remained favorable to his candidacy was a power in his favor in all sections. His friends were quick to detect the "concerted efforts" of the Calhoun men and equally quick in their efforts to annul them.[19] George C. Dromgoole and Thomas Jefferson Randolph, two of the most active and effective leaders east of the Blue Ridge, lined up behind his candidacy, while James McDowell now one of the most popular leaders in the whole state and in constant communication with his brother-in-law, Thomas H. Benton, led the Van Buren foices in the western counties. The movement for

[18] *Richmond Enquirer*, September, 1842.

[19] *Van Buren MSS.*, Benton to Van Buren, April 17, 1842.

Texas seems not to have entered into their calculations, and they now demanded the renomination of their favorite as a matter of right and justice.

William H. Roane wrote that Ritchie was put into "a narrow place" by these rival candidacies.[20] At all times Democratic success was uppermost in his mind, and there was no gainsaying the fact that its successes of 1841, in Virginia, had been due to an active co-operation between the Calhoun and the Van Buren factions of the party. In recognition of this fact Ritchie had not "for a long time breathed a sentiment of the slightest hostility to John C. Calhoun,"[21] and he had even praised his genius, his past services, and his recent espousal of the true republican doctrines of '98. The *Charleston* (S. C.) *Mercury* made bold to enlist him among those who favored Calhoun for the succession.[22]

But the *Richmond Whig* came nearer the truth in its prediction that "the past could not be forgotten" and that "Ritchie will not support the favorite of the South." Besides the Whig rule had necessitated the return of his friend Stevenson from the Court of St. James, and Ritchie now hoped to make him vice-president, governor of Virginia, or a member of the federal Senate. He preferred the vice-presidency for his friend, because such a promotion would not run counter to McDowell's ambitions to reach the Senate or the governor's chair. He also saw the impossibility of taking both the candidate for the presidency and the candidate for the vice-presidency from the South. Accordingly his preferences were for Van Buren for the first place and Stevenson for the second, but he did not dare openly to express a preference. In the strictest confidence and on the very eve of the gubernatorial election, in December, 1842, he did, however, declare himself to John Letcher, McDowell's close friend and political representative, as

[20] *Van Buren MSS.*, W. H. Roane to Silas Wright, February 14, 1843.

[21] *Richmond Enquirer*, August 12, 1842.

[22] *Ibid.*, December 8, 1842.

favorable to Van Buren's candidacy for the presidency and McDowell's candidacy for the governorship, and promised, furthermore, to declare himself openly for Van Buren after the spring elections of 1843. Considerations of Texas seem also not to have entered his mind at this stage of the campaign.

The first hand to hand contest between the rival factions within the party came in the Democratic State Convention held in Richmond on March 2, 1843. Led by James A. Seddon, the friends of Calhoun favored the latest possible date for holding the national Democratic convention, May, 1844, and insisted that the delegates thereto should be elected by congressional districts and that each delegate should have a vote on the floor of the convention. Led by George C. Dromgoole, the followers of Van Buren favored the earliest possible date for the convention, December, 1843, and adhered to the old method of appointing delegates thereto by state conventions and of allowing a majority of the delegates from each state to cast the vote of that state.[23] It was the old but ever recurring fight between the organization and the anti-organization forces. The former pled for an early nomination to prevent sectional and personal jealousies which they feared would arise in the next session of Congress. On the other hand, Calhoun's friends desired a late nomination for directly opposite reasons. Their only hope lay in the occurrence of the very things which the other faction feared. There were great possibilities in the Texas issue, and Calhoun's friends expected the South to line up against Van Buren on the tariff, even if Texas did not become an issue. The friends of Van Buren succeeded in controlling the convention and won all the points for which they contended.[24]

The action of the Democrats in Virgnia came as a stinging defeat to Calhoun's friends everywhere. Naturally

[23] *Richmond Enquirer*, March 7, 1843.

[24] *Richmond Enquirer*, March 7, 11, 1843; *Calhoun Correspondence*, Am. Hist. Asso. Rept. (1899), II., p. 516.

Ritchie received their severest criticism. The *Charleston Mercury* claimed that he had everything cut and dried for Van Buren days before the convention was held. In a long editorial Ritchie denied the charge but admitted his "deep interest in the contest."[25] The *Mercury* would not be appeased and defiantly placed at the head of its editorial column "JOHN C. CALHOUN, FOR PRESIDENT OF THE UNITED STATES, subject to the decision of a national convention to be held in May, 1844."[26] It was thus evident that the contest in Virginia was to be continued.

The next tilt between the rival factions came in the elections of April, 1843. From the beginning the friends of Calhoun despaired of success, and they made a strategic mistake by even entering the contest. They insisted that the Assembly had so gerrymandered the state as to prevent the election of representatives to Congress or of delegates to a national convention, who would be friendly to Calhoun's candidacy. Their consequent apathy injured only themselves and in a way they could ill afford. William O. Goode was defeated by George C. Dromgoole for a renomination for election to Congress; R. M. T. Hunter failed in his contest for a re-election; and William Smith (Extra Billy) went down to defeat before a Whig, Samuel Chilton.[27] As a result Calhoun had not a friend in Virginia's representation in Congress, except those who were also friendly to Tyler. Apparently the pro-southern cause had been defeated, but this contest, so far, was more personal than political; more anti-Calhoun than anti-slavery or anti-Texas.

True to his promises and in response to earnest solicitations, Ritchie now openly committed himself to the candidacy of Van Buren. A few weeks before he had associated with himself, as joint editors of the *Enquirer,* his two sons, William F. and Thomas, Jr., but he now desired it to be clearly

[25] *Richmond Enquirer*, March 18, 1843.

[26] *Ibid.*, April 4, 1843.

[27] *Richmond Enquirer*, April 7, 1843; *Ibid.*, April 16, 19, 1843; *Ibid.*, June 13, 1843.

understood that it was not only "the boys" but Father Ritchie as well, who desired the election of the "Little Magician."[28] This open stand was immediately felt in all directions, and many southern prints attacked the *Richmond Enquirer* without mercy.[29] With few exceptions the press of Virginia followed its course. The *Abingdon Banner* reminded the public of Calhoun's record in the days of Nullification and added that "it would be 'carrying coals to New Castle' to offer reasons and considerations to the voters of Little Tennessee why they should support Martin Van Buren."[30] The *Woodstock Sentinel* went for "Martin Van Buren and short Dutch cabbage against the world."[31] The conditions and Ritchie's ideas of the freedom of the press were such, however, that he admitted freely to the columns of his paper communications from those favorable to Calhoun's candidacy. He thus also thwarted the movement to establish a rival press in Richmond.

Their other political reverses and the open hostility of Ritchie did not deter the followers of Calhoun in Virginia, who at all times were conspicuous for their zeal and enthusiasm. Accordingly they flooded the state with another avalanche of speeches; "Calhoun's Plenipotentiary," Rhett, made another visit to "Van Buren's Secretary of the Southern Department," Ritchie;[32] from the press of South Carolina went up a sigh for "the proud Old Dominion under the feet of the Empire State;"[33] talk of a refusal to abide by the decision of a national convention and of throwing the presidential election into the House of Representatives was heard in the Calhoun camp. But it was evident to all that without some paramount issue their cause was doomed to

[28] *Richmond Enquirer*, July 18, 1843.

[29] *Ibid.*, September 15, 19, 1843.

[30] *Ibid.*, August 12, 22, 1843.

[31] *Ibid.*, July 27, 1843; *Ibid.*, August 1, 1843.

[32] *Ibid.*, September 15, 1843.

[33] *Calhoun Correspondence*, Am. Hist. Asso. Rept. (1899), II., pp. 527, 536.

failure, and that Van Buren would secure a third nomination.

Fortunately the issue was at hand. British interference in Texas and her consequent refusal to discuss further propositions for annexation to the United States aroused the dormant fears of all parties and shook off their apathy regarding that country. Texas had thus become a national and not a factional issue. Chief interest naturally centered in the South. Only ten years before England had freed the slaves in her West India possessions, and southern statemen, especially Calhoun and Upshur, now attributed her activities in Texas to a desire for the abolition of negro slavery not only there but also in the United States. Tyler and Upshur, now Secretary of State, decided to forestall English interference by more active efforts to conclude a treaty for the annexation of Texas. Incidentally they hoped to rally the friends of the administration in an effort to arrest the President's declining political fortunes. But his closest friends played fast and loose with him and Calhoun, and the followers of the latter decided to steal Tyler's political thunder. In the hope of committing Jackson to the annexation of Texas and with a possible view, also, to turning the political tables against Van Buren who, it was rumored, had agreed secretly with Clay to keep Texas out of the campaign of 1844, a letter written by Gilmer on the annexation of Texas had been sent to the "Old Hero" early in 1843. His reply, which urged the advantage of annexation from a military point of view and contemplated no sinister motives on the part of his informants, was forthcoming, but it was as readily laid by for future use. Mistrusting Van Buren's attitude toward Texas and conscious of its growing importance as a political issue, they had in hand the material which would alienate a large part of Jackson's following from him. Accordingly it was planned to commit Van Buren against annexation by skillful interrogations and to use his answers and the Jackson letter at the psychological time to destroy his candidacy.[34]

[34] *Van Buren MSS.*, John Letcher to Ritchie, September 23, 1843.

But the friends of Van Buren in Virginia were on the alert and quickly apprised their chieftain of the schemes of the rival faction. They knew that negotiations for the annexation of Texas were already in progress and now saw in the tactics to defeat their favorite only the proverbial straw in the sight of a drowning man. Ritchie insisted, therefore, that the midst of a presidential election was not a propitious time for the "free discussion and calm consideration of so vital a subject."[35] At the same time William H. Roane wrote to Van Buren that he had "long opposed the annexation of Texas," and that he now saw "nothing to change his mind." There is no denying, however, that Texas was, even now, a subject of the greatest concern to Ritchie and his friends, and that they were deeply concerned in the probable attitude of their candidate toward it. In the same letter, in which he showed such indifference toward Texas, Roane either displayed unpardonable ignorance or resorted to poor politics, when he informed Van Buren that "neither Ritchie nor I recollect your position in regard to it" (Texas), and assured him that any information on the subject "would be regarded in the strictest confidence."[36] Although Van Buren ignored all reference to Texas in his reply to Roane, there are no signs of a dampened ardor on the part of his friends in Virginia. The General Assembly, five to one, remained friendly to his candidacy, and the *Enquirer* continued to support him loyally.

Calhoun's friends resolved to make a final stand in the Democratic State Convention which met in Richmond, February 1, 1844. Meanwhile, R. K. Crallé, Calhoun's most ductile protegé in Virginia, and the *Petersburg Intelligencer* continued to complain of the "petulance," "dotage," and "dictatorship" of Father Ritchie.[37] On the evening before the meeting of the state convention Calhoun's address to his

[35] *Richmond Enquirer*, October 10, 1843; *Van Buren MSS.*, Stevenson to Van Buren, October 8, 1843.

[36] *Van Buren MSS.*, October 17, 1843.

[37] *Richmond Enquirer*, January 18, 1844.

"political friends and supporters" was made public in Richmond. It openly repudiated Van Buren but also resigned his own candidacy for the presidency. The effect was not to stampede the convention as some had expected. Both friends and antagonists took the address seriously and resolved to support the nominee of the Democratic party.[38] Had not the negotiations for the annexation of Texas by treaty been nearing a successful completion, the effect of this ultimatum might have been different. It certainly proves that little was expected from any *coup d'etat* in the nomination for the presidency.

From a scene of expected strife the Democratic State Convention was thus converted into a love feast. Although unwilling to be responsible for the effects of Van Buren's nomination, Calhoun's friends practically conceded it and for political reasons were now ready to vote for him. In return the convention adopted conciliatory resolutions and placed adherents of both factions on the electoral ticket.[39]

In the only important political speech of a life devoted almost exclusively to directing political movements, Ritchie welcomed this return of political accord and assumed full responsibility for the results.[40] The next number of the *Enquirer* proclaimed the Democratic party of Virginia "one and indivisible" and announced that "the Ark . . . which has been agitated on the billows of the sea of liberty . . . has now touched the summit of Mount Ararat—the rainbow of peace is brightening the Heavens—and the Dove has gone forth from the Ark to bring back the Olive Branch to all our party."[41] Calhoun was permanently out of the race, and the electoral vote of both Virginia and South

[38] *Van Buren MSS.*, H. A. Garland to Van Buren, February 7, 1844; *Ibid.*, W. H. Roane to Van Buren, February 3, 1844; *Richmond Enquirer*, 1, 6, 1844.

[39] *Ibid.*, February 6, 1844.

[40] *Richmond Enquirer*, February 6, 1844; *Polk MSS.*, Cave Johnson to Polk, February 6, 1844.

[41] *Richmond Enquirer*, February 3, 1844.

Carolina was counted for Van Buren.[42] On the other hand it was currently rumored and generally believed that Ritchie and his associates had committed themselves to Calhoun for the succession in 1848. Although he later denied these rumors, Ritchie now let them pass unnoticed.

The readiness with which Calhoun's friends gave up on this occasion was surprising, but their course was not wholly disinterested. Loyalty to their chieftain had sent Hunter, Goode, Gordon, and Smith down to defeat in 1843, and they were now doing yeoman service to avert their own ruin. Even Wise and others of the "corporal's guard," who had guided and misguided Tyler, were now ready to give up Calhoun for Van Buren. They insisted only upon the nomination of Polk for the vice-presidency, thus seeking to thwart Ritchie's plans for his friend Stevenson.

The days immediately following the Democratic State Convention were full of surprises. The opportunity to make political capital of Texas had come, and, as was so frequently the case in other things, Calhoun was not in a position to profit by it. The negotiations for annexation by treaty dragged on, and there began to be doubt about the attitude of the federal Senate toward any treaty for that purpose. Moreover, the publication of Senator Walker's letter on "re-annexation" made it impossible for Ritchie and his friends to maintain silence on so important a subject. There were many possible conditions, any one of which would inject Texas into the campaign as the leading issue. In a letter to James K. Polk, Aaron V. Brown expressed what was also the sentiment of most Virginians in the following words: "If the negro question (Texas) is settled wrong & if nothing can be done with the Tariff, we are a lost & doomed party."[43]

But there is no evidence that Ritchie and his associates even now deserted Van Buren or that they entered into any scheme to snatch the nomination from him by stealth. They had trusted the northern man with southern principles in

[42] *Van Buren MSS.*, B. H. Rhett to Van Buren, February 26, 1844.
[43] *Polk MSS.*, February 25, 1844.

1836, and they felt that they could do so again even under the changed circumstances. Calhoun had been beaten, and Van Buren had always been willing to play politics. Nor is it at all certain that Ritchie desired from him a public utterance of his attitude on Texas. He knew that the Democrats could not win without the electoral votes of New York and other northern states, and he also knew that there was a large and growing sentiment in those states against the annexation of Texas. He did, however, desire to convince Van Buren of the importance of the new issue and to make it impossible for him to go against Texas, should it be brought into the campaign for the presidency. To this end he wrote Silas Wright, Van Buren's closet political friend and adviser, as follows:

"I send you the following extract of a letter I received last night from Washington:

"'March 17—The Texas Question is destined to succeed. I think the treaty when made will certainly be ratified. . . . To-morrow evening a decisive article will appear in the *Globe*. General Jackson is most heartily with us, and *will go the whole*. He is the originator of this movement *and will see it through*. Unless forced to do so we must not make this a party question. Unless there is great imprudence or folly, Van Buren will be elected, but if he goes against Texas (which I deem impossible) all is lost.

"'I would send you the original, but it is marked 'confidential.' The writer is a member of Congress and a friend of Mr. Van Buren. Be so good as to consider its contents confidential, with the reservation only, that if you think it best, you may communicate them to Mr. V. B. I leave that disposition of them to your own discretion.'"[44]

Two days later and under date of February 12, 1844, instead of its correct date, February 12, 1843, Ritchie published General Jackson's letter to Aaron V. Brown, which had been called forth by Gilmer's letter and to which reference has already been made.[45] This anachronism and the subsequent developments have caused historians to give greater credence to the alleged existence of the above mentioned plot to keep the nomination from Van Buren, and such writers have not hesitated to connect Van Buren's friends

[44] *Van Buren MSS.*, Ritchie to Silas Wright, March 20, 1844.

[45] *Richmond Enquirer*, March 22, 1844.

in Virginia with the conspiracy.[46] Recent discoveries in the Van Buren manuscripts reveal, however, the fact that W. H. Roane had, five months before the publication of Jackson's letter to Brown in the *Enquirer,* informed Van Buren of the existence of such a letter and of the use proposed to be made of it.[47] Writers connecting Ritchie with the alleged plot also overlooked the fact that he himself corrected, in the very next issue of the *Enquirer,* the typographical error made in the original publication of the Jackson letter and called attention to the fact that an error had been made.[48] Whatever plots the "corporal's guard" may have been in, it is almost certain that Ritchie continued loyal to Van Buren and that he hoped to keep Texas out of the presidential campaign as a complicating issue.

Neither the publication of Jackson's letter nor the timely warning to Wright had the desired effect to convert Van Buren to the expediency of favoring annexation. The pact with Clay had to be kept; and Silas Wright counseled another course. Meanwhile it had become impossible to keep Texas from becoming an issue in the campaign. In his famous "Raleigh Letter," Clay had declared against annexation after a triumphal tour through the South; the northern as well as the southern press was full of comments upon Texas; and the legislatures of northern states were going on record as opposed to annexation. Van Buren's letter casting his lot with Clay and against the pro-southern program reached Richmond on April 30th, when the Junto was receiving the news of an unsuccessfully contested election for members of the General Assembly.

The effect of Van Buren's letter upon Richmond as upon the whole South was thrilling. With both of the presidential candidates opposed to annexation, the indications were that

[46] See Alexander, *Political History of the State of New York,* II., p. 66; Hammond, *Political History of the State of New York,* III., p. 447; McLaughlin, *Cass,* p. 215; Shepherd, *Van Buren,* pp. 401-406, etc., etc.

[47] *Van Buren MSS.*, Roane to Van Buren, October 17, 1843.

[48] *Richmond Enquirer,* March 26, 1844.

the Senate would reject the pending treaty and that Texas would be lost. The prospective market for negroes, then of consideration to Virginians, would be cut off, and the possibilities for a greater nationality would be blighted. To a race of expansionists, who, like Ritchie, now desired the Hawaiian Islands as a military basis for holding and governing the West, this was a sad disappointment. The effect of the letter is best described in Roane's immediate reply to it. "Your letter to Mr. Hammett," said he, "is just received here and has caused a sensation and is likely to produce an *effect* which no paper has caused or produced within my knowledge." He also informed Van Buren that the publication of his letter two weeks earlier would have given the House of Delegates to the Whigs by thirty or forty majority and added, "you cannot (I am grieved to the heart to think) carry this state next fall. Whether any Democrat can, God only knows."[49]

The members of the Junto were at a loss to know what to do. Various courses were suggested. Finally it was decided to hold a meeting of the Democratic Association in its hall on Shockoe Hill. At this meeting Ritchie was supreme. He drew, offered, and secured the adoption of resolutions which declared that the immediate re-annexation of Texas was a measure required by the best interests of the Union, that annexation was consistent with the soundest principles of international law; that the efforts being made in the North by Albert Gallatin and others to prevent the acquisition of more slave territory would, if successful, place the South under the ban of the republic; that the commercial and abolitionist activities of Great Britain in Texas furnished strong and additional grounds why we should repossess ourselves of that country; that Clay's letter opposing annexation was an attack upon the institution of negro slavery, and that the Democrats of Virginia be at once urged to express their opinion on the subject of Texas and on the propriety of relieving their delegates to the Baltimore convention of their

[49] *Van Buren MSS.*, April 30, 1844.

instructions.[50] Though he did not mention Van Buren by name this was his first repudiation of him, and it came openly and publicly.

While the meeting was in session on Shockoe Hill an admirer sent Van Buren the following anonymous letter:[51]

Richmond, May 1, 1844.

"*My Dear Sir:*

"You are deserted. Ritchie, Roane, Stevenson are *all out against you* on the Texas question; *positively, openly,* and *unequivocally against you.* Arrangements are *now, at this very hour,* being made to take up some other candidate, and of this be assured, if there be a God in Heaven.

"A faithful follower and a friend,

"Q in the Corner.
4 o'clock P. M."

From all over the state letters began to pour in upon Ritchie endorsing his course in the Shockoe Hill meeting and telling why Van Buren could not carry Virginia in November. With many the feelings of friendship for him were strong, but they simply considered him unavailable. Desiring to be perfectly frank and to apprise him of the sentiment in Virginia, Ritchie, on May 5th, sent him some of the communications which he was receiving together with a long personal letter from which the following extract is taken:

"I have refrained from writing you a single letter, during the present campaign, and I deeply regret, that the first one, which I shall have to write, would be one, which gives me as much pain to write, as any which ever came from my pen. I need not tell you, Mr. Van Buren, the feelings which I entertain toward you. Trusted at all times with a kindness, a liberality, a distinction far beyond my merits, I have conceived a sentiment toward you, which partakes not more of confidence in you as a politician, than of attachment to you as a man. I have received from you a hundred evidences of good feeling, which have left a reciprocal impression upon my heart. But I will not dwell upon particulars, nor will I deal in any profusions. You must know me well enough to believe them unnecessary.

"The last ten days have produced a condition of political affairs, which I had not believed to be possible. I am compelled to come to the conclusion that we can not carry Virginia for you. We have lost, I now believe, the joint vote in the Legislature. We have ten majority in the Senate, it is true, but in the H. of Delegates, where we had a

[50] *Washington Union,* April 3, 1847.

[51] *Van Buren MSS.*

majority of 16 at the last session, the Whigs have now a majority of about 12. But I do not attribute so much importance to this Revolution, as some of my friends. I have recovered from the temporary panic, which is so natural with such circumstances. I assure you, I do not write you under the influence of any feeling, which might cloud my judgment. But I write you under the effect of what I have heard from my friends and what they write me about your Prospects in November next. Judge for yourself, Sir. If I did not know that you are a man of honor, I would not put the enclosed letters in your hands. Read them, my dear Sir, but don't preserve their names—take no copies of them—but return me the originals. I will have no half confidence with you—some of them are my best friends. They are all your warm friends. I trust them in your hands, for, I know that you will not abuse the confidence I am now reposing in you. Read them, and judge for yourself. I am most anxious to spare your feelings, if I can, but I owe to you, as my friend, as the friend of our great Principles, to let you see what others have trusted to me, that you may determine for yourself.

"Whom we can get to supply your place, I know not, if you retire. You will see what my Correspondents say on that point. I can only tell you, that Mr. Calhoun's friends solemnly disclaim any wish to run him—that I have solemnly protested and will protest against any such idea as that and that I am actuated by no other motive under Heaven, than the desire to possess you of the views which these letters express. It is the same opinion, which is entertained by gentlemen, as staunch republicans as any in the state, who are around me, who have been late and are now your personal and political friends."[52]

Ritchie's admonitions regarding the use of his confidences were unnecessary. The Van Buren Manuscripts contain no record of them except that in Ritchie's own letter from which the above extracts have been taken. The stubborn and wily "Dutchman" returned them at once without even replying to the personal letter which accompanied them.[53] The insinuation that he should retire for a man who could win had doubtless added insult to injury.

Notwithstanding his indifference, Van Buren's friends in Virginia continued to speak kindly of him and, in some instances, to support his candidacy. In a public letter George C. Dromgoole condemned the action of the Democratic Association of Richmond;[54] Calhoun's friends showed their good faith in an address denying the charges of unfair dealing on their part and repudiating any alliances with the

[52] *Van Buren MSS.*

[53] *Richmond Enquirer*, July 24, 1854.

[54] *Ibid.*, May 10, 1844.

"anti-Van Buren Clique" at Washington, which had long plotted his overthrow; in an "Address to the People of Virginia" the Democratic Central Committee, which was made up largely from members of the Junto, praised his conscientious statesmanship and patriotism; and Ritchie himself promised to support his candidacy, should he be the nominee of the Democratic party.[55]

After the horse had been stolen, with the stable apparently locked, it was indeed a time for "conciliation and compromise." The electoral vote of New York was worth it, and it was evident to all that the tide had ebbed never to return, and that neither Dromgoole nor "a hundred *Globes*" could stop the current of public sentiment in favor of Texas.[56]

The choice of a new favorite for the presidency now became a matter of great concern at Richmond. Naturally many turned to Calhoun who, as Secretary of State since the untimely death of Upshur, was doing all in his power to secure Texas, but, true to his promise to Van Buren, Ritchie "solemnly protested . . . against any such idea as that." Benton, Buchanan, and Coloned R. M. Johnson were quickly eliminated from the running, as each had only a small local following, and Benton, the most formidable of the three, was pledged to Van Buren to the end. For a time Silas Wright was looked upon with favor. He combined all of Van Buren's political strength, being a northern man with southern principles and Van Buren's closest political friend, and it was thought he would profit by his friends' mistakes regarding Texas. But Wright declined all overtures. Finally a timely letter from Cass favoring the immediate annexation of Texas made him the favorite. It was with "great pleasure" that Ritchie published his letter in full in the *Enquirer*, but he very cautiously refrained from an open declaration in his favor, expressing himself as satisfied with any "Texas Man." There can be doubt, however, that Cass was already the choice of Virginia. His famous letter on Texas had put

[55] *Ibid.*, May 7, 1844.

[56] *Ritchie MSS.*, Ritchie to Howell Cobb, May 6, 1844.

him into the class of northern men with southern principles, for which the Virginians had a peculiar weakness, and besides he had always had a strong local following in the western counties, in one of which he had won a bride from one of the most aristocratic and influential families.

When the Democratic Convention met in Baltimore, Ritchie was in a strategic position. By yielding to the urgent demands for the abolition of the two-thirds rule, thus permitting Van Buren's loyal majority to effect his renomination, he had it in his power to accomplish that result. As the roll of states was called to hear the vote on this important proposition, all waited anxiously for Virginia, because she came last on the roll and had it in her power to control the situation. But her vote under the unit rule went against the abolition of the two-thirds rule and subsequently for Cass. When the first dark horse in American politics rode into the Democratic camp, Virginia was among the first to board the band-wagon, and the next issue of the *Enquirer*, her oracle, announced triumphantly that "a handful of Polkberries would kill any coon."[57]

Thus calmly and unostentatiously Ritchie had played a leading role through an important epoch in our history, without reverting to the methods of the "machine" or the "boss," but by loyal devotion to a great cause. In the moment of this, as in those of other triumphs, he was not exultant and refused to place himself in a position of authority. On the eve of the Baltimore Convention he declined to be a delegate thereto and advised his son, William F., who represented the Abingdon District, to go to that deliberation as "*no man's man*," not even his father's.[58] Meanwhile he remained at his post entreating the delegates from Virginia to act as free men and to lose no opportunity to effect such "a union of Democrats" as will defeat Henry Clay, "the greatest enemy of the country."[59]

[57] *Richmond Enquirer*, June 4, 1844.

[58] *Ritchie MSS.*, Ritchie to Howell Cobb, May 23, 1844.

[59] *Richmond Enquirer*, May 24, 1844.

While some were lamenting the course of the Baltimore Convention and conceding the election of Clay,[60] word came to Richmond that the Senate had rejected the treaty for the annexation of Texas. At once Ritchie voiced the slogan, "Polk and Texas." For the first time in the whole campaign he now believed Clay's chances ruined, so confident was he in the merits of the Texas issue. His political sagacity taught caution, however, and he now set himself firmly against the movement for a southern convention to resent the action of the North in preventing the annexation of Texas. Instead he proposed a national convention of the friends of annexation. This course would not only secure Texas;[61] but it would not endanger the Union. As rumor of English interference again spread over the country he reiterated his slogan and urged annexation as a condition of national security.[62] In reply, Whigs argued that annexation would lower the price of land and decrease the population in the older states. But Ritchie insisted that Texas would be a competitor in any event, and that she would be less dangerous in the Union than as a British colony.[63]

The subsequent contest was spirited and in doubt to the end. Whigs attacked the "despot," the "artful wirepuller," and the "miniature Talleyrand,"[64] Ritchie; they insisted also that he and others of the Junto were owners of lands in Texas, and that they were willing to destroy the Union for mercenary purposes;[65] they denominated the resolutions of '98 mere abstractions, and pled for a national bank as a means for increasing the currency and equalizing exchange;[66] they protested against the use of British gold to make the United States a free trade country,[67] and expressed great

[60] *Van Buren MSS.*, P. V. Daniel to Van Buren, June 11, 1844.

[61] *Richmond Enquirer*, June 11, 1844; *Ibid.*, June 18, 1844.

[62] *Ibid.*, June 28, 1844.

[63] *Ibid.*, July 19, 1844.

[64] *Ibid.*, September 10, 1844.

[65] *Ibid.*, September 6, 24, 1844.

[66] *Ibid.*, November 12, 1844.

[67] *Ibid.*, *October* 5, 1844.

fear lest the success of the Democratic party and the consequent repeal of the tariff act of 1842 would make it necessary for the laboring population of this country to live upon "free-trade bread," a black rye bread used by the laboring population of Germany;[68] and they went even so far as to invite John Quincy Adams to address a political meeting in Richmond.[69]

None of the personal attacks disturbed Ritchie quite so much as the appearance of John Quincy Adams in Richmond on a political mission. This he considered a disgrace to the Commonwealth. He would not deny that he and other Virginians owned lands in Texas, but he did insist that his and their interest in the preservation of the Union was paramount to all other interests;[70] he pronounced the rumors of disunion which had followed the Senate's rejection of the treaty for the annexation of Texas as "idle chimeras" started by some "hasty resolutions in South Carolina, which Calhoun regrets and reprobates;" by showing that rye-bread was then a wholesome and popular diet in Germany he proved the "black rye-bread" argument against the tariff a fraud; he held out the adoption of free trade in Europe as an example which should be followed in America;[71] and with the zeal of his younger days he returned to the old story of the "corrupt bargain" of 1825.[72]

Encouraged by their splendid showing in 1840 and the defection of the northern Democrats, the Whigs were hopeful of carrying Virginia. They had always been prominent in the lowlands among the "wise," and with "Harry of the West" as their standard bearer they now confidently expected to win in the western counties. Under the freehold qualification for suffrage the "wise" and "just" in that section shingled the mountain sides over with land patents to enable

[68] *Richmond Enquirer*, October 22, 1844.

[69] *Ibid.*, September 6, 1844.

[70] *Ibid.*, September 3, 1844.

[71] *Ibid.*, October 24, 1844.

[72] *Ibid.*, October 10, 12, 15, 1844.

the "slaves of Angus McDonald," the poorer whites who did not own land, to assist Henry Clay in his last effort to reach the White House. But the slogan "Polk and Texas" united the lowlands for the Democrats. As with one voice this section now spoke against the attempts of the North, in opposing the extension of negro slavery, to make the South a plague spot on the Union. On the other hand, Ritchie held the westerners in line by his repeated expressions of confidence in the "Tenth Legion" and other Democratic strongholds and by recalling the caricatures which the *Richmond Whig* had so thoughtlessly made upon the ignorance and stupidity of the "Suabian Dutch" for refusing to support General Harrison in 1840.[73]

The result was decisive. Polk carried the state by more than five thousand votes. With characteristic modesty, Ritchie attributed the victory to other causes than his own leadership and hastened to Brandon to enjoy it in the midst of his friends. The candidates and the issues doubtless determined the results for the country as a whole, but Father Ritchie's activity was the potent factor in Virginia.

[73] *Ibid.*, October 3, 1844.

CHAPTER IX.

THE NATIONAL SPOKESMAN.

Ritchie neither expected nor desired reward for his part in the political events of 1844. He had power in the South, where he was content to remain, an humble worker in the ranks, striving ever to maintain the ascendency of his beloved Virginia and to keep her right on great national questions. Ever mindful of his friends, he congratulated Polk upon his election and suggested Stevenson for a place in the Cabinet.[1] The fact that this was the second request of the kind ever made by him, proves that Ritchie was actuated on this occasion by motives of pure friendship and not by a desire to assist in dispensing the spoils of office.

But other councils were at work. Robert J. Walker, Aaron V. Brown, and Cave Johnson, who liked the flavor of political plums themselves, had decided that Blair, the editor of the *Globe* and the spokesman of the Democratic party since the days of Andrew Jackson, must go. His long standing hostility to Polk and the lukewarm attitude of the *Globe* in the campaign of 1844 left no difficulty in the way of convincing the President and his other associates of the wisdom of their plan. As the leader of the northern Democrats, Benton and Van Buren desired the retention of Blair as the editor of the party organ, and the expulsion of Calhoun from the Cabinet to make a place for Wright or Flagg of the "Barnburner" faction. On the other hand, southern leaders desired a southern spokesman and the retention of Calhoun. As a way out of the dilemma it was decided to place Ritchie in control of the party organ and to displace Calhoun by Buchanan, who held a semi-neutral position between the factions. The "Barnburners" were, however, to be treated con-

[1] *Polk MSS.*, November 20, 1844.

siderately, and to that end Wright was offered a place in the Cabinet, which he declined.

Thus Ritchie had been drafted without his personal knowledge or consent, and there was grave fear lest he would decline to come to Washington to supersede his old friend Blair. Accordingly Cave Johnson agreed to go to Richmond to see Ritchie personally. Fearing detection on the part of the northern Democrats he delayed his proposed visit and finally gave it up entirely, entrusting the negotiations to Ritchie's close personal friend, General Thomas H. Bayly, a representative in Congress from Virginia. In due time the finances for carrying out the proposed scheme had been provided by Walker's friend, Simon Cameron of Pennsylvania, and Bayly submitted a proposition. For days he and his associates earnestly awaited a reply from the great Democratic editor of the South, who had done so much to make Polk's nomination and election possible.

In the light of his subsequent failures, Ritchie's letter declining Bayly's offers and propositions is interesting as a whole despite its length. It was written from the midst of the Christmas festivities at Brandon and overflowed with love and devotion for Virginia. He wrote as follows:

"BRANDON, December 28, 1844.

"My dear General:

"I did not receive your very kind letter in time for me to answer it from Richmond. And here I am so much pressed with the gaities of a very large and social circle that I am not able to do full justice to the various conditions which induce me to decline the honor that my friends are preparing for me. Your own letter shows how well you know me—although you appreciate any good qualities I may possess much more than they deserve, I am free to say to you, my dear Sir, that tho' misunderstood by others, and the remissness of too many of my subscribers and my necessary inattention to my pecuniary affairs, have placed me and my family in such a situation as would make any improvement in our fortune very desirable. Indeed I have not altogether abandoned the scheme I once confidently communicated to you, viz.: as I jocularly told you to exchange the scepter of Dionysius for the female. I have talked the matter over & over again with my family, and my daughters are willing to do anything which may assist a father's interest. Still I confess to you frankly, I would rather resort to this expedient than undertake the too responsible office which you suggest.

"You refer to the proposition made to me 17 years ago to conduct the official paper under Gen. Jackson's administration. It was made to me jointly by Mr. Van Buren & Mr. Tazewell, in the kindest terms and the most taking form. I remember distinctly the reasons which I assigned for declining it: 1st that I and mine were deeply attached to Virginia and could not willingly leave our kindred and friends, 2nd that I would rather trust myself for support to a gracious people, than be dependent in any manner upon the favor of a Clique, however, respectable, or to the control which might be required over a Government Press, and 3d, that I doubted my qualifications for such an office—and particularly whether at my time of life, I was capable of enduring the physical fatigue and the cares which it would devolve upon me, reminding Mr. Tazewell of the saying of Old Partridge—'*Non suum qualis eram.*' Time, my dear Sir, has weakened not at all the two first arguments and certainly has added strength to the last, for though a gracious Providence has given me a very buoyant constitution, yet I am not equal to everything. There is a point of exertion and even of endurance to which I am not equal. These conditions alone would serve to induce me to decline the offer, but there are others which no wise man could fail to see in the circumstances of the times. I agree with you thoroughly that our party is in imminent danger. We have a strong, dogged, inexorable, indomitable party to encounter, conquered but not subdued, and if they can unite again upon H. Clay they will become more united than ever. On our side of the House we see the elements of discord too freely sown among us. We have scarcely won the victory and are called upon to do our duty, but we find stumbling-blocks in the way. We find Benton like a roaring lion in our path. We find Benton and Calhoun distrusting and opposing each other. I know that Benton does not like me and I am afraid that some of our New York friends are still dissatisfied with the course which Virginia boldly and wisely pursued in May last. With all the precautions which I employed at the time to explain our course to our N. Y. friends and especially to Mr. Van Buren, to whom I was not only politically attached, I shrewdly suspect that the impression still remains that Mr. Van Buren was superseded by an intrigue set on foot at Washington, principally by Mr. Calhoun's friends, and that I was directly or indirectly, a party to the movement. I doubt very much whether under the circumstances I should be the proper person to please and unite the whole party. I have no fear that I should not possess the confidence of Mr. Polk and his intimate friends, but it would not be a wise step to involve me in any of the objections, which these Gentlemen, however misguided *I know they are* and doing sore injustice to me by the very absurd suspicion they may have entertained, may indulge towards myself. And then there is the *Globe.* I could not buy out my friend, if he were even disposed to sell out, and if he continued at the head of the *Globe,* as I have no doubt he wishes to do, there would too easily get up a feeling of dislike and rivalry between the two establishments. The quarrel of the white and the red rose might then be expected and nothing would more strongly contribute to rend the party in twain. Thus, the very scheme you propose to unite and save the party might, more than any other, be the cause of its division and disruption.

"With many and most candid thanks, which you and our friends from Tennessee deserve at my hands, I must most respectfully decline the offer. I will do all I fairly and honorably can to support Mr.

Polk's administration and to keep our party together, but I had better try to do it here than shift the scenes to Washington.

"I am free to say to you that I think our Republican friends who are not altogether satisfied with the course of the *Globe,* ought frankly to tell Blair of it. Such a communication made in the proper spirit might have all the good effects which are desired. He must see as well as I do that Col. Benton is still taking a course to defeat the Administration and to do us much mischief by (*not legible*) and unnerving our party. But if the H. of R. of Missouri should concur with the Senate and defeat him the mischief may be averted, and we shall have much fewer difficulties to encounter. If our friends in Washington think that I could do any good in writing frankly to Mr. Blair, I would willingly undertake the office.

"I beg you to make a discreet use of this very hasty letter, and before I close permit me to recommend to you in the most earnest manner to resist this miserable and shuffling policy of procrastination. Strike home for Texas and for a reduction of the Tariff. The country demands both at our hands. We should be derelict in our duty, if we did not do *all* that our utmost energies can accomplish to secure both." [2]

"With best regards, your friend,

"THOMAS RITCHIE."

Following the refusal of its editor to enter national politics, the editorial tone of the *Enquirer* continued strictly Virginian. At home Ritchie was confronted with the shrewdly devised attempts of a Whig legislature to prevent the annexation of Texas and to bring about the re-lection of W. C. Rives to the federal Senate.[3] The legislature had been elected in May, 1844, when Henry Clay was at the height of his power and before "Polk and Texas" became the issue, and for political reasons it opposed practically everything endorsed by the Democrats. Ritchie pled in vain for a referendum on these questions and also suggested that the people be allowed to vote upon the proposed annexation of Cuba. The opposition remained persistent, sparring at every turn for party advantages. By keeping Texas constantly before the Assembly, Ritchie was able, however, to prevent the re-election of Rives or any other Whig, but he could not bring about the election of a Democrat.

[2] The original of this letter is in the possession of Mrs. George E. Harrison of Brandon, Virginia.

[3] *Richmond Enquirer*, January 7, 14, 21, 24, 1845; *Ibid.*, February 6, 1845.

The annexation of Texas, which occurred in the last days of Tyler's administration, simplified the situation in Virginia. It now mattered little what records a hostile opposition might make. The work had been accomplished, and a stream of praise went up from the *Enquirer* for those who had taken a friendly part in it. Ritchie now demanded a free hand for Polk in the use of the patronage and in the selection of his cabinet. The Oregon question remained to be settled, and the pledge to the people for a reduction of the tariff was to be made good. It was therefore necessary to give the newly elected President a free hand. Evidently this was a warning for the Benton, the Buchanan, and the Calhoun factions.

Buoyant over the annexation of Texas and fully confident that it would put an end to much of the factional discord within the Democratic party, Ritchie launched a war of extermination upon the Whigs in Virginia. Since the annexation of Texas he had received more kindly the repeated proposals for his coming to Washington, but he could not think of leaving the "Old Dominion" in the hands of the enemy. The country had launched upon a new era in which she was to play a part, and a federal senator, a much needed asset to the new administration, was an immediate stake. The response to his leadership was immediate and overwhelming. Forgetting their former affection for Van Buren and their inclination to follow the leadership of New York and Pennsylvania, the Democrats of the western united with those of the eastern counties, whose numbers had already been increased by the accession of "Texas Whigs," in an alliance which swept the state in 1845 and retained undisturbed control until 1861. Hitherto the representation of Virginia in the federal Congress had been almost one-third Whig; now it included a solitary representative of that party.

This Democratic triumph marked a new era in the politics of Virginia. It was the first direct and important result of the Democratic State Convention of February, 1844, when Calhoun's friends had given up his candidacy and reluctantly consented to follow the leadership of Van Buren. Meanwhile epoch-making events had ushered in a new national era, each turn of which had strengthened the Calhoun following. Even in the midst of success, Ritchie had lost to his old time enemies. R. M. T. Hunter, Henry A. Wise, James A. Seddon, William O. Goode, William Smith, and others of their school had never been reckoned as among the political friends of Ritchie, and they were now the leaders in Virginia. Though hesitating to urge it, Ritchie had never denied the ultimate right of a state to secede. Those who now led the Democracy of Virginia not only recognized that right, but in some instances, were anxious to exercise it. The *Richmond Whig* attributed the Whig Waterloo of 1845 to the presence of a "Grouchy in the field," James Lyons, the leader of the "Texas Whigs;"[4] the *Richmond Enquirer* rejoiced over the general result, but found especial joy in the fact that the "Gibraltar of Whiggery," Richmond, had fallen; but the *Charleston* (S. C.) *Murcery* spoke of it as of "the greatest value to the South."[5]

Meanwhile those desirous of bringing Ritchie to Washington had taken new courage. With Texas out of the way, one of his own chief objections to the change had been removed. For a brief time after his first refusal there had been hope that Benton would go "right on Texas," and, with Calhoun out of the Cabinet, it had been thought possible to retain the *Globe*.[6] But Benton did not go right, and in their chagrin at the slight done their own chieftain, the friends of Calhoun, backed by Duff Green, who had himself been displaced by Blair, demanded a new editor. To Walker, Johnson, and Brown their demands, sanctioned as they were by the President, seemed imperative.

Ritchie, however, continued to hesitate and to urge the appointment of his friend Stevenson to a place in the Cabinet. For local reasons he also considered it unwise to offend

[4] *Richmond Enquirer*, April 29, 1845.

[5] *Ibid.*, May 6, 1845.

[6] *Polk MSS.*, A. V. Brown to Polk, January 1, 1845.

the Democrats of western Virginia by displacing Blair, whom they loved as the spokesman of Jacksonian Democracy, which, after all, was the basis of Ritchie's strength in Virginia. Then, too, the practical difficulties which he had already suggested in his first refusal had not been removed. Blair would not sell, and Ritchie could not buy at any price. Besides the proposed change had called forth the fury of General Jackson, now quietly but eagerly watching the movements on the political chess-board from his home at the Hermitage. Though friendly to Polk, the "Old Hero" could not gracefully give up his cherished plan to have Van Buren succeed him in the presidency for eight years and Benton to follow for an equal period. He had plainly told Polk that Blair's removal would be the signal for the complete disruption of the Democratic party.[7] Naturally both Benton and Van Buren shared Jackson's feelings and opinions. Besides there was no assurance that Blair would not continue to edit the *Globe* in any event.[8]

But the Italian hand of Robert J. Walker continued its work. The ravings of "Old Hickory" he completely ignored, and Jackson himself finally advised Blair to sell the *Globe*. Later Wright, Benton, and Van Buren concurred in this advice. An interview was arranged between Blair and Ritchie, who agreed to continue their former friendly relations, happen what would. On his way home, Calhoun stopped in Richmond, dined with Ritchie,[9] and it was believed gave him assurances of his support. Meanwhile Simon Cameron, by a careful manipulation of the federal funds at his disposal, had provided the wherewithal for the purchase of the *Globe;* Blair had agreed to sell; and a business manager in the person of John P. Heiss of Tennessee had been engaged to run the new establishment. What part Walker had

[7] *Van Buren MSS.*, Blair to Van Buren, March 29, 1845.

[8] *Polk MSS.*, Brown to Polk, January 17, 1845; *Ibid.*, Ritchie to Polk, February 17, 1845.

[9] *Richmond Enquirer*, March 14, 1845.

in all these arrangements can not be determined, but that he played the chief part can not be denied.

Under these circumstances Ritchie was invited to Washington for a personal interview with the President. He was made to believe that his services were needed to unite the party and possibly to save the Union, and that he had a clear and friendly field before him. The call came as the call of his country, and nothing remained but to accept.

That the public might know that a new regime had begun in the editorial as well in the political world, Ritchie deemed it expedient to effect a complete change in the character of the party organ. Not only were weekly and semi-weekly issues to be added to the regular daily editions, but these new issues were to be furnished at popular prices. Then, too, the very name of the journal was to be changed, not that there was so much in a name, but that the power and prestige of Blair might sooner be forgotten. To this end the *Washington Enquirer* was at first suggested as a suitable name, but it was finally rejected that the *Richmond Enquirer,* now to be continued under the joint editorship of Ritchie's two sons, might have an independent existence free from all suspicions of outside influence. Various other names were suggested. Finally, after a conference with the "Calhoun men" of Richmond it was agreed to call the new party organ *The Union* and to adopt for its motto, "Liberty, the Union, and our Country," instead of the motto desired by Ritchie, "The Union, it must be preserved."

The "Prospectus" of *The Union* breathed the spirit of the times and could have emanated from none other than a patriot. In the success and preservation of our institutions its author saw a torch which would eventually carry the "flame of Liberty over the Eastern World." In the enterprise fostered by our free institutions he saw the power which was erecting schools, executing canals, building railroads, felling the forests, redeeming the prairies, scattering cities and towns throughout the West, multiplying our population, and doubling the number of our states. Well could he exclaim in the words of the poet:

> "Westward the course of empire takes its way;
> The first four acts already passed;
> A fifth shall close the drama with the day,
> Time's noblest offspring is the last."

With the success and preservation of our free institutions, the extension of discovery, and further conquests of the steam engine, he confidently predicted that the course of empire would continue westward.

After a characteristic recapitulation of his theories regarding the character and nature of our government, Ritchie then came to more practical things. On the subject of the tariff the "Prospectus" was most guarded. It stood only for a "system adjusted on a scale consonant with all the great and varied interests of the Union without sections," looking to a revenue standard only. The rash and meddlesome disposition of the abolitionists to interfere with the great compromises of the constitution were soundly condemned, as calculated to destroy our public counsels and endanger the Union. Regardless of the evident disposition on the part of English journals to ridicule and deprecate our claims to Oregon, he was certain that the President would omit nothing, "demanded by a proper spirit of conciliation, and due regard to the rights and interests of our country," to defend our just claims to that country. With all questions connected with the annexation of Texas finally settled and the tariff system brought to a proper revenue point, he expected a return of tranquillity in the Democratic party, and he, furthermore, let it be known that he came to Washington determined to avoid all remote contests for the succession, pledged to no candidate or clique, prejudiced against no portion of the party, and anxious to extend the right hand of fellowship to every section and to every honest Democrat.

Ritchie's correspondence with his partner regarding the "Prospectus" for their proposed paper is both interesting and instructive, and furnishes a complete justification of the fears entertained by Calhoun and others regarding the attitude of the administration toward the tariff. "You will see," said he, "that of all subjects the tariff is the most difficult." To avoid a storm of protests and a loss of moral force he knew that the subject could not be passed over equivocally. Therefore he spoke "frankly but guardedly, leaving the question of protection, discrimination, the minimum principle, the ad valorem, etc., untouched."[10] In the same connection he later informed Heiss that the tariff was the one question upon which "we," "our friends in Washington," and "especially Mr. Polk and Mr. Walker ought to make up their minds."[11]

These preliminaries settled, the passing courtesies of the retiring and the incoming editor were in order. In an apparently frank and honorable statement, which, however, can be judged better in the light of subsequent developments, Blair expressed unbounded confidence in the "ability, integrity, and patriotism" of the man who was now to preside over the establishment and expressed himself as willing to make any further sacrifices for the "continued union and success of the Democracy."[12] On the other hand, Ritchie praised in the highest terms the "manly and magnanimous and liberal conduct" of Blair and J. C. Rives in transferring the party organ to him, mentioning in particular the liberal terms upon which the transfer had been made. As a double precaution he quoted from Van Buren's letter of April 24th to Rives, in which the former President had also praised the liberal and conciliatory course of his former spokesman, Blair.

Declining a public dinner tendered him by the citizens of Richmond, Father Ritchie now bade adieu to Virginia and to the readers of the *Enquirer*. The characteristic tone of his valedictory is sufficient apology for the following lengthy extracts from it:

"On this day forty-one years ago (9th May, 1804), I appeared before my country as the editor of the *Richmond Enquirer*. The same day

[10] *Polk MSS.*, Ritchie to Hiess, Aprill 13, 1845.
[11] *Ibid.*, April 17, 1845.
[12] *Richmond Enquirer*, April 16, 1845.

of the month, which brought us together, is about to separate us—not in my affections, nor in my principles, but in my person and in the press. My lot is now cast on a different theater. The star of my destiny seems to point, at least for a time, in a different direction—but I can never forget Virginia, or her people. Sooner would my 'right hand forget its cunning;' sooner would my heart forget to beat, than I cease to honor the time-honored Commonwealth—to love the soil where my cradle was rocked, and my coffin will be deposited. She has cherished me in her bosom—trusted me beyond my deserts—and made me what I am. I should indeed be unworthy of bearing the proud name of a Virginian, if I did not carry with me a heart filled with gratitude and overflowing with affection.

"I should have remained with you, altogether, if the interest of those, who are dearer to me than life itself, did not call me away from you. But though the sacrifice is bitter enough—though to part with friends who have been endeared to me by so many years, be one of the bitterest sacrifices which man can make, yet it is imposed upon me by a sense of duty which I cannot control. I shall try not to add to it the sacrifice of the principles which I imbibed almost with my mother's milk.

"It would have given me a pain which I have no words to describe, if I had left my political friends amid disaster and defeat—if the sun of Virginia's glory were at all eclipsed—if, in any respect, the Old Dominion had been wrapped in sackcloth and ashes. Far different, however, is her condition. I leave her in the midst of her triumphs. In November last, she carried out her great principles, in the election of a Republican President by a majority of near six thousand. During the last month she has followed up this victory by another, and one of the most brilliant achievements which has ever graced her annals. The laurel is still green upon her venerable brow—and I can leave her without the slightest suspicion of treachery, or any taint of disgrace. Younger, but not more zealous, hearts—stronger, but not more eager arms, are ready to support her banner. To their prudence, and to their firmness, I commit that portion of the responsibility which has hitherto fallen upon my shoulders.

"I leave the old '*Enquirer*' with feelings similar to those with which the veteran soldier surrenders his arms, but I have the consolation of reflecting, that I not only leave my political associates in the proud possession of the field of battle, but that I transfer my sword to my own sons. I give to them in charge, to defend the post which their father has attempted to guard for forty-one years—to maintain your principles, and to uphold the character of Virginia. On my own account, as well as on theirs, I ask of you to extend to them the same confidence and kindness which you have uniformly given to me. I know they are deeply dyed in the wool of the Republican faith—anxious to serve their country, and I hope competent to discharge the commission which I now entrust to their hands. More I could not ask of you, than to treat them as you have treated me. In a political life of forty-one years, I have probably made some few personal enemies—few, I trust, they are—perhaps few as most men may have made. I have brought, perhaps, some prejudices around the *Enquirer;* but I ask, in the name of charity and justice, visit not my political sins upon my sons.

"It is not necessary for me at this time to recapitulate the articles of my faith. They are your own. They are the same I have professed for so many years. They are the same with those of the present editors of the *Enquirer*, and it is therefore with some confidence that I invoke on their behalf the support of the people.

"Were I to venture to leave with you one piece of advice, of more importance than the rest, it would be to guard with more than vestal vigilance the purity of the right of suffrage. It is the right conservative of all the other rights. Let this precious privilege be corrupted, and you poison Liberty at her very fountain. Destroy this corner-stone of the building, and the whole structure of your political institutions is in danger of falling into ruins.

"Henceforth, my own name will be stricken from the firm of the *Enquirer*, and I leave it to my sons, to make the best arrangements for your interests, as well as their own.

"Eight hours only separate me from my late abode; but I know not how long it will be before my pressing engagements will enable me to breathe, even for a day, the air of Virginia. Yet, I am happy to say, that I find warm hearts on *this* side the Potomac as on *that*—not as many of them, perhaps. I have met with kindness and confidence in the few days during which I have sojourned in the Metropolis. There is full scope and verge enough for any man who wishes to serve his country—great interests to maintain in opposition to the claims of foreign nations—and great power invested in the federal government, for weal or for woe. I find men here willing, I honestly believe, and able, I know, to maintain our rights and our interests—to 'put the government on the Republican track,' and to administer the executive power under the constitution, according to the Jeffersonian standard. I come here prepared to co-operate with such men in the support of such principles: and I trust, when the time of settling up their trusteeship shall arrive, you will not repent of bringing them into power, nor I of exchanging Richmond for Washington. I have political duties to discharge here, that may require all my energies, and almost all my time. Besides, I do not mean to confine '*The Union*' altogether to politics. I should not properly employ the facilities which my position may give to me, if I did not at least attempt to call around me, for the benefit of the *Union*, most of the lights which may be in possession of the government, or which may be obtained through its enlightened agents in foreign parts. It will become the duty of the press to bring the *people of the states* (to whom this government belongs) well acquainted with its transactions, as well as with the events, prospects and views of other countries. How far I may be able to succeed in making the press here a 'brief abstract and chronicle of the times' will depend upon circumstances, which I may not be able to understand or to calculate. I will attempt, however, to do my duty. And one thing more I will attempt to do, which is, if I do not elevate, I will not debase the dignity of the Press—that 'miraculous organ,' to which free government, on an extended scale of empire, is so much indebted for its creation and preservation.

"I cannot close this hasty Valedictory, without again expressing the sentiments of gratitude and affection, with which I am so profoundly penetrated.

Yours faithfully,

"Thomas Ritchie.

"*Washington, D. C.*"

As his valedictory would indicate, Ritchie entered upon the discharge of his new duties with the vigor, ambition, and enthusiasm of a man of half his years. External indications pointed to a brilliant success. He was in charge of one of the greatest presses in the country; training and inclination fitted him for his new position; and his fellow editors applauded his deserved promotion. The *Charleston* (S. C.) *Mercury* thought his selection "far the best choice Mr. Polk has yet made for office," and henceforth began to have a little "generous confidence" in the administration. On the other hand the *Albany Argus,* representing the other extreme of the Democracy, spoke of the choice as the most fortunate that could have been made. Then, too, the spirit of the times inspired confidence in an editor called to this responsible position. The country had said to the newly elected President "carry out your program," which embodied the annexation of Texas and Oregon and contemplated the acquisition of Cuba and Mexico. It was a glorious program, filling all patriotic hearts with the spirit of 1803 and that of 1812, and inspiring the oldest patriots with new enthusiasm and confidence.

In this new position with all its possibilities, Ritchie was a Sampson shorn of his locks. Great in his former sphere, his idiosyncrasy was not national. Both in the North and the South the political thunders continued to rumble, and the old man's strict construction doctrines and constitutional abstractions were placed in the catalogue of provincialisms. Though professing friendship and good wishes for the new editor, Blair confidently expected his arrival in Washington to divide the party on sectional lines "before the middle of the next session."[13] Drafted as a conciliator and pacifier, Ritchie had been too long a free man now to play the role of a politician on a national scale or to assume the livery of a parasite on any scale. He had opinions of his own, a self-respect, and a regard for the rights of the people which made it next to impossible for him to flatter the vanity of officials

[13] *Van Buren MSS.*, Blair to John Van Buren, March 29, 1845.

in high position or to sacrifice principle for personal gain or favor.

Also, there is ample proof that Ritchie did not grasp fully the situation before him. As the "Prospectus" of *The Union* indicates, he looked backward instead of forward. The contests of the future were not to be fought out, as he expected, along old lines or even upon old battlefields. Contrary to expectations the tariff had ceased to be the important issue; the fight for the acquisition of Oregon and Texas was practically won; but new issues, which did not readily admit of compromise, were to be raised in the coming contest between the slave-holding and the non-slaveholding sections. Efforts directed toward a settlement of the differences between free traders and protectionists proved inadequate for a solution of the differences between those who desired free labor and those who desired a monopoly upon labor. But Father Ritchie was not the only man who failed to penetrate the future at this important period of our history, to see that the contest with Mexico would be pressed to the sword's point, and that important consequences would follow, and to realize that the tariff and our boundary disputes were not the most important questions before the country.

Already the signs of more momentous questions could have been read in the contest between the slaveholding and the non-slaveholding portions of the great national churches. The very year that witnessed the election of Polk and ushered in a new political era, the Methodist Church had split from bottom to top on the question of whether a bishop should own slaves. Ritchie regarded such divisions and dissensions as so many links struck off from "the chain which binds the glorious Union," but, like those accustomed to view problems of statecraft from the standpoint of the tariff, banks, and internal improvements, he did not despair of the republic and confidently looked to the good sense of the body politic to bear safely the ark of the covenant.[14]

Ritchie's first task as an editor was to win the northern

[14] *Washington Union*, May 15, 1845.

Democrats, because the impression yet lingered that both he and the President were the creations of the "Calhoun faction." In his selection of Buchanan over Calhoun to be Secretary of State, the selection of Marcy to be Secretary of War, and Bancroft to be Secretary of the Navy, his chieftain had already taken a long step in the direction of conciliation. It remained for Ritchie, as his spokesman, to aid in the further wooing. Accordingly *The Union* defended earnestly our claims to the "whole of Oregon" and said little about Texas, except to give the doubtful assurance that Benton and Van Buren had each acquiesced in its annexation, though they could not approve the methods by which it had been made.[15] Furthermore, Ritchie denied the report of Dame Rumor to the effect that he was committed to Calhoun for the succession, and he called both James A. Seddon and R. M. T. Hunter, leaders of the Calhoun following in Virginia, to testify to his truthfulness.[16] As a last precaution he visited Blair in his country home at Silver Spring, Maryland, and returned to praise the hospitality and the amiable qualities of his predecessor. So far did the pendulum swing in the direction of the North that *The Union* was currently reported to favor Van Buren for the succession.[17]

In trying to please the North, Ritchie naturally offended the South. His conciliatory attitude won his election to the office of public printer by a practically unanimous vote of the Democrats in Congress, but it was evident, even before Congress met in December, 1845, that his mission of reconciliation would be unsuccessful. Calhoun remained distrustful of Polk's attitude on the tariff, and was willing to compromise our claims to Oregon. On the other hand, the North did not like the indefinite statement of the Prospectus of *The Union* on the Oregon question and was conse-

[15] *Washington Union*, May 5, 1845; August 4, 1845; *Ibid.*, September 4, 1845; *Ibid.*, November 17, 1845.

[16] *Ibid.*, December 2, 1845.

[17] *Ibid.*, May 22, 1845.

quently distrustful of the administration. The introduction of the resolution providing for a notice of termination of the Convention of 1827 whereby we held Oregon in joint occupation with England, brought matters to a crisis. Without urging our claims to 54° 40′ Ritchie tried to advise and to scold the Senate into passing the resolution, insisting that such a course would not be followed by war with England and that it was necessary to protect and defend our just rights.[18] But Calhoun and his small following remained deaf to those tactics which had appalled the Assembly of Virginia. In due time a characteristic assault was made upon Calhoun. When the desired resolution finally passed both houses of Congress in face of his opposition, Ritchie was exultant.[19] He spoke of the event as an epoch-making incident in our history, which would fix the eyes of Europe upon us and stand as an eternal reproach to those who had opposed it. The result was immediate. The followers of Calhoun could now strike the President through his spokesman, Ritchie, who was frequently reminded that he was not running Congress.

Fearing that his course, as an editor, would defeat their plans for acquiring Oregon or any part of it by alienating Calhoun and possibly precipitating a foreign war, northern leaders took alarm. Ignorant of all the circumstances surrounding Blair's removal and of Polk's well-founded objections to the *Globe,* Senator Allen of Ohio and Secretary Buchanan called upon the President to tell him of the intense dissatisfaction with Ritchie and to ask that Blair be associated with him as joint editor of *The Union.* Allen was confident that "Ritchie could not get five votes out of the Calhoun faction in either house of Congress." The President took no alarm, however, and assured his callers that Ritchie was honest and actuated by no other desire than to serve the Democratic party. It was true that the old man made mistakes, but it was also true that he was ready and

[18] *Washington Union,* January 7, 12, 29, 1846.
[19] *Ibid.,* March 25, 1846; *Ibid.,* April 23, 1846.

willing to rectify them. Failing to enlist the sympathy of the President, the dissatisfaction continued, and finally led to a movement to set up an independent press with Blair as its editor. Senator Cass agreed with Polk that such a course would not only defeat the ends of the northern leaders, but that it would also result in a disruption of the Democratic party. Accordingly he and other leaders arrested the movement and turned their energies to the task of making Ritchie a more acceptable editor.[20]

The politicians had a difficult task, because Ritchie was not of the malleable type. Nor is it at all certain that his chieftain now desired him to be all things to all men. With a foreign war upon his hands and the prospect for an extension of the South's boundary to the Pacific, and with Oregon not yet won, he saw his only chance of maintaining union and accord between the factions in adhering to a semi-independent course in dealing with each. Accordingly Ritchie continued to defy England, now even to the point of the sword, and he made bold to read the *Charleston* (S. C.) *Mercury* out of the party,[21] as a print that was unfriendly to the greatest interest of the West at a time when it was ready to unite with the South to procure a reduction of the hated tariff. Thus by adhering to the middle ground he hoped not only to save the party but also to work for a greater Union.

The sound of the war trumpet temporarily diverted attention from Ritchie and gave him a free opportunity to give expression to that patriotism with which his soul continually overflowed. In reply to an editorial of the *London Times* commenting upon the fact that the United States had no standing army and that she could not therefore carry on a successful war with Mexico, he assured the hated Englishmen that volunteers would start up like Cadmus' men from the sowing of the dragon's teeth to fight our battles, that a bugle sound in the West and the Southwest would call forth thousands of men who would go forward with the cry "West-

[20] *Polk's Diary*, I., 350-361.

[21] *Washington Union*, May 1, 6, 1846.

ward Ho," and that Americans would not only take the capital of Mexico in a single campaign, but would carry their wives and children to the region of Santa Fe in one season and to Colorado and California in the next.[22] This was the brand of patriotism which had deposed Van Buren, won Texas, and stood ready to fight for Oregon and California.

Ritchie did not long find protection under the war cloud, which at no time became menacing or interrupted the progress of ordinary legislation. His caustic editorials on Oregon had sunk deep into the memories of southerners, and their untimeliness and boldness had alienated those whom they were meant to serve. Henceforth he was a marked man; a scapegoat for Polk; and a football for the politicians. Calhoun opposeed the manner of conducting the war with Mexico, and the North remained indifferent to it. But as its staunch defender Ritchie made many enemies and few friends.

From a settlement of the Oregon question and its preparation for the war with Mexico, Congress proceeded immediately to a discussion of the tariff. Ritchie followed cautiously. In lenghty editorials overflowing with the teachings of the classical school of political economists he exploded the protectionist theories and sustained a revenue tariff, but he now, as in the past, found a practical way out of the difficulty by accepting the compromise tariff of 1846. He saw in this bill a complete triumph for the Democratic party and the long desired union between the West and the South for the benefit of agriculture, but he did not fail to give credit to the Democrats of the Middle and New England states, who had supported it. In the affirmative votes from Pennsylvania he professed to see a return of the day when the Keystone State and the Old Dominion would be united again as of old.[23]

Generalizations and pleas for conciliation and compromise did not conceal the fact that the tariff of 1846 was not

[22] *Washington Union*, June 9, 1848.

[23] *Washington Union*, July 8, 1846.

merely a revenue tariff. Accordingly it found favor neither in the North nor in the South, and in supporting it Ritchie made almost as many enemies as he had made in discussing the Oregon question. Calhoun's predictions had come true. In the moment of her triumph, as in 1832, the South was again betrayed in the house of her friends for the sake of the party. Some of her leaders saw a return of the day, when, under the leadership of Ritchie, Virginia, Pennsylvania, and New York would again control their party for the spoils of office and the advancement of their favorites. Discouraged at the prospects, Yancey withdrew from Congress, vowing his purpose never again to attend another Democratic convention.[24] On the other hand, Blair, Benton, and the Van Burens were exultant; subscriptions to *The Union* were discontinued; and reports came thick and fast of how Ritchie's ardor for free trade was disrupting the Democratic party in Pennsylvania and other northern states.[25]

At no time in our history have politicians been over scrupulous in the selection of their sacrifices. Polk had disappointed all parties on the tariff, and some atonement had to be made. The lot fell to Ritchie without even the formality of the usual casting. This time the way was to be paved for a rival independent press in Washington by first providing a financial basis for it. The opportunity came when Garrett Davis of Kentucky, a Whig, wishing to strengthen his own party and to widen the breach within the Democratic party, introduced a resolution to let the public printing to the lowest bidder. The dissatisfied Democrats seized the proposition with avidity, defending it as a means of putting the public printing upon a non-partisan basis and of emancipating the executive from the clutches of the editors. The resolution finally became law and did have wholesome effects, but it was enacted to humiliate and embarrass Thomas Ritchie, at a time when he stood for the interests of

[24] *Washington Union*, August 11, 1846.
[25] *Ibid.*, July 28, 1846.

the whole country as opposed to those of any particular sections. His offence was a too ardent devotion to the interests of his party. In the nomenclature of this day he was a "standpatter."

Ritchie accepted this mark of disfavor with that composure which comes only from confidence. After assuring the public that he was no interloper, having been invited to Washington in 1804 and again in 1827 to become the editor of the national Democratic organ, his plans for putting the press upon a more popular basis and divorcing it from complete dependence upon the government were carried into execution. The daily *Union* was now offered at $10 per year, the semi-weekly at $5, and the weekly at $2. Besides a *Congressional Register* resembling the present *Congressional Record,* but published only weekly, was promised to the public.[26] Thus not only the government, but the press as well profited in the long run by the exigencies of this occasion.

The adverse results of the autumnal elections of 1846 only complicated Ritchie's difficulties. Instead of attributing their defeats to other and more potent factors, the disappointed politicians traced them to the unwise leadership of "Old Nous Verrons," as Ritchie was now contemptuously called by Blair and others. Naturally many of "the wise" returned to the next session of Congress resolved to rectify Polk's mistake in the selection of a spokesman for their party. The contemplated withdrawal of the public printing was not enough, he was to be driven completely from his position of leadership.

Not ignorant but fearless and firm in his conviction of the justness and wisdom of the causes in which he fought, Ritchie remained defiant. The unpatriotic equivocation of Calhoun and the political designs of Benton were alike disgusting to him, and he continued to urge a vigorous and unrelenting prosecution of the war with Mexico. He spoke of the *National Intelligencer,* which opposed that course, as

[26] *Washington Union,* July 1, 11, 1846; *Ibid.,* August 7, 1846.

the Mexican paper in the federal capital, and Calhoun and his followers in the Senate were classed among the "friends, compatriots, and fellow soldiers" of Santa Anna and Ampudia. The crisis came, when immediately following the defeat of the "Ten Regiment Bill" their appeared in *The Union* a communication signed "Vindicator" and entitled "Another Mexican Victory." In no unmistakable references to Calhoun this writer described the battles then waging in Congress in behalf of the Mexicans and pled for a more genuine and unselfish patriotism.[27]

Smarting under the attack of "Vindicator," and thinking that his utterances had been inspired by the President, Calhoun and his small personal following in the Senate, now called the "balance of power party," did not hesitate to reply. On the day following "Vindicator's" appearance, Senator Yulee of Florida introduced the following resolutions, which the balance of power party, composed of the two Senators from South Carolina and the two Senators from Florida, aided by the Whigs, were able to pass:

> *Resolved*, That the editors of the *Union*—a newspaper published in the city of Washington—having in a publication contained in a number of that paper, dated the 9th of February, issued and published a public libel upon the character of this body, be excluded from the floor of the Senate.
>
> "That the report of the proceeding of the Senate of the 8th day of February in relation to the bill entitled 'An act to raise, for a limited time, an additional military force, and for other purposes,' is partial and unjust to this body and that the reporters for that paper be excluded for the residue of the session from a place in the gallery of the Senate."[28]

The debate which followed the introduction of the above resolutions affords ample proof of Ritchie's abilities and of the high esteem in which he was held. Senator Allen of Ohio, who had desired his removal only one year before, now threatened the Senate with an unfriendly visitation of the sovereign power of the people should they see "the hands

[27] *Washington Union*, February 13, 1847.

[28] *Cong. Globe*, 29th Cong., 2d sess., p. 366.

of Fifty-six Senators clinched in the gray hairs of Thomas Ritchie," should they be forced to witness a cowardly and unnecessary assault upon "an old man, almost twice as old as the Senate itself."[29] Sevier of Arkansas thought the resolutions unnecessary to protect the dignity of the Senate, and predicted that the result would be a "Ritchie victory," if not a "Mexican victory,"[30] and Turney of Tennessee saw in them simply a revolt against an honest effort to fix responsibility where it belonged and against the freedom of the press.

The resolutions were defended on the undemocratic ground that the Senate had the same right to protect itself in its home that a private individual had to protect himself in his home. Any intention of an attack upon the freedom of the press was disclaimed, as were all feelings of political animosity. Equally ridiculous and ludicrous with these declarations was a denial on the part of Calhoun that he was then or ever had been a candidate for the presidency, and that he entertained personal feelings toward Ritchie.[31]

The reflections of Van Buren's friends upon Ritchie's predicament were more amusing than instructive. They show an utter incapacity to understand the importance of Texas and to concede to others honesty and sincerity in politics. Silas Wright had already discovered a rebuke for Ritchie in the election of Hunter to represent Virginia in the federal Senate, but he now saw in Ritchie's expulsion from the press privileges of that body a "retributive justice" for the wrongs done Van Buren in 1844. He, also, observed that in every crisis Ritchie had allowed his fears to drive him "off in a tangent" from which his personal fidelity had eventually brought him back "weak and wound, and powerless." Accordingly, he now confidently expected his return to his first love, Van Buren, and as a relief to "the good old

[29] *Cong. Globe*, 29th Cong., 2d sess., p. 392.

[30] *Ibid.*, 395.

[31] *Ibid.*, 395-417.

man," Wright now magnanimously considered renewing his subscription to the *Enquirer,* which he had not seen since 1844.[32] John C. Rives, former business manager of the defunct *Globe,* jocularly compared Ritchie's situation to that of the father and son who, to avoid the jeers of the crowd, had carried their jackass to market instead of both riding him, and had been rewarded by even greater criticisms.[33] Meanwhile Blair confidently expected Van Buren to be the Democratic nominee for the presidency in 1848, and looked forward to the re-establishment of the *Globe* with himself as editor.

Following a complete disavowal of all responsibility for "Vindicator" on the part of the President, Ritchie launched a characteristic attack upon the Senate. He regarded his expulsion as a cowardly attack upon the administration and as an outrage upon the rights of the press, and he invited the people to rally to a defence of their constitutional rights. Calhoun was described as the ambitious leader of a "little clique professing to belong to the Democratic party." He defied both him and his followers, and appealed to the people to right his wrongs. "They will not," said he, "desert the cause. What becomes of us is of little account. We are but atoms in a powerful community of twenty millions of people." In large black letters he printed the names of A. P. Butler, John C. Calhoun, James D. Westcott, and David L. Yulee, Democrats who had voted for the resolutions of expulsion, on the front page of *The Union,* together with the resolutions for which they had voted.

Whatever his attitude toward others, it was now evident that Ritchie would not support Calhoun for the succession. Accordingly northern leaders began to share the opinions entertained by Silas Wright and to hope for a renomination for Van Buren. Polk had pledged himself not to seek a re-

[32] *Van Buren MSS.*, Wright to Van Buren, January 28, 1847; *Ibid.*, April 14, 1847.

[33] *Van Buren MSS.*, Wright to Van Buren, January 28, 1847; *Ibid.*, Rives (J. C.) to Van Buren, May 12, 1847; *Ibid.*, Blair to Van Buren, July 7, 1847.

election; Texas had been won; the war with Mexico was on the point of a successful termination; and it was generally conceded that an old-time alliance between the northern and southern Democrats was all that could save them in 1848. Thus they saw no reason for a refusal to return to the days of Jacksonian Democracy. In his adherence to the national nominating convention, now attacked by Calhoun as an undesirable method of selecting candidates for the presidency, in his pleas for accord within the party, and in the persistency of his attacks upon the "prince of nullifiers," the northern leaders now scented the return of Father Ritchie to those halcyon days.

Although there was no evidence of a turning to Van Buren, Calhoun's treatment of Ritchie and his course in general met with disapproval in Virginia, and for a time rendered uncertain the hold of his followers upon the state. In many instances where avowed Calhoun men presented themselves as candidates for Congress and the Assembly in 1847 they were successfully opposed by administration candidates. This was true in the Richmond district, where James A. Seddon and W. D. Leake were candidates for Congress. The regular nomination went to the former, but, with only two dissenting votes, the convention adopted the following resolution: "That in the nomination of Mr. Seddon this convention does protest against its being considered as giving, directly or indirectly, any color of approval to the political course of the Hon. J. C. Calhoun, or any pledge to support him for the presidency." Seddon, always an ardent follower of Calhoun, considered this resolution a reflection upon his course and resigned his candidacy.[34] The nomination then went to Leake, but, as in most cases, where similar lines were drawn, the Whig candidate was successful at the polls. Such experiences had the effect of riveting more firmly the hold of the pro-southern statesmen upon Virginia, because it had become impossible for the Democrats to win without them.

[34] *Washington Union,* April 3, 1847.

In another, yet a most important field, Ritchie seemed willing to co-operate with the North. Calhoun's schemes for uniting the South and connecting it with the West by a network of internal communications had long been known to the leading statesmen of both sections. The political, commercial, and industrial possibilities of such a South were beyond conception. They might enable Calhoun to reach the coveted presidency. They would certainly divert the lines of trade from the North and from the central waterways of Virginia. The only way to counteract them was at once to bind the West by arteries of trade to the East. Accordingly a convention met in Chicago, July 5, 1847, to devise means for improving the navigation of the rivers and lakes in that region and for connecting the upper Mississippi valley with the Oregon country. Letters sympathetic with the movement were read on this occasion from Clay, Van Buren, Benton, and Wright. Later Ritchie spoke enthusiastically of the proceedings and seems to have been willing to brush aside his scrpules regarding the power of Congress over internal improvements with a mere reference to former decisions, vetoes, speeches, and state papers. He now admitted that it involved a "doubtful power" and that there was much well-founded "difference of opinion" on the constitutional power of the general government over internal improvements. Evidently he was again ready to "conciliate and compromise." The problems of our greater nationality had necessitated a growth in the organic law, which could be made only in the spirit of compromise. To what extent Ritchie was actuated by hostility to the schemes of Calhoun, the desire to protect the interests of the Border, a desire to co-operate with the North, or the spirit of nationalism which characterized the epoch can not be determined.

Developments in the North soon made it impossible, however, for Ritchie to co-operate with its leaders in anything. A more momentous question than the tariff, or the freedom of the press, or individual rights, that of the extension of slavery into the territories, was now engaging the attention of its people. It had become evident that they would not give up the principles of the Wilmot Proviso. Other efforts at conciliation were attempted. Ritchie being readmitted to the privileges of the floor of the Senate and entrusted with the editorship of a special organ, *The Campaign,* established to fight for the presidency in 1848. But the Herkimer convention with its radical resolutions upon the subject of negro slavery and the power and duty of Congress to exclude that institution from the territories and the persistency of the abolitionists, as seen in the ecclesiastical and political gatherings at the North, forced Ritchie to beat a retreat in the direction of the pro-slavery camp. At the first mention of the Wilmot Proviso he had calmly suggested that it would be time enough to govern and administer our territories after they had been acquired. Later he had proposed the extension of the line of the Missouri Compromise, as a suitable boundary between slavery and freedom in all newly acquired territory. But the increasing bitterness of the abolitionists in their attacks upon the South, their unreasonable demands regarding the exclusion of slave property from the common territory, and their boldness in shouldering the abolitionist propaganda upon Thomas Jefferson, brought from Ritchie a vigorous defence of the rights of the slave owner in the common territory and a flat denial that the Sage of Monticello was not at the time of his death in sympathy with negro slavery as it existed in the South.

Blows now fell upon the venerable editor from another direction. Following the cue of the *New York Evening Post,* the northern prints insisted that *The Union* had become a pro-slavery organ. The defeat of the Democratic candidates in the autumnal elections of 1847 in New York were attributed to its changed attitude. In February, 1848, David Wilmot rose in his place in the House and demanded the retirement of the "old man," then "in his second childhood," for a more impartial and disinterested spokesman.[35]

[35] *Cong. Globe,* 30th Cong., 1st sess., p. 182.

Defeated and disappointed, Ritchie was ready, in May, 1848, to surrender all and to retire to his beloved Virginia;[36] but other councils prevailed and he remained. From this point things went from bad to worse. The Barnburners, Freesoilers, and other third parties held conventions and nominated separate candidates for the presidency; Van Buren himself accepted the nomination of the Freesoil party; and the Democracy which Ritchie had come to Washington to unite and preserve was rapidly going to pieces, and that, too, at a time when there was every necessity for unity and strength.

From the very beginning Ritchie despaired of success in the presidential campaign of 1848. That valiant leader, Lewis Cass, a northern man with southern principles, whom Ritchie himself had preferred for the presidency in 1844, could not inspire confidence. With the Democratic vote of New York divided between Cass and Van Buren, Ritchie knew that there was little chance for his favorite. Experience had taught him to attach a high value to that vote in presidential contests. In a reminiscent mood he referred to Van Buren's former wooings of the South, reviewed the incidents of 1844, and pronounced a well done upon his own patriotic course in deserting him. Thus prepared he went down, "defeated but not daunted, beaten but not overwhelmed."

[36] *Van Buren MSS.*, Blair to Van Buren, May 23, 1848.

CHAPTER X.

THE GREAT COMPROMISE.

Though honored and respected for his venerable services and sterling character, Ritchie did not always share the complete confidence of his political chieftain. His intense desire to appear to others as the real spokesman of the administration and his mania for publicity made it difficult, and at times, impossible for him to keep a secret.[1] These traits greatly annoyed the President who, however, attributed them to habits of the editorial profession and not to defects of character in his spokesman. To complaining politicians he defended Father Ritchie, insisting that he always meant well. Thus Polk made it possible for the party organ to retain its place as the representative of his own following and as the spokesman of his party through the stormy days of the Great Compromise and after he himself had retired.

As spokesman of the minority, Ritchie's trials and troubles were not lessened. In the very midst of the campaign in which his party had gone down to defeat, the debate on the question of establishing a territorial government for Oregon had again brought into review the whole subject of negro slavery. The leadership of Lewis Cass had failed to reconcile the sections and even to produce accord within his own party. At the North there were Democrats who desird to apply the Northwest Ordinance of 1787 to Oregon, and at the South there were those, led by Calhoun, Davis, and others, who insisted upon the constitutional right of Congress to protect and defend the slave-holder in the possession of his property in the common territory. The enactment of the bill excluding slavery from Oregon was the be-

[1] *Polk's Diary*, III., 237, 474; *Ibid.*, IV., 214-216.

ginning of another great crisis. Before Calhoun's mournful prophecy, "The great strife between the North and the South is ended" could become true another political contest was to be waged between the sections, and Ritchie, as the spokesman of the conservatives of the Border, was again to be harrassed and cajoled by the warring factions entrenched in the extreme North and the extreme South.

When Congress met in December, 1848, it heard in Polk's optimistic message, which Ritchie had already approved, simply an ardent plea for peace and accord within the party. But there was to be no peace. Exultant over their victory in the contest for Oregon and armed with resolutions from their state legislatures endorsing the Wilmot Proviso and demanding the exclusion of slavery and the slave trade from the District of Columbia, the North had returned to the national councils resolved to fight the further extension of slavery, cost what it would. Alarmed because of their previous defeats and concessions and because of the aggressiveness of their rivals the representatives of the lower South, aided by recruits from other parts of the slave-holding section, had also returned resolved to fight for a perpetual franchise over the labor of negroes, which, they said, was guaranteed them by the constitution. Thus, standing on the constitution they demanded their "bond" regardless of the principles involved and the possibility of compromise. The necessity for a regular government for California and her subsequent request for statehood had precipitated the fray, and it was evident that the peaceful councils advised by the retiring President and his venerable spokesman would not prevail.

Contrary to his usual course, Ritchie did not face squarely the demands of either section. Formerly he had favored the extension of the line of the Missouri Compromise as a solution of the slavery question, but he now advised the immediate admission of California without requiring her to pass through the territorial stage, and with full power to determine for herself whether or not slavery would exist within her borders. Circumstances made delay impossible.

In the immediate admission of California to statehood, Ritchie saw defeat for any movement looking to an independent republic on the Pacific, also the impossibility of a repetition of the foreign complications experienced in our dealings with Texas. Such a course would also make a revival of the Wilmot Proviso impossible and make it unnecessary to compromise the honor and dignity of the South. Besides it would then be unnecessary to debate the conflicting theories regarding the power of Congress over slavery in the territories.

Although willing to dodge the real issue in dealing with California, Ritchie's sympathies were with the South. He thought, however, that additional constitutional guarantees, later demanded by Calhoun, were unnecessary and did not take kindly to the suggestions for a dual federal executive. In their mad haste for power and ascendency and conscious of the embryonic nationality of their respective sections, the leaders of the extreme North and the extreme South had long calculated the value of the Union, and in so doing had lost confidence in the constitution. But Ritchie, like most of the leaders in the Border and like those who had ordained and established the federal government, saw in the strict interpretation of that document full security for the guaranteed rights of the South and for the perpetuity of the Union of the fathers. He found in the conservatism of the Border the leaven which was to destroy two prospective nationalities for the preservation of a greater nationality. Consequently he did not even now despair of the republic. There was yet security for all in "the Rights of the States and the Union of the States."

Adherence to the letter of the constitution did not, however, preclude possibilities of compromise. Ritchie's theory of the nature of the federal government had been wrought out at the time it was made and in a spirit of conciliation and compromise, later to be fostered by the genial influences of a conservative environment, the great Border section. He did not now understand why new problems involving the national life and security could not be met and solved in the same spirit. To-day centralization is the slogan of greater nationality; with Ritchie that slogan was compromise. He regarded good faith, kindness, and forbearance as necessary for the preservation of the federal compact, and held him a traitor who assumed a different attitude. He could understand Calhoun and Davis who would have been satisfied with the letter of the law, but, in the light of the great compromises upon which the Union was founded and the long struggle to maintain them, the attitude of Garrison and Seward was beyond his conception. In answer to the charge, now frequently made, that he had become the spokesman of a section instead of a great political party, he reiterated his devotion to the constitution with all its compromises, which he insisted were as old as the government itself and as dear to all real patriots.[2]

Liberal concessions in regard to California intermingled as they were with pleas for a strict interpretation of the constitution, did not satisfy all the leaders of the North. Of California they were reasonably certain, and they had already identified strict construction with a defence of negro slavery. After a caucus attended by fifty or more members of Congress and encouraged and abetted by interested pressmen, Senator Allen of Ohio waited upon the venerable editor, then in his seventy-second year, to express dissatisfaction with his course in general and with his pro-slavery leanings in particular.[3] Of this interview Blair, who was always jealous of Ritchie and never free from a desire to supersede him, said: "Ritchie remonstrated, wept, and at times defied—said he would stand no matter what happened—that he meant not only to maintain his press here during his life, but would leave it to his son as a successor."[4] After agreeing to associate with himself Edmund Burke, as joint editor of *The Union,* Ritchie was retained as the

[2] *Washington Union,* January 13, 20, 27, 1849.

[3] *Polk MSS.,* Cave Johnson to Polk, March 17, 1849.

[4] *Van Buren MSS.,* Blair to Van Buren, March 4, 1849.

LOWER BRANDON

spokesman of the party, but dissatisfaction with his course never ceased.[5]

The proposed admission of California brought prominently to the front the subject of internal communication. Already, as seen in the deliberations of the Chicago Convention of 1847 and in the gigantic schemes of Calhoun, leaders of the rival sections were calculating the advantages to be derived from connecting their own growing nations with the great West. That the interests of the whole country might be served more patriotic spirits would have connected the Atlantic and the Pacific by a canal crossing the Isthmus of Panama or the Isthmus of Tehuantepec. But all recognized that the day when the iron horse would cross the Rockies was near at hand. No power could keep the immigrant out of the West, national ownership of which had necessitated a sectional contest for its control.

True to his ideals of a greater nationality for the whole country, Ritchie endorsed the "grand idea" of bringing China to our door. Since this great task involved the rights and interests of the sections, even the existence of the slaveholding power itself, it too, like the other great questions which had confronted the fathers in 1787, was to be undertaken in a spirit of conciliation and compromise. In such a solution the constitution was to find adjustment to the demands of a growing and changing nationality. The acquisitions of 1845, 1846, and 1848 had inspired a feeling of true national greatness which even the constitution could not be permitted to retard. True, Ritchie, like Jefferson in 1803, preferred a constitutional amendment to meet the exigencies. In lieu of that he was now willing to invoke the true spirit of the constitution, the only liberal construction known to a strict constructionist, the spirit of compromise, as a solution of the difficulty and as a guarantee of the rights of all.

These conditions and these facts made it possible for Ritchie to face the facts boldly. Accordingly he suggested

[5] *Washington Union*, June 2, 1849; *Polk MSS.*, Ritchie to Polk, April 10, 1849.

routes for three trans-continental railways: one to connect the southern point of Lake Michigan with the mouth of the Columbia river, another to connect St. Louis and Monterey, and still another to connect New Orleans with some point farther south on the Pacific. The fact that he had fought for both Oregon and Texas and that he would have waged international war for 54° 40′ almost as readily as for the Rio Grande boundary, made a preference of routes impossible.[6]

Thus far Ritchie had spoken the sentiments of President Polk, which he himself most heartily endorsed. But Polk had retired, Congress had adjourned without admitting California, and the South, as a last resort, was trying to enlarge the slave-holding territory by adding a part of New Mexico to Texas. The contest between the sections was to continue and even to increase in bitterness. Both at the North and the South Democrats demanded a more clear-cut statement of principles by their editor. Accordingly he now declared for the policy of non-intervention, fathered by the new leader of the party, Lewis Cass of Michigan. By non-intervention Ritchie denied to Congress the expediency of legislating upon the subject of negro slavery in the territories and reserved to the people thereof the right to determine the regulations and laws under which they became states.

Ritchie had not, however, ceased to be a compromiser. This declaration had simply placed him in accord with the dominant element of the Democratic party without changing his principles. Non-intervention was in full accord with his ideas of government, and it offered a possibility of removing the contest for the new West from the legislative halls to the federal courts. Besides, acceptance of this policy might bring about a life-long ideal, party unity.[7]

The months immediately following this declaration marked a period that tried men's souls. The opinion was general that the next session of Congress would either save

[6] *Washington Union*, April 17, 1849.

[7] *Ibid.*, June 9, 1849.

or destroy the Union. All parties groomed for the contest. A convention of southern members issued an address in which they complained of the difficulty of recovering fugitive slaves and of the action of the abolitionists, demanded the right of immigrating into the territories with their slave property, and inveighed against the action of the House in attempting to exclude slavery from California and New Mexico. The legislature of Virginia had no difficulty in selecting a course between submission to the Wilmot Proviso and resistance to federal aggression, and feeling ran at fever heat in the cotton states. In the North feeling ran equally high. State legislature after legislature put itself on record in resolutions defending the power and duty of Congress to prohibit slavery in the territories and urging it to abolish the "curse" in the District of Columbia. Party lines were broken down and little heed was paid to time-honored party principles. With each succeeding day the political horizon became darker, and, when Congress met in December, 1849, echoes of the gathering storm resounded from the federal capital.

Under such conditions no political editor who attempted to maintain a neutral position could escape attack. There was no neutrality. Northern leaders continued to regard Ritchie as pro-southern, and the South could not find in him a safe custodian of its rights and interests. Of the trials of this period Ritchie himself said: "Never did my poor bark weather so fearful a tempest."[8] But he rejoiced, and succeeding ages my rejoice with him, that the bark rode the storm and emerged "with the flag of the Union still flying." In the time of a great crisis, the greatest that he had ever seen, Father Ritchie, now the spokesman of Jefferson and Madison, had risen to his greatest stature.

The meting of Congress brought the expected crisis, but Ritchie was ready. On the very day that Clay came forward with his first set of resolutions looking to a compromise

[8] *Richmond Enquirer*, September 10, 1852.

of the differencies between the sections, Ritchie disappointed the "fire-eaters" of the lower South and the "fanatics" of the North by throwing the power of *The Union* for conciliation. Following a review of our struggle for independence, of the conciliatory and compromising spirit which had made the federal government possible, and of the blessings which had flowed from the Union, he pictured a glorious future for our republic, "rising on a new continent—stripped of the antique prejudices and the aristocratic privileges which defaced the ancient world—with an immense surface of young and unappropriated land, capable of supporting a teeming population and of furnishing an asylum to all the oppressed emigrants of Europe—abounding in rivers and sea-coast, and all the facilities of commerce and manufactures—blessed with liberty—and, on all these accounts, productive of an energy and character which has never been equaled by the proudest republic of antiquity, and of an ingenuity and enterprise which are calculated to advance the improvement of the country to an indefinite extent." Then he issued a call for patriots, men whose spirits were equal to the storm which threatened the nation, who would sacrifice office for the good of their country and die for the fatherland. The editorial closed with the assurance that there were Suffolks in Congress, who, like the English statesman of that name, would deem themselves unworthy of the name, if asked to ward off an impending blow to their country.[9]

One week later Clay began his great speech in favor of the compromise resolutions. Ritchie praised his motives and many of his utterances, but could not approve his plan for excluding slavery from the new territory by extending the laws of Mexico to it, on the ground that they were already the laws which governed it. He searched in vain for a concession to the South in such a proposition, and then assured Clay that it could not be palmed off as a compromise.[10] Then by a shrewd use of those arts of which he was master,

[9] *Richmond Enquirer*, September 10, 1852.
[10] *Ibid.*

those arts which gave him his political power, Ritchie began to cast about for "clearer," more "generous," and more "intrepid" spirits than Clay who could be relied upon to save the Union. With an eye upon the great man whom he professed to be abandoning, he assured the public that there were other men in Congress "who have the ability and patriotism to risk themselves for the glorious Union—who, like Curtius, would plunge into the fiery gulf for the salvation of this country!"

At this jucture Clay realized that he could accomplish little without Ritchie's assistance. Accordingly he expressed a desire to confer with his old-time assailant. As all intercourse between them had long ceased, and as they were each recognized leaders of opposing parties, extreme caution was necessary in effecting a meeting. Through the kindness of a mutual friend, James W. Simonton, it was finally arranged for Ritchie, accompanied by General Thomas H. Bayly of Virginia, to call upon Clay in his rooms in the National Hotel at 4 P. M. on Sunday, February 10th. The meeting was cordial, and began by pleasant references to the old days in Richmond, when they had attended the same frolics and paid court to the same ladies. Although the *Enquirer* had been his most bitter assailant when he had sought the coveted presidency, Clay assured Ritchie that he had never ceased to read it and to be interested in its editor.

After a short conference, both were convinced that nothing but patriotic motives had brought them together. Accordingly they proceeded at once to a discussion of the compromise resolutions. Clay defended them as originally proposed, but at length he agreed to strike the provision regarding the Mexican law from them and to insert instead a provision leaving it to the territories to decide for themselves whether or not they would have slavery. Through a mutual friend, Senator Foote of Mississippi, Ritchie had already suggested to Clay the reference of the whole matter to a special committee of thirteen. Now, as a means of effecting the proposed changes in the original resolutions, he renewed his suggestion which Clay received with favor and later accepted.[11] After discussing the claims of Texas to a part of New Mexico, the necessity for a more stringent fugitive slave law, the expediency of abolishing slavery in the District of Columbia, and the possibility, in the last resort, of extending the line of the Missouri Compromise, they parted resolved that "everything or nothing" should be settled by a "fair and liberal compromise," at once and forever, to secure "the peace, the union, and the prosperity of our country." In the light of subsequent events the importance of this meeting can not be overestimated.

Henceforth Ritchie was one of Clay's most valuable lieutenants in the fight for compromise. Cordial relations were resumed extending even to the joking point. Shortly after this meeting it is reported that Ritchie, in the presence of a number of public men, promised Clay to forgive him for his course in 1825, if he would only save the Union and cease to aspire to the presidency. To which Clay replied: "Tom Ritchie, you never believed a word of that bargain story." But Ritchie's aid was not conditional in support of the Compromise resolutions. He attacked bitterly the unconciliatory attitude of Calhoun's speech of March the 4th, and pronounced Webster the "lion of the day."[12] Despite the chidings of friends he entreated the President to join Clay and Webster in their efforts to save the Union, and, if necessary to maintain the findings of the select committee of thirteen, he himself was willing to drain the cup of poverty to the last dregs.[13] Alternately he begged and scolded in an effort to induce Congress to act, the North to give up the Wilmot Proviso, and the South to cease its agitation for disunion. With the resolutions of the Nashville Convention upon the

[11] Foote, *Casket of Reminiscenes*, p. 24; *Richmond Enquirer*, September 10, 1852.

[12] *Washington Union*, March 6, 8, 1850; *Ibid.*, May 10, 1850.

[13] *Ibid.*, May 10, 1850.

nature of the federal government and the ultimate right of state to secede he was in full accord, but he condemned its ultimatums and particularly its independent attitude toward the northern Democrats.[14] As in the days of Jackson and Van Buren he continued to value his northern allies. He now classed Rhett, Yancey, and Toombs with Garrison, John Van Buren, Phillips, and Seward as disunionists. A true representative of the Border he, like the Great Compromiser, loved the Union of the fathers and deplored the movements which now threatened its destruction.

As at other times, notably in 1832, Ritchie paid dearly for his devotion to the Union. Contending that he had surrendered the party of Jackson to its arch enemy, Calhoun, Douglas and Richardson of Illinois, acting as the representatives of a number of others, tried to induce Blair to set up an opposition press.[15] A few weeks later forty-four southern members of Congress adopted an address to their constituents recommending the establishment of a newspaper in Washington to be devoted to "the support and defence of southern interests." Ritchie was accused by them of placing party welfare before their rights and interests, the old charge so frequently made by Calhoun. The severest attack came from his beloved Virginia, when R. K. Meade, a representative in Congress from that state, assailed his course in support of the Compromise. Meade urged the impropriety of permitting the young men of Virginia to call Father Ritchie "Old State Rights," and demanded that he cease to fight for "Onachar who had drunk the milk of the white doe," and that he return to the leadership of her stalwart sons or desert completely to the camp of the Philistines. He was opposed to all concessions, to all compromise, but did not represent the sentiment of Virginia. He, like many others, was alarmed for the future of the South when the balance between the states had been destroyed by the admission of California, Utah, New Mexico, and Oregon, as free states.

[14] *Washington Union*, June 15, 18, 1850.

[15] *Van Buren MSS.*, Blair to Van Buren, March 24, 1850.

"Then," said he, "the pressure on our sides will cause southern respiration to grow thick and short: the serpent's fold will become tighter and tighter, and the days of our fair land with its wonderful civilization will be numbered."[16]

But Ritchie did not think this a death struggle for the South. In dissolution he saw death, but in view of his understanding with Clay that contingency was impossible. Accordingly he continued buoyant and steadfast in his course. Knowing that the northern leaders would in time understand his position and adjust themselves to it, he paid little attention to their attacks, but those from the South, and particularly those from Virginia, disturbed him no little. He frankly admitted the right of any person to establish a press at Washington, but he reviewed his record on the Wilmot Proviso, abolition, and the political contests of 1844 to prove his loyalty to the South and her institutions. Moreover, he denied outright the charge that he had lulled the South into a "false security" by keeping her attached to the North for the sake of political union and party successes. To Mr. Meade he gave the assurance that the "glorious edifice on which we dwell might yet survive us and bless our children, for it is founded upon a rock."[17]

In national affairs the compromise resolutions which were finally adopted one at a time did not produce even a truce, and the war upon the venerable editor continued. After one year Burke retired from the co-editorship,[18] and Ritchie was left to bear the burdens alone. Occasion for further attacks came when he petitioned Congress for relief for losses sustained in the execution of his contract to do the public printing. When the contract was made, it was thought to include the printing of the census of 1850, but the politicians through some hook or crook kept that work from going to Ritchie. He was now accused of holding up Congress for a contribution for his share in bringing about

[16] *Washington Union,* June 9, 1850.

[17] *Ibid.,* May 14, 15, 18, 1850.

[18] *Ibid.,* May 31, 1850.

the Compromise. The debate which followed his petition and the newspaper comment upon it brought into review the questionable acts attending the establishment of *The Union* and General Jackson's various expressions of disapproval of Ritchie.[19] James L. Orr of South Carolina denied the desired relief, alleging that the contract had been entered into with a view to prevent the establishment of an independent press in Washington, and that the parties to it should thus suffer for their political sins.[20] Ritchie's poor financiering afforded a rare opportunity for Blair and Rives, who had hounded him ever since his arrival in Washington. Unable to destroy him as an editor, they now hoped to accomplish his downfall by attacking him in his most vulnerable spot, his weakness as a financier. To secure the appropriation Blair now accused him of courting the favor of the Hunkers, but he was confident that "the old scavenger will be left to perish in his sink," unless "Cass & Co." and "Buck & Co." considered "the central organ with its Polk prestige" worth the price.[21]

From this final testing Ritchie emerged with character unsullied.[22] It was shown that he knew nothing about the financial deals and arrangements by which Simon Cameron, Robert J. Walker, Cave Johnson, and Aaron Brown had founded *The Union,* that his whole career had been honest and straightforward, and that his petition for relief was just.[23] Accordingly the House voted the desired appropriation which was defeated by Calhoun's friends but later granted by the Senate.[24] Thus, vindicated before the whole country and apparently sustained and endorsed in his support of the Compromise, Father Ritchie decided to retire. Calhoun had passed to the great beyond, and Clay and Web-

[19] *Washington Union,* January 2, 1851.

[20] See speech in the House of Representatives, February 12, 1851.

[21] *Van Buren MSS.,* Blair to Van Buren, September 20, 27 and December 26, 1850; *Ibid.,* January 22, 1851.

[22] *Cong. Globe,* 31st Cong. 2d sess., p. 838.

[23] *Washington Union,* January 2, 16, 1851; *Ibid.,* March 15, 1851.

[24] *Cong. Globe,* 32d Cong, 2d sess., XXVI, p. 935.

ster were about to follow. With the passing of these great lights with whom he had worked for the good and glory of their common country, his opportunity for the greatest usefulness had ended. Throughout the whole Border and notably in Virginia, his influence had been a power in reconciling the dissatisfied to the last great effort to save the Union.[25] In his own mind and in the mind of others, the object of his mission in coming to Washington had been attained.[26] Henceforth the ship of state was to be entrusted to newer and younger pilots. That they might be able freely to select their own bearings, he was now willing to retire. Accordingly it was announced that after April 15, 1851, Andrew Jackson Donaldson assisted by General Robert Armstrong would edit *The Union*, and that Father Ritchie would write no more editorials.[27]

Ritchie's farewell, closing a period of forty-seven years as an editor, is deserving of more than passing attention. Speaking as it were from his "political death-bed, with all the solemnity and responsibility which surrounded the confessions of a dying man," he told the story of how his influence in the South had been shorn from him after coming to Washington because of his efforts to save the Union. He rejoiced, however, in the fact that loss in one theater had been met by gains in another, which he had been able to use in the service of his country at the time of its greatest crisis. As a father would council his children, he warned his "countrymen at the North" not to deceive themselves, "because" said he, "the South is in earnest." It would certainly insist upon a faithful execution of the fugitive slave law. "For otherwise," said he, "the Union will topple to the ground. It is idle to talk about the Union alone. We must preserve all the three great pillars of our prosperity—the *Liberty of the People, the Rights of the States, and the Union of the*

[25] *Washington Union*, March 11, 1851.

[26] *Goldsboro* (N. C.) *Republican*, March 25, 1851; *Milledgeville* (Ga.) *Union*, March 25, 1851.

[27] *Washington Union*, March 15, 1851.

States." To this end he thought it imperative that they should keep their hands off of the institutions of the South, put down freesoilism, and, in keeping with his own ideas of party unity, permit no man to reach the presidency who would not disavow "all participation with fanatics."[28]

His advice to his own section was equally paternal and prophetic. First of all it was to observe the Compromise and to discountenance any man "who would now rush into secession." Conscious of the growing nationality of the South he advised loyalty to the federal Union, "until the southern people are so far united by common wrongs as to be given into a common struggle and until the issue is fairly made between a dissolution of the Union and a government without limitation of powers."[29] Thus the man who had lived by the Virginia and Kentucky Resolutions was ready to die by them. He had never doubted the ultimate right of a sovereign state to secede.

The work of reorganizing the Democratic party he left to younger and abler hands. He was certain that local and clashing interests would arise, but saw no reason why they could not be adjusted by the "standard of the constitution." He also saw the possibility of demagogic leaders arraying section against section in contests over the presidency, but he was certain that a united party, for which he had always stood and made many a sacrifice, could repress ambitious leaders and settle all party contests in deliberative conventions, until such a time as the selection of the President could be referred directly to the people.

Very appropriately the "Napoleon of the Press," as Ritchie was called in his day, directed his last paragraph to his fellow editors. From the very beginning of his editorial career he had regarded a free and unsubsidized press as the life of the republic. To him the editorial profession was one of honor and dignity, if not of emolument. To meet this

[28] *Washington Union,* April 15, 1851.
[29] *Ibid.*

high standard he insisted that it must be conducted with talent, independence, liberality, courtesy, and decency. He assured his fellow editors that there was much of drudgery and sacrifice before them, but begged that they carry into their work an indomitable spirit which would quake under no fear, except that which came from a neglect of duty and a reproof of conscience. He considered energy of character insufficient to make an editor; the profession required enthusiasm. A survey of his life and of the comments made upon it at the time of his retirement affords ample proof that he lived his precepts.

The three remaining years of Ritchie's life were passed in retirement in his own home at Washington or in his daughter's home on the James. The politics of the pressroom there gave way to the joys of the domestic circle and the delights of social intercourse. None knew better than he how to use leisure, another proof of his greatness. The Bible which had been his constant companion through life, the classics, and even music now became sources of comfort and delight, and his beautiful grandchildren became his constant companions. Meanwhile he was not forgotten by the public which he had served so faithfully. Among the many honors which came, his election to honorary membership in the State Historical Society of Wisconsin, through the influence of his friend, Lyman C. ~~Proper~~ Draper, was keenly appreciated.

The death of Henry Clay, which occurred in 1852, called Ritchie again into the press, but only as a contributor. In the presence of a large company of distinguished men he had jokingly promised to plant a laurel upon Clay's grave, if the Compromise of 1850 were accepted. Now that the venerable statesman had passed away and he survived him, Ritchie took his promise seriously. It afforded an opportunity to right himself with the only man whom he had ever hated and consequently treated unjustly. The article which he prepared for the press on this occasion reviewed the history of the Great Compromise and again held it up as a document to live by. In terms of praise and admiration which will live longer than any floral tribute could live, it pictured also the virtues and talents of the Great Compromiser in a spirit which made it certain that the past had been forgotten and that Ritchie could die at peace with all men.

CHAPTER XI.

THE EDITOR AND THE MAN.

Ritchie was not a genius. Either of the others of the great "Democratic Triumvirate" of political editors, Francis P. Blair of the *Washington Globe,* or Edwin Croswell of the *Albany Argus,* was his equal in natural ability. Possibly John Hampden Pleasants, Duff Green, and even others surpassed him in one or more of the qualities requisite in a great editor. In versatility, broadness of vision, soundness of judgment, and constructiveness, any of a half score of modern editors surpass him. Why then was he justly called the "Napoleon of the Press"? Some would say that it was because he was the first of the great editors, but that answer is not satisfactory and does not adhere to the truth. No less distinguished an editor than Benjamin Franklin preceded him. There was something of worth in the man himself, which caused him to live and to bear this title of distinction. As his numerous nicknames, "Thomas Nous Verrons," "Old Nous Verrons," "Momentous Crisis Ritchie," "Obita Principiis Ritchie," "Old State Rights," "Father Ritchie," etc., indicate he had a distinct personality.

Success and distinction came to Thomas Ritchie because of his superior tact, his sound judgment, his genial temper, his persuasive manner, and his ability to work. He knew how to improve a victory and equally well how to recover from a defeat, characteristic Napoleonic traits; he seldom distrusted a friend and was as rarely deceived by an enemy; he never surrendered but chivalrously flung away his sword the moment he heard the cry of quarter; he counseled with the aged without becoming obsolete and carressed the young without becoming an enthusiast; he enjoyed the confidence of the sages of the "Mother of Commonwealths" and was admired for his sterling character and devotion to principle throughout the nation; he united Parisian manners with republican simplicity and possessed versatility without caprice, wit without malice, grace without affectation, courage without Quixotism, zeal without bigotry; and he combined with his broad patriotism an intense love for Virginia. Like our greatest and most successful lawyers, he never fought without an object and beyond the pale of his conscience.[1] Then, too, he did not enter the field of national politics until after he had distinguished himself as the recognized spokesman of a great state in the center of the border section. From this strategic point his vision extended to the very outskirts of the nation whence it gathered facts later to be boiled down in the crucible of conservatism and national patriotism. Thus he became an oracle for the whole country and a guide for all other editors less favorably situated and constituted. It should also be borne in mind that he won his prestige when the American press was comparatively in its infancy and when Virginia and her sons were directing the affairs of the nation. After Jefferson and Madison passed from the stage of action Ritchie was, through some of our greatest crises, looked to as the oracle whence they continued to speak.

Historians and casual readers have done Ritchie a grave injustice by handing him down to posterity as a political boss and by overlooking the importance of his editorial career. Such a verdict is not surprising, however, in the light of contemporary comment of which the following from the *New York Express* is a sample: "If anybody ever understood the politics of the Old Dominion it was Father Ritchie, for he had sounded the depths of all the abstractions of that old Commonwealth from the Resolutions of '98 to the resolutions of 1844, when a new era seemed to dawn upon the Democracy of the country."[2] From this and simi-

[1] Claibourne, J. F. H., *Life and Times of General Sam Dale*, p. 200.

[2] *Richmond Enquirer*, July 7, 1854.

lar comments it was easy to confuse a thorough knowledge of political principles, conditions, and methods with adeptness in the use of political machinery, at which art Ritchie was as ignorant and as helpless as a child. True, there are brief periods in the history of Virginia when his influence and organizing power seemed to dominate, but it is also true that he was more frequently opposed to the leading politicians of that state than in accord with them. The methods of the boss were unknown to him. During the twelve years from 1829 to 1841, when he was a power at the federal court, he recommended only one person for a federal appointment, and during the whole term of his service as national spokesman for his party, he scrupulously refrained from any part in the distribution of the patronage. Certainly Ritchie's editorial career in Washington, when he became the political football in the contest between the North and the South over the goal to be reached on the Pacific, argues him anything else than a practical politician. With him knowledge and art were not synonymous.

If destined to live among the sons of men, Ritchie must be known as a great editor. His influence upon men came not from a skillful use of political machinery but from an enthusiastic adherence to fundamental principles, from his power and versatility as a writer, and from his unselfish and patriotic love of the Union. He was not a Tweed. A contemporary of opposite political faith has given the following explanation of his great power: "It proceeded from a knowledge on the part of the public that he was aiming with his whole soul to promote, as far as he thought right, the public interest and particularly to sustain Virginia in her highly prized principles, and to sustain her in the ascendency among the states. It strengthened in the confidence felt in his disinterested devotion to these things and his freedom from selfish aspirations for himself and his friends."[3] Had the "Virginia doctrines" lived as the popular theory of the

[3] *Richmond Enquirer*, July 25, 1854.

nature of the federal government, the motto, "The Rights of the States and the Union of the States," would to-day have been as popular as that other motto, "The Union, now and forever.' As in other great contests so in this, failure attracted attention to the minor incidents by which it was sustained and not to the principles involved. In the light of modern developments, when section is being arrayed against section and interest against interest, who can not see the possibility for a resurrection of this great apostle of the rights and interests of the sovereign states of America and of the classical school of thinkers in politics and economy? Should that time ever come, it would be as impossible to think of Ritchie as a mere politician as it is now impossible to think of Webster in that role.

To Ritchie more than to any one of his contemporaries the press of to-day owes a debt of gratitude for the high ethical conceptions which he brought to and made a part of his profession. Although caustic and at times severe in his attacks upon public men he never rioted in an unnecessary massacre of private character and always proceeded to such attacks with the recollection that he too had a character of generosity and liberality to maintain and that abuse and scurrility are not always antidotes for ignorance and vice. When he entered the editorial profession the Billingsgate of foreigners was its chief characteristic, necessitating as it had done the enactment of the sedition laws and rendering the profession dangerous to life and limb. Actuated by a high conception of his calling and the importance of a free press as the basis of popular government, he sought to remedy these conditions by proposing to his fellow editors a code of rules, which served to elevate the tone of the press of the whole country and to put the editorial profession upon a higher plane.[4]

Ritchie's exertions did not end with an effort to purify editorial ethics. Throughout his whole career he lost no op-

[4] See *Richmond Enquirer*, November 7, 1806.

portunity to elevate the personnel of the press and to increase its usefulness. It was he who called and presided over the first convention of editors held in this country. A review of his address on that occasion (the convention met at Richmond in January, 1838) furnishes ample evidence of his multitudinous services to his profession. After humorous references to the fact that he was already called "the venerable," he dwelt at length upon the magic power of the press in promoting the progress of art, extending the sphere of science, and in keeping alive a spirit of vigilance over the republic. The irksomeness of tasks "still beginning, never ending" in rolling the stone of Sisyphus up the mountain and in listening to the going and returning footsteps of "the poor Devil" had not stolen the joys of his prison house, the editorial department, and he admonished his co-editors, each as poorly paid as himself, to aim for something higher than fortune, for a position of distinction and power as constructive members of society. In the distinction, high standing and power of the editors of the *London Examiner* and the *Edinburgh Review* he saw encouragement for every patriotic American editor who was willing to devote his best to his profession and to cast off the maliciousness and licentiousness of the press in an honest effort to raise the tone of the public morals and to strengthen the character of the public councils.[5] Thoughts of our present subsidized and commercialized press seem never to have crossed his mental vision.

As in most other things Ritchie lived his precepts of industry and application. The demands upon him were great. During the period of his residence in Richmond he was the moving spirit in almost every public gathering, the manager of public balls and dinners, the toastmaster for great occasions, such as that when Charles Dickens, on his second visit to America, was received as the guest of the city, the hospitable host of the politicians, and the faithful reporter

[5] *Richmond Enquirer*, January 17, 23, 1838.

of the proceedings of the General Assembly and of all conventions whatsoever, except those in which the hated Whigs held their councils of war. After a night spent in conviviality or in study (he did not retire before three in the morning), an attenuated form, thin and wand and apparently wasted to a shadow, appeared clad in civilian suit with white Marseilles vest, thin pumps, and white socks on schedule time at the office of the *Enquirer*. Through heat and cold, snow and rain, mire and dust, Father Ritchie was always the same both in dress and manner. When Congress and the General Assembly were in session, work piled upon him thick and fast, and he then frequently carried to his home large bundles of exchanges and copy bound in his white cambric handkerchief. Under such circumstances it was his habit to retire to an upper apartment of his residence, for the time ceiled to the world, where in dressing gown and slippers and frequently upon the flat of his back with two large candle sticks at his head, he examined exchanges and produced those editorials which shaped the political thinking of others and won for their modest and retiring author the name of a "managing politician."[6]

This disinterested devotion to duty and to principle largely explains that stoicism and heartlessness with which Ritchie could change his course and strike down a friend without remorse. As his editorials constantly show, the immortal examples of Roman patriotism were his constant sources of inspiration, inspiring as they did others of the fathers who, like Ritchie, could have played the role of a Brutus. Thus it was that he favored the abolition of negro slavery in 1832, following the Southampton insurrection, and the retention of the state banks as depositories of the federal moneys, later to become the very Cerberus of the South's "peculiar institutions" and a most violent opponent of W. C. Rives who continued friendly to the "pet banks."

[6] Hudson, *History of Journalism*, p. 270; *Richmond Enquirer*, July 24, 1854.

Thus it was that he struck down Van Buren in 1844, without, so far as he himself was concerned, going beyond the pale of his friendship or the possibility of a reconciliation. It is not strange that his ideas and principles, when acted out in the life of that body politic which he did more to shape than any other, except possibly Thomas Jefferson, carried eastern Virginia out of the Union in 1861 and kept western Virginia loyal to it.

In one very essential particular Ritchie was a complete failure as an editor. Though himself the impersonation of honesty and square dealing, he was ignorant in matters of domestic and business economy. His accounts went uncollected until they aggregated thousands and were then frequently forgotten. After Van Buren had ceased to be his political friend, he was forced to a use of strategy in an effort to pay his arrears to the *Examiner*. With a large and extravagant family to maintain and educate, with a home a center of the hospitality of hospitable Richmond, and with tastes better suited to spending than to accumulating a fortune, Ritchie was kept constantly to the wall. At times his dependence upon friends and banks for loans embarassed him as an editor, and, in an evil hour of his fame, it was the hope of remedying his finances that induced him to go to Washington. Had it not been for the timely and deserved relief extended by Congress, he would doubtless have died in poverty.

Ritchie's home life was ideal. At the age of twenty-nine he had married Miss Isabella Harminson Foushee, daughter of Dr. William Foushee, a distinguished physician of Richmond. To this marriage were born twelve children: Isabella, always referred to by her father in his correspondence as "my dear Bell," Mary, John, William Foushee, Robert Ruffin, Margaret, Thomas, Jr., Charlotte, Frances, Anne Eliza, George, and Virginia. In the midst of this large and charming family circle Father Ritchie appeared at his best, the *beau ideal* of a gentleman of the model of the old French school and a kind and indulgent parent. The sons received the best education obtainable in this country, and William F. spent some years abroad in a study of the modern languages. The daughters received training in the private schools of Richmond and under the direction of their father who spent many an hour in their instruction. To them he was peculiarly tender and affectionate. When speaking of them to friends and acquaintances, it is said, that his eyes sparkled with that pleasure which evinces true satisfaction and pride. He also loved his grandchildren, and a large part of his holidays and of the period of his retirement was spent in romping with them upon the green lawn or in the halls of the palatial home of his dear Bell at Brandon. Both children and grandchildren had his first thoughts and deepest interests. On the occasion of the birth of his fifth daughter and eighth child he wrote his brother Archibald as follows: "What a load upon a man to do justice by such a crowd and give them all a good education. However, they must do as well as they can for themselves (the boys, of course, I mean). As to the girls, they must behave well and try to fix themselves as well as they can, or live contentedly without extravagance in their father's house."

It is needless to say that children thus carefully reared rarely fell short of their father's expectations. Isabella married George E. Harrison and became the mistress of Brandon, whence her famed hospitality extended throughout the states and even to Europe; Mary became Mrs. Thomas Green. William F. became the editor and proprietor of the *Enquirer,* which he continued to edit with marked ability even into the period of the War between the States, always adhering to the conservative and conciliatory policy of his father. Robert Ruffin was a distinguished physician and practiced in the vicinity of Brandon. Margaret became the wife of Robert King Stone, a celebrated physician of Washington and a friend of Abraham Lincoln. Until his death, which occurred on May 22, 1854, about six weeks before that of his father, Thomas, Jr., was associated with his brother as joint editor and proprietor of the *Enquirer.*

It was he who accepted a challenge in an affair of honor which resulted fatally to John Hampden Pleasants and cast a shadow over his own life to the time of his death. Charlotte married John Gittings, and Anne Eliza, a famous beauty, became Mrs. William B. Cross. George died while yet a young man, and Virginia never married but, after her sister's death, continued to reside at Brandon and to share in the distribution of its hospitality.

Thus Ritchie had lived to see most of his children happily married and some of them on the road to service and even to fame; he himself had a comfortable living; friends were respectful and appreciative; and the joys of the several firesides around which he was called grandfather were sources of true comfort and delight. These were certainly suitable blessings for a stormy life spent in the service of others, and human justice would have continued them indefinitely. But the God of nature decreed otherwise. Beneath the outer cover of cheer and vigor the iron constitution of the venerable editor was wearing slowly away. When his final illness came he expressed the belief that he would never recover; nevertheless, he was calm and poised, patient and benevolent, conversing freely and frankly upon public affairs and uttering his counsels and warnings with his usual tone and power, and declaring, as he had ever done, that his solicitude for his country was high and buoyant.

On many notable occasions the pealing anthems of our national anniversary have mingled with the requiem and the dirge of statesmen and patriots, but never did they fall upon a nobler, purer soul than that of Thomas Ritchie. He died at 12 o'clock noon, July 3, 1854. Following a brief funeral service which was attended by the President, members of his cabinet, scores of senators and representatives in Congress. and a vast concourse of loving admirers, his remains were taken to Richmond and laid to rest in Hollywood at a beautiful spot overlooking the James which he loved and by the side of which his greatest battles had been won. The inscriptions upon his monument are those that Ritchie himself might have selected. In one side this appears: "In memory of Thomas Ritchie, founder of the Richmond Enquirer, and for more than forty years, the controlling spirit of that Journal," and on another this expressive characterization: "He never turned his back upon his country, was always devoted to his friends, and never dreaded his enemies."

Regardless of party affiliations the press of the whole country hastened to pay tribute to the venerable dead. His political enemies, for he had few others, had never hated him personally, the charm of his personal purity having made even them to be "at peace with him." Of the many tributes paid to him the following from the *Washington Sentinel*, then edited by a man whom he had practically reared, is the most appropriate for this biography:

> "No impure thought ever found a resting place in that old man's heart. The world thought that he was shrewd and cunning, but the world did not know him. Mr. Ritchie was a plain, free spoken man with intense personal attachments, and, we believe, without an animosity toward a living man. For fifty years he has been an active combatant. He has gone down to the tomb without an enemy." [7]

Ritchie died as he had lived, a patriot, loyal to the whole country and true to his original conception of the nature of the federal government. At the time of his death all efforts to compromise the differences between the North and the South seemed futile, and he was distressed to see the states again estranged and the stars of the great constellation of commonwealths dimmed and unstable in their spheres. Unlike the venerable George Mason he did not, however, despair of the republic. In the closing paragraph of his last will and testament,[8] which is its own apology for quoting here as the closing paragraph of this biography, he, in a patriotic retrospect of the past and vision of the future and in a concise statement of his own political philosophy, dedicated his sons to the public service. Said he:

[7] *Richmond Enquirer*, July 7, 1854.

[8] *Ibid.*, July 25, 1854.

"I hold it to be the duty of every citizen to watch over the interests of the country of which he is a member, and such a free and glorious country as *this is!* Who is not proud of her destiny? Who is not willing to give his services and even his life to the maintenance of the great principles on which her *free* and *federal* institutions are based? America has made one of the greatest political discoveries which the world has witnessed: a form of government which reserves to the states and their people the power of regulating most of the functions which appertain to government, leaving but very few powers, and they only of the most general and yet important character, to the jurisdiction of the federal authortities. Hence the specification which is made in the constitution of those powers, which the United States are to exercise in their legitimate sphere; and hence the necessity of watching over the operation of the machinery and repairing its excesses, when it threatens the rights of the States. We are already the greatest power among the nations. We are destined to be greater still, but let us not be too ambitious, or too rapid in our advances. Let us fill up the immense territory which we own. Let us not be too anxious to step our foot from the mainland to the islands, unless indeed, as in the case of Cuba, we are threatened by the barbarization of that beautiful island and its conversion into a black and hostile neighborhood. Let us not deny to the inhabitants of other lands (evidently a warning against the Native American movement and the Knownothings) a free asylum into our own shores; but let us confine ourselves to the operation of natural causes. In this way we may best acclimate the emigrant to our free institutions. Preserve both the Rights of the Union and the Rights of the States. These are the two great pillars of American prosperity and glory."

APPENDIX I.

Genealogy of William Roane and Mary Upshur.[1]

1. *Thomas Roane* x *Mary A. Hipkins.*

Children: Sarah x Archibald Campbell who left a son Hugh x Nancy Gatewood and Mary Fleet; *Margaret* x A. C. Harwood and Thomas Garnett and left, by the first marriage, Archibald R. and Thomas Harwood and, by the second, Henry, James, John R., Annie M. and Emily C. Garnett; *Alice* x Sterling Ruffin whose children were Judge Thomas Ruffin of N. C. x Annie Kirkland, Minerva x Edward Delany and George McNiel, father of Rev. George and Rev. James McNiel, Mary R. x William Cain, William , James H. of N. C. and Ala. x Susan Williams; *Molly* and *Mary; Rebecca* x Richard Barnes; *Martha Hipkins* x Archibald Ritchie whose children were Janet x Richard Rowzee, Juliet x Dr. Clopton and Mr. Roy, and Archibald x Miss Spindle; the eight child (————) never married; *Lucy* x Edwin Upshur; *Catherine* x Archibald Ruffin of N. C.: *Archibald; Thomas* x Mary A. Wilson and left Charlotte, Maria x Dr. A. B. Westmore, Isabella x Horace Waring, Lawrence and Thomas; *William; Samuel; and John* x Agnes Kazier.

The children of *Janet (nee) Ritchie and Richard Rowzee* were *Mary* x Mr. McDonald, *Juliet* x Dr. James Latané, and *Archibald* x Katharine Lewis. *Dr. James Latané* left four children: *Anne Burwell* x R. L. Ware whose children are Edward M., Robert L., Wm. L., Henry H., Burwell, Ritchie, John, and Catsby; *Janet Roane Ritchie* x William Campbell whose children are Janet x Alfred Bagby, Anne x R. C. Williams, Mary, Wade H., and Courtney x R. G. Neale; *Rev. William Catsby Latané x* Miss Wilson and left Wilson, Janet Ritchie, Henry A., William C., Lawrence W., James, and Bettie W.; and *Mary S.* x M. S. Sale whose children are Mrs. Meriwether Smith, Charles, Dandridge, Latané, Ritchie, Lewis, and Mrs. Alger Shaw.

2. *John Roane* x *Miss Jones* of Middlesex.

Children: John of King William county, who was for many years a representative in Congress, and *Molly* x James Ruffin who left Robert x Lucy Roane and Miss Haskins, John, James x Agnes Dandridge, Lucy x Mr. Haskins, Thomas, and Sterling.

3. *William Roane* x *Judy Ball* of the Northern Neck.

Children: Thomas; Spencer, President of the Virginia Court of Appeals and father of W. H. Roane who was a representative and senator in Congress; *Judy* x Mr. Proudfit; *Sarah* x James Dykes who left a daughter, Sarah x William Bernard.

The children of *William Bernard* and his wife, *Sarah,* were *Eliza*

[1] For years this genealogy has been preserved on a piece of cardboard in Lower Brandon. Few additions have been made to it, and these only by parties who were themselves interested.

Frances x Thomas Semmes, Professor at V. M. I. x Louise Brockenbrough whose children are Mrs. Howard Jones, Bernard, Alice x Corse, Louise x Brooks, and Thomas, and *Sarah Ann* x Judge John A. Meredith who had twelve children, William B., James, Walter, Mary Ella, Sarah Roane, Eliza B. x J. Preston Cocke, Charles V. x Sophy G. Rose, Edward D. x Lelia Withers, John, Julian, Wyndham R. x Ann Marson, and Lelia B. x Richard I. Manning. J. Preston Cocke's children are Ella M., Edmonia Madison Randolph, Sarah B., and Elizabeth P. Chas V. Meredith's children are Katie Rose x Max L. Talbot, Sophie R., Sarah B., and Bernard. Wyndham R. Meredith's children are John A., Marion, and Alice. Richard I. Manning's children are Sarah B. x Rev. Alfred Berkeley, Richard I., John M., Wm. S. x Barbara Brodie, Vivian M. x Adair McDowell, Bernard, Wyndham M., Elizabeth, St. George S., Laelius M., Burwell D., John Adger, and Preston Cocke.

4. *Molly Roane* x *Archibald Ritchie.*

Children: Col. Archibald, who commanded in the Second War with Great Britain, x Martha Hipkins Roane (see descendants of Thomas Roane); *Margaret* x William Ruffin of N. C.; *Janet* x Dr. Buckner of Ky.; *William, Captain John,* who fell in an engagement near Lunday's Lane; *Thomas,* founder of the *Richmond Enquirer,* x Isabella Harminson Foushee; and *Molly* x Mr. Hopper and Gov. Robert Brooke, of Va.

To *Thomas Ritchie* and his wife, Isabella, twelve children were born: *Isabella H.* x Goerge Evelyn Harrison of Brandon; *Mary Roane* x Thomas Green; *John; William Foushee* x Anna Core Mowatt, nee Ogden, the celebrated actress; *Dr. Robert Ruffin; Thomas; Margaret F.* x Robert King Stone, the friend and physician of Abaham Lincoln; *Charlotte Carter* x John Serret Gittings; *Frances Gantier; Ann Eliza,* the celebrated beauty, x Wm. B. Cross; *George Harrison;* and *Virginia.*

George Evelyn Harrison and his wife, *Isabella,* had two children, *George Evelyn* x Guhilma Clifford Gordon of Savannah, Georgia, and *Isabella Ritchie. George Evelyn Harrison* and his wife, *Guhilma,* left five children: *Guhilma Gordon* x Richard Cuyler; *George Evelyn* x Mary Walker and left two children, Evelyn Byrd and Virginia Ritchie; *William Gordon* x Sadie King and left two children, William Gordon and George Evelyn;*Isabella Ritchie* x Stephen Decatur Mayo; and *Robert Clifford* x Eliza McKay Huger and left two children, Isabella and Joe Huger.

Thomas Green and his wife, *Mary Roane,* left six children: *Isabella Foushee* x Wm. Jessup Ward whose children were Mary Roane, Wm. J., Charles R., and George x Eliza Byrd Page; *Thomas Ritchie; Julia Peyton ; William Carter; Emily Smith* x Sydney Ashe Legare of South Carolina whose children were James, Sarah Seabrook who married Morton Waring Simmons, Balie Peyton x Liefji von Herwerden, Sydney A., Thomas Green, Marie Stone, and Sydney Claude; *Bernard Peyton.*

Dr. Robert King Stone and his wife, *Margaret F.,* had three children, *Jane Southall* x Dr. George Byrd Harrison, *Isabella,* and *Thomas Ritchie* x Lelia Whitney. Dr. George Byrd Harrison left two children, William Evelyn and Margaret Ritchie, and Dr. Thomas Ritchie Stone left two children, Lillian Garnett x George Appleby and Robert King.

5. *Sarah Roane* x *John Brockenbrough.*

Children: John, President of the Bank of Virginia, x Mrs. Mann Randolph; *William,* Judge of the Court of Appeals of Virginia, x Judith White; *Lucy* x James Cox; *Arthur; Thomas;* and *Dr. Austin.*

Sarah Jane, eldest daughter of Judge Wm. Brockenbrough, x *Edward Colston* whose children were *Elizabeth Marshall* x R. Alfred Williams whose children were Alfred B. x Mary Brice, Edward Dandridge, Rosalie B. x Wm. E. Page; *Mary Brockenbrough* x Wm. Leigh whose children were Benj. Watkins, Edward Colston, Wm. Robinson, Elizabeth M., and Thomas; *Raleigh,* killed in the War between the States; *Wm. B.* x Minnie Summers and left children, Susan, Jane, Elizabeth Marshall x Wm. Trapnell, and Sophia Hunter x Wm. Cornwall; *Lucy B.* x Bennet Taylor; *Minnie* x Dr. Michie; *Edward* x Sally Stevenson and Mary Stevenson.

Judge Wm. Brockenbrough's second child, *John W.,* Judge of the U. S. District Court for western Virginia, x *Mary Bowyer* and left Bowyer x Alice Murrell, William x Miss Major, Willoughby Newton x Miss Thomas, Louisa x Thomas M. Semmes, Robet L. x Miss Grasty, and Frank.

Judge Wm. Brockenbrough's third child was *Elizabeth* x *Mr. Philips,* and the fourth, *Mary, x Willoughby Newton* to whom was born John B., x Roberta Page Williamson; Hon. Willoughby whose children were Mary Mann Page and Wm. B., Sally x John Phillips Smith whose children were Willoughby Newton, Mary Newton, William Newton, and Raleigh Colston.

Judge Wm. Brockenbrough's fifth child was *William* and the sixth, *July x Rev.* J. *P. McGuire* whose daughter, *Fenton* x Rev. Kinlach Nelson. His second daughter, Emily, x Phillip Nelson.

6. *Lucy Roane* x *Richard Barnes.*

Children: Richard x Rebecca Roane to whom was born Lucy x Mr. Branham, Maria x Phillip Claiborne, Charlotte x Mr. Wright, Thomas, Richard, and Arthur.

6. *Lucy Roane* x *Moore Fontelroy Brockenbrough.*

Children: Col. Moore F. x (————) whose children were Walter, Littleton, John M. of the C. S. Army, (————) x W. R. Aylett, Ella, and Edward; and two daughters.

INDEX

"A. B." plot, suggested by Edwards, 93.

Abolition, beginnings of, 100; opposed in Virginia, 165; considered a political move, 167; in local politics, 175; attacked by Ritchie, 207; influenced by Texas agitation, 222.

Adams, Dr. John, 16.

Adams, John Quincy, author of Monroe Doctrine, 84; candidate for presidency, 85; popular in New England, 88; characteristics, 89; elected President, 99; first message to Congress, 101; use of General Survey Act, 115; visited Richmond, 244.

Agriculture, chair of in University, 221.

Albany Regency, loyalty to Crawford, 94; influence upon Ritchie, 153.

Alexander, Nath., opposed gradual emancipation, 166.

Allen, Senator William, opposed Ritchie, 261; defended Ritchie, 266; dissatisfaction with Ritchie, 276.

Ambler, Jacqueline, Justice Marshall's father-in-law, 16.

Ambler, Major John, 16.

American System, popular in Virginia, 87; popular in western Virginia, 149.

Anderson, John T., letter to Mr. O'Callaghan, 213.

Archer, Wm. S., democratic leader, 139; opposed Proclamation, 152; joined Whig party, 161.

Atlanta (Ga.) *Chronicle*, comments upon Ritchie, 173.

Baker, John, Federalist, 56.

Baldwin, B. G., member of constitutional convention, 121.

Baltimore and Ohio Railroad Co., chartered, 115.

Bancroft, George, Secretary of Navy, 260.

Banks, Linn, speaker of H. of Delegates, 164.

Banks and banking, first bank in Virginia, 26; proposed re-charter of Bank of U. S., 51; movement for, in western Virginia, 66; banks incorporated at Winchester and Wheeling, 67; bank of U. S., re-chartered, 72; branch bank of Bank of U. S. in Richmond, 72; attacks upon Bank of U. S., 74; Richmond monopoly, 177; independent treasury, 194; "free banking" system opposed by Ritchie, 208.

Barbour, James, supported Adams, 89; member of cabinet, 103.

Barbour, P. P., elected to Congress, 73; member of anti-tariff convention, 143; candidate for vice-presidency, 146.

"Barnburners," political faction, 246.

Bayly, Gen, T. H., negotiations with Ritchie, 247; accompanied Ritchie to see Clay, 281.

Benton, Thomas H., for annexation of Texas, 129; hard money policy, 187; popular in Virginia, 191; "Great Expunger," 192; suggested for presidency, 211; for Van Buren, 1844, 227; suggested for presidency, 241; opposed annexation of Texas, 251; friend of Blair, 252; interest in internal improvements, 271.

Biddle, Nicholas, ridiculed by Ritchie, 149.

Blair, F. P., editor, 69; editor of Jacksonian organ, 109; editor of *Globe*, 137; efforts to depose, 246; retired from *Globe*, 255; supported Van Buren for presidency, 1848, 268; rejoiced in Ritchie's failures, 276.

Boston Repertory, opposed embargo, 46.

Brandon, on James, 207.

Breckenridge, James, Federalist, 56.

Brockenbrough, Dr. John, marriage, 15; social leader, 15; banker,, 27; for war with Great Britain, 43; war-hawk, 57; member of anti-tariff convention, 143; consulted Van Buren about financial conditions, 193; suggested independent treasury, 194; supported Van Buren, 205; suggested for governor, 212.

Brooke, Judge, Clay's friend, 137.

Brown, Aaron V., comment on Texas, 235; hostility to Blair, 246.

Buchanan, James, favored treasury system, 194; suggested for presidency, 241; secretary of state, 246.

Burke, Edmund, associate editor of *Union*, 276; retired, 284.

Burr, Aaron, interest in the West, 37.

Burwell, Lewis, 16.

Butler, A. P., Calhoun follower, 268.

Butler, B. F., attitude toward negro slavery, 172.

Cabell, William H., life in Richmond, 15; elected governor, 32; interest in manufacturing, 45.

Calhoun, member of 12th Congress, 56; proposed for cabinet, 57; opposed Jackson's conduct in Florida, 69; nationalist, 72; candidate for presidency, 85; candidacy unpopular, 87; incurred enmity of Ritchie, 88; again popular in Virginia, 106; favored alliance between New York and Virginia, 108; political friends in New York and Virginia, 114; accused of disloyalty, 114; disappointed in Jackson, 131; breach with Jackson, 135; urged as Jackson's successor, 137; internal improvement schemes, 141; fathered nullincation, 141; efforts to win West, 156; political ambitions, 161; aided sectional discord, 167; supported independent treasury, 199; internal improvement schemes, 207; reconciled to Van Buren, 212; suggested for presidency, 227; candidate for presidency, 228; retired from contest for presidency, 234; neglected by Polk, 246; visited Richmond, 252; mistrusted Polk, 260; opposed occupation of Oregon, 261; drove Ritchie from Senate floor, 266; repudiated by Va., 269; planned to unite South and West, 270; strict construction, 276.

California, desired statehood, 274.

Cambreleng, C. C., visited the South, 111.

Cameron, Simon, hostility to *Globe*, 252.

Campbell, Alex., member of constitutional convention, 121.

Campbell, David, elected governor, 185; interest in education, 219.
Carrington, Col. Edward, 16.
Cass, Lewis, letter on nullification, 153; suggested for presidency, 241; Texas letter, 241; defended Ritchie, 262; failures, 272; for non-intervention, 278.
Charleston Patriot, supported Marshall, 80.
Chesapeake, attacked by *Leopard*, 42.
Chesapeake and Ohio Canal Co., chartered, 115.
Cheves, Landon, member of 12th Congress, 56.
Chilton, Samuel, a Whig, 230.
China, trade of, 277.
Church Hill, home of Adamses, 16.
Clay, Henry, influence upon Ritchie, 23; at inauguration of Madison, 49; member of 12th Congress, 56; proposed for Cabinet, 57; interest in Spanish America, 72; nationalist, 72; candidate for presidency, 85; visit to Richmond, 87; a nationalist, 88; popular in Va., 88; popular in West, 88; characteristics, 89; favored by Va. for vice-presidency, 94; choice of Junto for vice-presidency, 98; breach with Ritchie, 99; candidate for presidency, 137; efforts to win South, 156; unpopular in Va., 157; political ambitions, 161; Whig orator, 215; opposition to Tyler, 223; retired to private life, 225; opposed annexation of Texas, 232; "Raleigh letter," 237; interest in internal improvements, 270; compromise of 1850, 279; speech on compromise, 280; eulogized by Ritchie, 288.
Clinton, DeWitt, candidate for presidency, 85.
Cohens vs. *Virginia*, authority in case, 81.
Coles, Betsy, letter to A. Stevenson, 99.
Compromise of 1850, proposed, 279; defended by Clay, 280.
Congressional Caucus, favored Crawford, 91.
Conservatives, beginnings of, 197; successes in Va., 202; balance of power in Va., 208.
Constitution, spirit of, 22.
"Construction Construed," written by John Taylor, 80.
Conventions, Staunton, 68; Harrisburg, 113; Va. constitutional convention of 1829-30, 119; anti-tariff convention of 1831, 142; Southern proposed, 173; educational, 219.
Conventions, political, national nominating convention proposes, 86; national convention endorsed by Van Buren, 107; Baltimore convention, 1835, 170.
Cooke, John L., joint editor of *Enquirer*, 118.
Cooper, Dr., teacher of Manchester doctrines, 124.
Corporal's Guard, 223.
Courts, decisions of Federal Supreme, 73.
Crallé, R. K., Calhoun protegé, 233.
Crawford, W. H., candidate for presidency, 64; nationalist, 72; currency report of 1820, 76; candidate for presidency, 85; candidacy nation-wide, 86; popular in South, 88; political record, 90; caucus nominee for presidency, 92; followers support Jackson, 117.

Cuba, desired by the U. S., 71.

Daniel, P. V., war-hawk, 57; member of Junto, 139; suggested for U. S. Senate, 144; on political conditions in Va., 158; defeated for council, 164; accepted independent treasury; criticized Van Buren, 204; supported Van Buren, 205; estimates of Ritchie, 206.

Davis, Garrett, Whig, 264.

Davis, Jefferson, strict construction, 276.

"Decius," essays by, 35; commended Jefferson, 36.

Dessalines, black chieftain, 25.

Dew, Thomas R., writing on negro slavery, 167.

Dickens, Charles, entertained by Ritchie, 294.

Distribution Bill, passed, 182.

Doddridge, Philip, member of constitutional convention, 121.

Douglas, Stephen A., opposed Ritchie as editor, 283.

Dromgoole, George C., local democratic leader, 110, 139; member of anti-tariff convention, 143; supported Van Buren, 205; for Van Buren, 1844, 227, 229; loyalty to Van Buren, 240.

Duane, attacks Ritchie, 30, influence with Madison, 56.

"Dutch," in Valley, 217.

Eaton, John, influence with Jackson, 136.

Eaton, Mrs. John, 135, 139.

Edwards, Ninian, attacks Crawford, 93.

Elections, presidential of 1808, 46; presidential of 1816, 63; presidential election of 1820, 85; presidential election of 1824, 86-88; importance of that of 1828, 126; presidential election of 1832, 146-149; local elections of 1835, 169; presidential of 1836, 179; local in Va., 1838, 202; local of 1840 in Va., 214; presidential of 1844, 226, 242-245.

Embargo, proposed, 43; repealed, 45, 55.

Erskine, Minister to U. S., 53; recalled, 54.

Essex Junto, reproduced in Va., 27.

Eustice, Dr. William, Secretary of War, 60.

Examiner, organ of reform party, 18.

Exposition, work of Calhoun, 114.

Federalists, defend Burr, 38, 40; crushed in Va., 74.

Florida, occupation of, 28; impotency of Spain, 29; trouble with Spain, 32; purchase suggested, 36; invaded, 69.

Floyd, John, elected to Congress, 73; as a leader, 103; suggested for cabinet, 127; disappointed in Jackson, 131; opposed by Jackson, 134; letter to Col. John Williams, 135; deserted Jackson, 135; comments upon Jackson, 136; comments upon Ritchie, 138; forced to support Jackson, 139; comments upon Ritchie, 145; comments upon Ritchie and Junto, 153; attempted to win Clay, 156; loss of influence, 169.

Foote, Senator, suggested committee of thirteen, 281.

Foushee, William, interest in manufacturing, 45; war-rawk, 57.

France, interest in Florida, 33; attacked American commerce, 41; Berlin decrees, 43; reprisals upon commerce, 163.

Gallatin, Albert, election of 1808, 48; for re-charter of bank of U. S., 51; cabinet official, 57; nominated for vice-presidency, 92; endorsed by Va. for vice-presidency, 94; abolitionist, 238.

Gamble, Major Robert, owner of Gray House, 15.

Garland, Hugh A., editor, 201.

Garland, James, Conservative leader, 200.

Garnett, James M., interest in education, 220.

Garrison, W. L., abolitionist, 283.

Gazette, Federalist organ in Richmond, 19.

Genealogy, See Appendix.

"General Survey Act," used by Adams, 115.

Georgia, dispute with Indians, 100.

Giles, W. B., election of 1808, 47; opposed for Secretary of State, 50; war-hawk, 57; retired from Congress, 58; as a leader, 103; attempts to re-enter public life, 105; message on federal relations, 113; accused of disloyalty, 114; favored election of Jackson, 116; member of constitutional convention, 121; loss of influence, 169; opposed right of instruction, 178.

Gilmer, Thomas W., deserted Jackson, 135; attempted to displace Ritchie, 136; Democrats attempt to win, 201; left Whig party, 222; member of "Corporal's Guard," 223.

Gladstone, comments upon nature of our government, 22.

Globe, criticised Stevenson, 188; sold to Ritchie, 253.

Gooch, C. W., letter to Van Buren, 95; joint editor of *Enquirer*, 118; letter to Van Buren regarding Ritchie, 122; on political conditions in Va., 158.

Goode, Wm. O., local Democratic leader, 111; affiliated with Democrats, 214; nominated for Congress, 230, Calhoun supporter, 251.

Gordon, William F., suggested independent Treasury, 194.

Great Britain, attacked American commerce, 41; industrial conditions, 42; orders in Council, 43; industrial conditions, 44; orders in Council, 54; interest in Florida and Northwest Territory, 61; interest in Florida and Cuba, 71; importations of, 76; interest in South America and Cuba, 83; interest in Texas, 232, 238, 243.

Green, Duff, editor, 109; editor of *U. S. Telegraph*, 111; supported Calhoun for presidency, 137; attacked Ritchie and Van Buren, 144; attempts to defeat Van Buren, 156; aided sectional discord, 167; opposed Blair, 251.

Grey House, 15.

Gray, Edwin, "Quid," 16.

Grundy, Felix, member of 12th Congress, 56.

Gwin, Dr. W. McK., received letter from Van Buren, 172.

Hammett, W. H., 238.

"Hampden," letters of, 80.

Harrison, George E., 297.

Harrison, Randolph, member of anti-tariff convention, 143.

Harrison, Gen. W. H., nominated for presidency, 179; renominated for presidency, 212; abolitionist, 214; opposed annexation of Texas, 223, death of 223.

Harvie, John, built Grey House, 15; Revolutionary soldier, 16.

Hay, George, election of 1808, 48; war-hawk, 57.

Heiss, John P., Ritchie's associate, 252.

Hopkins, George W., Conservative leader, 200.

Hunter, R. M. T., Speaker of H. of R., 212; Life of Calhoun, 227; defeated for re-election to Congress, 230; Calhoun supporter, 251.

Hunter vs. *Martin,* Virginia's court reversed, 80.

Immigrations, westward, 65; effects upon East, 65-66.

"Index," attacked Jefferson, 28.

Independent treasury, proposed by Brockenbrough, 194; rejected by Rives, 195.

Ingham, Samuel D., favored alliance between N. Y. and Va., 108.

Internal Improvements, following war with England, 64; Chicago convention of 1847, 270; between East and far West, 217.

Italy, revolution in, 83.

Jackson, General, invasion of Florida, 69; candidate for presidency, 85; endorsed by Penn., 92; Ritchie's estimates of, 93; leader of opposition in Va., 99; favored by Va. and N. Y. for presidency, 105; favored by Va. politicians, 111; popular in western Va., 115; elected President, 117; an innovator, 128; renominated, 130; toast on Federal Union, 131; vetoed Maysville Bill, 132; breach with Calhoun, 135; forced resignation of cabinet, 138; vetoed Bank Bill, 149; re-elected to presidency, 149; issued Proclamation, 151; denounced nullifiers in Va., 152; censured by Senate and protested, 159; policy in dealing with France, 174; supported independent treasury, 199; for Van Buren, 1844, 227; on annexation of Texas, 232, Texas letter, 236; friend of Blair, 252.

Jefferson, Thomas, interest in founding *Enquirer*, 18; anti-salvery sentiment, 25; breach with Randolph, 30; peace policy, 33; friend of Miranda, 36; published writings upon banking, 67; particularist, 73; praised Ritchie, 81; party leader, 82; Monroe Doctrine, 84; friendship for Adams, 98; comments about the West, 102; birthday celebrated, 131; father of nullification, 142; on negro slavery, 271.

Johnson, Cave, hostility to Blair, 246; negotiations with Ritchie, 247.

Johnson, Chapman, member of constitutional convention, 121.

Johnson, Richard M., member of 12th Congress, 56; suggested as Speaker, 156; nominated for vice-presidency, 171; repudiated by Va., 180; unpopular in Va., 184; suggested for presidency, 241.

Jones, Skelton, editor of *Examiner*, 18.

Kendall, Amos, influence with Jackson, 136.

Kentucky Reporter, supported Marshall, 80.

Kerchival, Samuel, Jefferson's letter to, 68.

King, Rufus, opposed Missouri Compromise, 78; candidate for presidency, 85.

"Kitchen Cabinet," beginnings of, 112.

Leake, W. D., candidate for Congress, 269.

Leib, Michael, influence with Madison, 156.

Leigh, B. W., resident of, 16; attack upon Nicholas, 47; member of constitutional convention, 121; elected to Federal Senate, 157; re-elected to Senate, 159, 164; suggested for vice-prsidency, 162; attempts to drive him from the Senate, 162; driven from Senate, 178.

Letcher, John, friend of McDowell, 229.

Lewis, Joseph, Federalist, 56.

Lewis, William B., influence with Jackson, 136.

Liancourt, Duke de La Rochefoucauld, description of Richmond, 13.

Livingston, Edward, author of Proclamation, 151.

Louisiana purchase, political issue, 28; exchanged for Florida, 36.

Lyons, James, Texas Whig, 251.

Lowndes, Wm., candidate for presidency, 185.

McClurg, Dr. James B., 16.

McDonald, Angus, 245.

McDowell, James, favored Special Circular, 192; supported Van Buren, 205; leader of Va. Democracy, 210; suggested for governorship, 211; suggested for U. S. Senate, 212; abolitionist, 214; supported for presidency in 1844, 227; candidate for governor, 229.

McDuffie, George, visited Richmond, 111.

McRea, Alex., 16.

Macon, N., friend of Randolph, 31; for war with Spain, 32; interest in Burr, 37; author of "Macon Bills," 55.

Madison, James, candidate for presidency, 31; candidacy effected by local conditions in Va., 34; nominated for presidency by Va., 47; adhered to peace policy, 53; particularist, 73; Monroe Doctrine, 84; elector on Adams ticket, 116; member of constitutional convention, 121.

Madisonian, Conservative Organ, 197; Tyler Organ, 225.

Mann, Horace, educator, 12.

Manufacturers, protected by tariff, 44.

Marcey, W. L., Secretary of War, 260.

Marshall, John, relations with Ritchie, 17; dined with Burr, 40; the Burr trial, 41; political activity, 116; member of constitutional convention, 121.

Maryland, interest in internal improvements, 64.

Mason, J. M., conservative leader, 200; deserted Rives, 206.

Mason, John Y., local Democratic leader, 110; suggested for U. S Senate, 213.

Masons, political party, 116.

Maysville Bill, vetoed, 132.

Meade, R. K., attacks upon Ritchie, 283.

Mercer, C. F., opposed war with Great Britain, 42; member of constitutional convention, 121.

Methodist Church, dismembered, 259.

Mexico, revolution in, 71, 83, 129.

Miranda, General, leader of Spanish patriots, 36.

Missouri, admission of, 77-79; negro slavery in, 85.

Monroe Doctrine, suggested, 36.

Monroe, James, candidate of the Quid party, 91; treaty with Great Britain, 42; nominated for presidency by Va., 47; elected to presidency in 1816, 63; particularist, 73; re-election and Missouri Compromise, 79; veto of 1822 and "Views," 82; message on South America, 83; elector on Adams ticket, 116; member of constitutional convention, 121.

Moore, Bishop, 16.

Morgan, W. S., conservative leader, 200.

Nashville Convention, ultimatum, 282.

Napoleon, banishment to Elba, 60; returns from Elba, 62.

Nationalism, effect upon the West, 68.

National Intelligencer, organ of Jeffersonian party, 19; favored Mo. Compromise, 79; supported Marshall, 80; parties in Va., 82; supported Monroe, 85; favored Clay for vice-presidency, 95; comments upon Ritchie, 113; on nullification, 114; opposed annexation of Texas, 130.

Negro slavery, reaction against abolition of, 25; fight for extension Missouri, 77; defended by South, 100; abolition opposed by Ritchie, 120; discussed in Congress, 164; in District of Columbia, 176; agitation revived, 259; westward extension, 270; attempt to exclude from D. of C., 274; fugitive slaves, 279.

New England, opposed embargo, 46; opposed war of 1812, 62.

New York, activity in internal improvements, 64; political relations with the South, 85; with Va., 87; political ally of Va., 107; effect of alliance with Va., 169; opposed Rives for vice-presidency, 171; differences on slavery, 222.

Nicholas, Judge P. N., resident of 16; war-hawk, 57; bank director, 72; letter to Van Buren, 106.

Nicholas, W. C., part in election of 1808, 47; bank director, 72.

Niles, Hezekiah, comments upon Va., 105.

Nullification, fathered by Calhoun, 124; activity of leaders, 131. 133; aided by Tariff Bill of 1832, 149; ordinance adopted, 150.

Ohio, taxed U. S. bank, 75.

Oregon, territory of, 83; claims to, 261; attitude of North toward, 273.

Orr, James L., attacked Ritchie, 285.

Panama canal, proposed, 72, 277.

Panama Congress, proposed, 100.

Panics, causes of , 1819, 77; causes of, 1837, 193.

Park, John, editor, 46.

Parker, R. E., accused of disloyalty, 114; member of Junto, 139; supported Van Buren for vice-presidency, 145; letter to Van Buren, 183; elected to Senate, 185; accepted independnt treasury, 195; "gum-shoe" politician, 201; criticized Van Buren, 204; supported Van Buren, 205.

Particularism, reaction toward, 72.

Pendleton, Edmund, author of the "Danger Not Over," 23; essay republished in *Enquirer*, 125.

Pennsylvania, interest in internal improvements, 64; supported Calhoun for presidency, 85; deserted Calhoun, 92; renominated Jackson, 130. z

Phillips, Wendell, abolitionist, 283.

Pinkney, William, Minister to England, 54.

Pitt, William, influence on neutral commerce, 33.

Pleasants, John Hampden, editor of *Lynchburg Virginian*, 90; wrote Ritchie's obituary, 95; efforts to overthrow Ritchie, 103; leader of Whig press, 162; opposition leader, 192; comments upon Suabian Dutch," 217;; killed in duel, 298.

Pleasants, James, popular in Va., 116.

Pleasants, Samuel, war-hawk, 57.

Poinsett, J. R., report on militia, 214.

Political Parties, origin of National-Republican and National-Democratic, 83; Whig party formed, 155; Conservatives, 197.

Polk, James K., suggested for vice-presidency, 235; nominated for presidency, 242; elected, 245; defended Ritchie, 262, 273; message of 1848, 274.

Porter, Peter B., member of 12th Congress, 56.

Press, freedom of, 166; effected by public printing, 265; tone of, elevated by Ritchie, 293.

Printing, public, job printing, 264.

Proclamation, 151.

Prussia, educational system, 220.

Public lands, speculation in, 65; sales of, 182.

"Quids," party of discontent, 31; principles of, 35; defend Burr, 39.

Randolph, John, anti-slavery sentiment, 25; opposed Yazoo claims, 30; attacked Madison, 31; for war with Spain, 32; opposed peace policy, 33; speech on Gregg's resolution, 34; alliance with Federalists, 35; author of "Decius," 35; interest in Burr, 37; opposed non-intercourse act, 42; opposed embargo, 43; "Constant Reader," 48; opposed war with England, 58; apostle of republicanism, 73; elected to U. S. Senate, 103; power as opposition leader, 105; member of constitutional convention, 121; secessionist, 124; minister to Russia, 129; endorsed Van Buren for vice-presidency, 144; supported Van Buren for vice-presidency, 145; first suggested independent treasury, 194.

Randolph, Peyton, interest in manufacturing, 45; war-hawk, 57.

Randolph, Thomas Jefferson, favored Specie Circular ,192; entertained Van Buren, 204; supported Van Buren, 205; for Van Buren, 1844, 227.

"Republican Blues," 43.
Resolutions of 98, authorship, 50; interest of nullifiers in, 134.
Rhett, B. H., visited Richmond, 231; disloyal, 283.
Richmond, in 1800, 13; social and intellectual center, 14; political and social life, 17; Federalist stronghold, 17; fondness for disitinction and rank, 17; Wirt's comments upon Richmond, 17; aided Miranda, 36; in campaign of 1840, 216; educational convention, 220; captured by Democrats, 251.
Richmond Compiler, founded, 63.
Richmond Enquirer, founded, 19; Jeffersonian organ in Va., 19; account of Burr trial, 40; increased its influence, 121; Conservative organ, 199.
Richmond Junto, distribution of spoils, 82; political factor, 90; loyalty to Crawford, 94; power in Va., 156; repudiated Van Buren, 238.
Ritchie, Archibald, Scotch merchantman, 9; a tory, 10; member of Committee of Public Safety, 10.
Ritchie, Archibald, military service, 59.
Ritchie, John, killed at Bridgewater, 59.
Ritchie, Thomas, Jr., joint editor of *Enquirer*, 230.
Ritchie, William F., joint editor of *Enquirer*, 230; delegate to Baltimore Convention, 1844, 242.
Ritchie, Thomas, born, 9; maternal influence , 10; relatives and connections, 11; education, 11; became a teacher, 12; bookseller, 12; relations with Justice Marshall, 17; founded *Enquirer*, 19; principles and influenced as an editor, 20; strict constructionist, 22; influence of Madison and Pendleton, 22; anti-slavery movement, 25; foreign slave-trade, 26; interest in banks, 27; Louisiana purchase, 29; Yazoo claims, 30; failure to win the Quids, 31; defeated for public printer, 32; for war with Spain, 32; deserted Randolph, 34; defended peace ragine, 35; mistrusted Miranda, 37; confidence in Burr, 37; deceived in Burr, 39; wrote "Cursory Reflections," 41; criticized Marshall, 61; defended embargo, 43; for protection, 44; desired war with England, 45; opposed disunion, 46; defense of Union, 46; election of 1808, 46; attacked John Taylor of Caroline, 49; for war with Great Britain, 53; interest in Congressional election of 1812; early friendship for Calhoun, 56; favored war with England, 57; a soldier, 59; part in the war of 1812, 59; opposed peace, 60-61; spokesman of the new era, 61-62; friend of internal improvements, 64; attitude toward West, 65; opposed state banks, 67; opposed Jackson in Florida, 69; opposed war with Spain, 70; favored independence of Spanish America, 71; acquiesced in nationalism, 72; a particularist, 73; attacked bank of U. S., 74; opposed tariff, 76; opposed Missouri Compromise, 77; commends Roane, 80; comments upon "Construction Construed," 81; party leader, 82; on occupation of Cuba, 83; espoused cause of Greeks, 84; suggested Monroe Doctrine, 84; endorsed Monroe Doctrine, 84; opposed re-election of Monroe, 85; supported Crawford, 86; friendship for Clay, 87; comments upon candidates, 1824, 89; member of Junto, 90-91; comments upon caucuses, 92; estimates of Jackson, 93; Calhoun's political enemy, 93; loyalty to Crawford, 94-98; concedes Jackson's election, 1824, 95; political obituary, 96; breach with Clay, 99; comments upon abolition, 100; favored internal improvements and schools, 100-101; repudia-

ated Adams, 100-102; letter to A. Ritchie on political condition in Va., 104; comments on Federal relations, 105; reluctance to accept Jackson, 106; refused editorship of National Organ, 108; lost an opportunity for service, 110; loyalty to N. Y., 112; hostility to Clay, 112; concedes legality of tariff, 113; visited Albany, 113; opposed nullifiers, 114; witnessed Jackson's inauguration, 117; spokesman of Jacksonian democrats, 118; champion of local reform, 119; Gooch's opinion of, 122; strengthened by constitutional convention of 1829-30, 123; opposed nullification, 124, 134; distrust of Jackson, 125; devoted to Va., 125; advice to Jackson, 126; confidence in Van Buren, 127; condemned office-seekers, 128; for annexation of Texas, 130; for Jackson's re-election, 131; comments on Maysville veto, 132; comments on West India trade, 133; successful Democratic leader, 139; desired retirement of Van Buren from cabinet, 139; internal improvements, 141; denounced Calhoun and nullification, 141; opposed Clay Compromises, 143; endorsed Van Buren for vice-presidency, 144; suggested for Minister to England, 144; attacked Duff Green, 144; supported Van Buren for vice-presidency, 145; political leader, 146; confidence in Van Buren, 148; comments on South Carolina, 150; as a conciliator, 150; accepted Proclamation, 152; attempts to destroy influence of, 152; devotion to Union, 153; comments on Whigh party, 155; efforts to remove as public printer, 157; on political conditions in Va., 158; political activity and defeat, 159; comments upon election of 1834, 160; comments upon Whig party, 160; concern about Jackson, 163; defeated for public printer, 164; minority leader, 164; favored gradual abolition, 165; called an abolitionist, 167; "corrupt bargain," with Van Buren, 169; political arbiter, 169; comments on Rives' candidacy for vice-presidency, 170; opposed Southern convention in 1835, 173; placed party success before sectional interests, 173; efforts to control Jackson, 174; re-elected public printer, 174; moderation in dealing with abolitionists, and love of Union, 176; opposed increase of state banks, 177; for independence and annexation of Texas, 181; opposed distribution of land sales, 182; interest in election of 1836, 183; mentioned for governor, 183; commended by Van Buren, 184; denounced abolitionists, 184; at height of power, 185; letter to B. F. Butler regarding Stevenson, 188; defended credit system and state banks, 191; panic of 1837, 193; rejected independent treasury, 196; proposed banker's convention, 197; letter to Van Buren on independent treasury, 198; continued opposition to Calhoun, 199; proposed Special Deposit System, 200; letter to Rives, 200; supported Rives, 200; supported Van Buren, 202; responsible for victory of Conservatives, 203; letter to Van Buren, 203; pled for compromise, 205; underestimated popularity of independent treasury, 205; deserted Rives, 206; as described by Daniel, 206; opposed Calhoun's internal improvement policies, 207; opposed "free banking," 208; renewed loyalty to Democrats, 210; efforts to redeem Va. from Whigs, 210; political abilities acknowledged, 211; declaration for independent treasury, 212; abolitionist, 214; political activity in 1840, 215; edited *The Crisis*, 215; political leader, 217; interest in education, 219; pro-slavery advocate, 222; praised Tyler's vetoes, 224; defended the Virginia doctrines, 225; county named for, 226; denounced by friends of Calhoun, 230; supported Van Buren, 230; attempted to prevent Texas from becoming a political issue, 233; letter to Wright regarding Texas, 236; published Jackson's Texas letter, 236; an expanionist, 238; letter to Van Buren, 239; favored Cass for presidency, 241; raised "Polk and Texas" cry, 243; a miniature Talleyrand, 243; owned Texas lands, 244; comments on campaign of 1844, 244; devotion to Va., 246; suggested for national spokesman, 247; letter to Gen. Bayly, 247; refused to leave Richmond, 249; on annexation of Texas, 250; war upon Whigs, 250; lukewarm on secession, 251; editor of Democratic organ, 253; established *Union*, 253; on the tariff, 255; farewell to Va., 255; opportunities in Washington, 258; difficulties, 258; comments on negro slavery, 259; a conciliator, 260; visited Blair, 250; offended South, 260; on occupation of Oregon, 260; difficulties as national editor, 261; reply to *London Times*, 262; made new enemies, 263; influence upon press, 265; efforts to depose, 265; attacked U. S. Senate, 268; interest in internal improvements, 270; readmitted to floor of Senate, 271; Wilmot Proviso, 271; publicity mania, 273; for extension of Missouri Compromise line, 274; adhered to conservatism, 275; spokesman of border section, 275; Garrison and enigma, 276; interest in Chinese trade, 277; changed views on internal improvement, 277; internal improvement schemes, 278; endorsed non-intervention, 278; considered pro-southern, 279; disappointed "fire-eaters" and "fanatics," 280; praised Clay, 280; supported Compromise of 1850, 281; conference with Clay, 281; praised Webster, 282; condemned Nashville Convention, 282; placed party above sectional interest, 283; loyalty to South, 284; petitioned Congress for relief, 284; financial failures, 285; vindicated by Congress, 285; retired, 286; editorial farewell, 286; eulogized Clay, 288; claims to distinction, 290; not a political boss, 291; as a great editor, 292; influence upon editors, 294; entertained Dickens, 294; a stoic, 295; financial failures, 296; marriage, 296; children and descendants, 296 (see also appendix); death, 299; will, 299.

Rives, John C., retired from *Globe*, 255; comments upon Ritchie, 268.

Rives, W. C., local Democratic leader, 110; minister to France, 129; suggested for governor, 144; elected to U. S. Senate, 152; retired from Senate, 157; candidate for vice-presidency, 170; re-elected to Senate, 178; endorsed Van Buren for presidency, 180; leader of Conservatives, 187; popular in Va., 192; "Little Expunger," 192; author of essays by "Camillus," 197; prevented from becoming Whig, 201; entertained Van Buren, 204; underestimated popularity of independent treasury, 205; adhered to Conservatives, 207; Conservative candidate for Senate, 209; deserted Ritchie, 210; suggested for governor, 211; affiliated with Whigs, 213; Whig orator, interest in agriculture, 221.

Roane, Spencer, lawyer, 11; influence upon Ritchie, 23; president of Va. Court of Appeals, 27; for war with Great Britain, 43; warhawk, 57; wrote letters of "Algernon Sydney," 69; influence upon Ritchie, 70; president of Va. Court of Appeals, 73; death of, 73; opposed bank of U. S., 75; as "Hampden," 80; party leader, 82; influence on National-Democratic party, 83.

Roane, William H., member of anti-tariff convention, 143; leader of Van Buren forces, 146; elected to Senate, 185; for Van Buren, 1844; 228; letter on Texas, 233; opposed annexation of Texas, 237; letter to Van Buren, 238.

Robinson, Conway, 16.
Ruffin, Edmund, editor of *Farmer's Register*, 221; editor of *Southern Magazine*, 222.
Russia, encroachment upon Northwest, 83.
Rutherford, Thomas, bank director, 72; on political conditions in Va., 158.

San Domingo, insurrection in, 25.
Santa Anna, Gen., planned to invade U. S., 181.
Scott, Gen. W. S., suggested for presidency, 213.
Scott, William, decision on neutral carriers, 33.
Sectionalism, factor in elections, 85.
Seddon, James A., Calhoun leader, 229; Calhoun supporter, 251; friend of Calhoun, 269.
Sergeant, John, candidate for vice-presidency, 146.
Sevier, Sen. A. H., defended Ritchie, 267.
Seward, W. H., Governor of N. Y., 200; refused to extradite fugitives, 222.
Sheffey, Daniel, Federalist, 56.
Shepherd, Samuel, elected public printer, 164.
Simonton, J. W., intermediary between Clay and Ritchie, 281.
Shockoe Hill, social center, and seat of Richmond Junto, 15.
Slave-trade, prohibited, 26.
Smith, Adam, influence upon Ritchie, 20, 75.
Smith, George William, 16.
Smith, Robert, influence with Madison, 56.
Smith, William, supported by Va., for vice-presidency in 1836, 184.
Smith, William (Extra Billy), defeated for Congress, 23-; Calhoun supporter, 251.
Smyth, Gen., Adams' letter to, 89.
South Carolina, pro-slavery, 26; opposed tariff of 1828, 114; opposed tariff of 1828, 130; Union Party, 150; efforts to detach Va. from N. Y., 231.
Spain, interest in Louisiana, 29; violates treaty, 69; delay in sale of Florida, 70; revolt of American colonies, 71; revolution in, 83.
Spanish Association, exposed, 38.
Special Deposit System, suggested by Ritchie, 200.
Specie Circular, 187; efforts to repeal, 193.
Stone, Robert King, 297.
Stevenson, Andrew, director in branch bank of Bank of U. S., 72; elected to speakership, 113; accused of disloyalty, 114; endorsed Van Buren, 139; supported Van Buren for vice-presidency, 145; leader in Baltimore Convention of 1835, 171; comments upon Bank of U. S., 187; candidate for vice-presidency, 210, 212; returned from Court of St. James, 228; suggested for vice-presidency, 228; suggested for cabinet, 246.
Summers, Judge Lewis, member of constitutional convention, 121.
Sydney, Algernon, letters of, 69; nom-de-plume of Spencer Roane, 70.

Tappahannock, commercial center, 11.

Tallmadge, N. P., leader of Conservatives, 187; opposed independent treasury, 195; nominated for vice-presidency, 211.

Tariff, desired in 1808, 44; opposed by particularists, 76; "Bill of Abominations," 114; declared unconstitutional, 131; Clay Compromise, 143; opposition to injured Va., 207; issue in 1844, 244; of 1846, 263.

Taylor, Col. John, part in election of 1808, 49; opinions of Ritchie, 50; knowledge of Federalist, 51; attacks new nationalism, 51; a particularist, 73; author of "construction Construed," 81; party leader, 82; influence on National-Democratic party, 83; proposed amendment to constitution, 85; in election of 1824, 89.

Taylor, W. P., a Democrat, 214.

Tazewell, L. W., candidate for Federal senate, 95; communication of 1827 with Ritchie, 108; member of constitutional convention, 121; suggested for cabinet, 127; proposed for Minister to England, 129; disappointed in Jackson, 131; opposed by Jackson, 134; deserted Jackson, 135; forced to support Jackson, 139; elected governor, 158; loss of influence, 169; message of 1835 to Assembly, 175; opposed right of instruction, 178.

"Ten Regiment Bill," defeated, 266.

Tenth Legion, location, 183; praised by Ritchie, 216, 245.

Texas, annexation proposed, 129; annexation desired, 180, 222; political issue in 1843, 229; national issue, 232; treaty of anexation rejected, 243; annexed, 250.

Tidewater, became Democratic, 226.

Toombs, Robert, disloyal, 282.

Troup, George M., member of 12th Congress, 56.

Tucker, Henry St. George, a nationalist, 103.

Turner, "Nat," leader of insurrection, 165.

Turney, Sen. H. L., defended Ritchie, 267.

Tyler, John, elected to Congress, 73; elected to U. S. Senate, 106; friendship for Clay, 111; favored election of Jackson, 116; member of Constitutional Convention, 121; deserted Jackson, 135; forced to support Jackson, 139; elected to U. S. Senate, 152; letter to Floyd, 155; suggested for vice-presidency, 162; driven from Senate, 178; nominated for vice-presidency, 179; attempts of Democrats to win, 201; nominated for vice-presidency, 212; President, 223; first message, 224; strengthened Democrats, 226; interest in Texas, 232.

Union (Washington), established, 253; prospectus of *Union*, 254; proslavery organ, 271.

Upshur, Abel P., member of constitutional convention of 1829-30, 121; Democrats attempt to win, 201; left Whig party, 222; member of "Corporal's Guard," 223; interest in Texas, 232; death of, 241.

Van Buren, John, abolitionist, 283.

Van Buren, Martin, use of federal patronage, 85; a political organizer, 105; father of alliance between N. Y. and Va., 107; visited the South, 111; influence with Jackson, 128, 136; rejected as Minister to England, 145; candidate for vice-presidency, 145;